Praise for *Going First*

"Nell's call to 'Go First' has arrived at the perfect time. We have seen the power of our I-WE-IT approach to drive SheEO's world-changing work, so I'm thrilled that Nell is sharing her Me-We-World framework in such an action-oriented way for leaders to transform the way we do business."

~Vicki Saunders, founder and CEO of Coralus (formerly SheEO)

"Nell shows you step by step how to make purpose an actionable part of your work and life—and how doing so will make you happier, healthier, and more successful."

~Klay S. Williams, Transformation and
Change Communicator, Plan A With Klay

"Rethinking how we work and live, and why it matters, is an invaluable part of the challenging task of moving toward a more inclusive and sustainable economic system. We can all use Nell's powerfully simple framework to optimize the impact of all that we do and how it benefits our teams, our businesses, society, and the planet."

~Anthea Kelsick, C-suite business leader driving impact
through innovation; previous CEO of B Lab/B Corp, US & Canada

"Nell Debevoise's approach and methodology to purposeful leadership could not arrive at a better moment in time. In her new book, she creatively demonstrates the many concrete ways in which purpose drives performance while providing the necessary tools for success and the inspiration required to make positive change."

~Susan McPherson, author of The Lost Art of Connecting; *corporate social impact leader*

"Combining inspiring vision with pragmatic and actionable tools is not easy, but this is exactly what *Going First* manages to achieve. It should be viewed as essential guidance in the movement toward stakeholder capitalism."

~Martin Whittaker, CEO of JUST Capital; member of Forbes Finance Committee; 2020 NACD Directorship 100; Business Insider's 2020 List of 100 People Transforming Business

"Nell has developed powerful and practical tools for purpose-driven leaders looking to be part of the shift to stakeholder capitalism. She shares these resources in *Going First*, giving CEOs and other leaders of teams the inspiration and guidance to go further in incorporating social, environmental, and financial priorities into their business performance. Nell shows you how to evaluate your business with balance and perspective."

~Lorna Davis, board member of Seventh Generation, B Lab; Former CEO of Danone North America

"I aspire to be a purposeful CEO and deeply value Nell's business-aligned perspective on purposeful leadership. Her framework and tools inspire me and my team to mindful action in terms of the impact we wish to achieve in the Me, We, and World dimensions."

~Sylvana Sinha, founder, chair, and CEO of Praava Health

GOING FIRST

Finding the Courage to
LEAD PURPOSEFULLY
and **INSPIRE ACTION**

GOING
FIRST

NELL DERICK DEBEVOISE

For permission requests, write to the publisher, addressed "Attention: Permissions Coordinator," at the address below.

Publish Your Purpose
141 Weston Street, #155
Hartford, CT, 06141

 **Publish** Your Purpose

The opinions expressed by the Author are not necessarily those held by Publish Your Purpose.

Ordering Information: Quantity sales and special discounts are available on quantity purchases by corporations, associations, and others. For details, contact the publisher at hello@publishyourpurpose.com.

Edited by: Nancy Graham-Tillman
Cover design by: Phoebe Miller
Typeset by: Medlar Publishing Solutions Pvt Ltd., India

Printed in the United States of America.

ISBN: 979-8-88797-048-6 (hardcover)
ISBN: 979-8-88797-047-9 (paperback)
ISBN: 979-8-88797-049-3 (ebook)

Library of Congress Control Number: 2023904361

First edition, May 2023.

The information contained within this book is strictly for informational purposes. The material may include information, products, or services by third parties. As such, the Author and Publisher do not assume responsibility or liability for any third-party material or opinions. The publisher is not responsible for websites (or their content) that are not owned by the publisher. Readers are advised to do their own due diligence when it comes to making decisions.

Publish Your Purpose is a hybrid publisher of non-fiction books. Our mission is to elevate the voices often excluded from traditional publishing. We intentionally seek out authors and storytellers with diverse backgrounds, life experiences, and unique perspectives to publish books that will make an impact in the world. Do you have a book idea you would like us to consider publishing? Please visit PublishYourPurpose. com for more information.

Contents

Table of Figures

Why I Think You're Here

Here's what I imagine about you: you're in a leadership position or aspire to be, and you want to lead with purpose. You care about the people you work with and want to keep growing as a leader. You also want to keep growing as a person, for that matter, so you can be the best partner, friend, parent, kid, and neighbor you can be. For one reason or many, you're concerned about the state of the world. Though you want to help make it better, you feel overwhelmed. You keep seeing articles and books about purpose. You've even read some of them, which felt aspirational but vague. Though others make you ashamed of your role in the problems, you're still intrigued by purpose because it feels like if you could find yours, it would be a magic bullet to nirvana and success. You're clearly looking for something related to leadership, purpose, or impact, or you wouldn't have picked up this book.

Now that you're here, here's what I have to offer: I want to demystify the concept of purpose. It's neither an amorphous, passing trend nor a mandate to give up all your earthly belongings for a life of selfless devotion. Purpose is simply a reason to get up in the morning. Identifying yours will unlock the fullest potential impact you can have on yourself, your family, your friends and colleagues, and the world beyond that. We'll talk more about the opportunities of living purposefully, but for now consider this: Going First as a purposeful leader will bring you true and deep happiness. The Greeks understood the difference between *hedonia* (pleasure, or what we call happiness) and *eudaimonia* (true fulfillment; deep happiness in a long-term, satisfying way). Leading and living purposefully is the path to the latter—profound and sustainable contentment.

Your Mission, Should You Decide to Accept It

Regardless of your training, role, skills, age, geography, or any other element of your background, by virtue of being human, you have what it takes to contribute to solving a problem you care about. Making those contributions, noticing you're doing it, and then finding ways to do it more or better will bring you eudaimonia—that deep sense of satisfaction—*and* change the world.

Unfortunately, modern life presents some major obstacles to this natural purpose-seeking state of being. For one thing, most of our approaches to training and career development don't recognize or harness the power of purpose. Our schools and work structures invest little in the process of uncovering our own purpose and the best ways to live it. Has a mentor, boss, or friend ever asked you what your purpose is? Have you ever asked anyone in your family or on your team? Are you clear on the purpose of your business?

Failure to explore and nurture our purpose leaves so much on the table! Leaders who leverage purpose see the payoff in their individual and organizational performance. When we're connected to purpose, we're more motivated, creative, and collaborative—all things that are good for our teams, organizations, and the world beyond.

Purposeful leaders are the heroes who are Going First. They're doing things a bit differently in their own careers and on their teams.

The good news is that the rewards to this approach are becoming increasingly more obvious. Even better, every one of us has the opportunity *today* to Go First in some way and start connecting our work and lives to purpose.

The Timeliness of This Approach

When it comes to living and leading more purposefully, there's no time to waste. Our physical and mental health require us to invest differently than we have before in all the factors that keep us well, including sleep, food, mindfulness, social connections, and movement.

Professionally, the only path to success in the 21st-century economy is one that considers our effects as individuals and organizations on the people around us and the planet we share. As our work lives and personal lives become more intertwined thanks to technology, remote and hybrid work, and longer working lives, we hold ourselves and our businesses to a higher bar as professionals, consumers, and investors. If we want to be part of the future of our roles or industries, we'd better do it in a way that has a positive impact on all of our stakeholders.

The social and environmental crises that we're facing in local and global communities are existential. If we don't take immediate and serious action to change the way we live and work, we'll do irreparable damage to our collective well-being in terms of our natural resources and global community.

Halla Tómasdóttir founded an investment firm that was one of very few to survive Iceland's financial crisis of 2008. Then she ran for president. Now she's a deep thinker and global movement leader of purposeful business as CEO of the B Team. When I interviewed her, she told me she sees the 2020s as a "portal moment. It's not just a paradigm shift in the way we do business; we're headed into a whole new reality in which humanity comes first."

If that resonates with you, you're here for all the reasons I thought, and this is the right place for you to be!

Why I'm Here

This book is the result of my purpose: wrangling ideas and people to make work purposeful for all of us, leading to fairer and healthier workplaces and, ultimately, a more just and equitable world. That drive has led me to study, practice, and create. The results of that journey are the ideas, stories, and tools in this book.

My Invitation to You

This book is designed to share the stories of purpose pioneers as well as provide specific tools to make your own purpose journey more approachable. I want to make it easy for you to start or continue living purposefully, join this community in Going First, and help the people around you do the same. To that end, I include a variety of resources at the end of this book, and on the book's page on my website (www. inspiringcowgirl.com/goingfirst). These are great (free!) ways to deepen your engagement with this content and set yourself up for the success and satisfaction that comes from leading and living with purpose. And there's a dynamic community you can join—with free full access as thanks for buying the book!

Because of the incredible upside that awaits those who spend the time, effort, and attention required to work and live purposefully,

I'm calling this a Purpose Party. None of it works unless you work it, though, so I've also created a *Going First* Purpose Party Playbook as a companion volume to this one (see www.inspiringcowgirl.com/playbook). For optimal results, I hope you'll follow along in it. If you choose not to, you can find the reflection questions and suggested processes here, but in a briefer, less guided, and not as interactive way.

Find the courage to
LEAD PURPOSEFULLY
and INSPIRE ACTION

GOING FIRST

Purpose Party Playbook

The indispensable companion to *Going First* by
NELL DERICK DEBEVOISE

You're invited. I'm thrilled to be your host, and I couldn't be more excited to welcome you to the next steps in your journey toward working and living purposefully.

I want to start by sharing a brief overview of the road that culminated in this book so you can see what has informed, influenced, and contributed to it. I want you to understand where I'm coming from, which I see as a critical first step in any conversation. And I do hope this book provokes conversation, whether between you and me directly, or between you and your colleagues, friends, family, and neighbors.

In the Books

I studied learning, human development, and neuroscience as an undergrad at Harvard, cross-registering at the Graduate School of Education to study with the legendary Howard Gardner, among others. After a few years of teaching abroad, I went to Cambridge and wrote a master's thesis about the risk of external rules and controls eroding our internal sense of morality, drawing on political and pedagogical theory. Next, I earned a master's in intercultural communication at the Università di Roma, studying cultural differences and the way they influence personal and professional interactions.

Finally, I did an executive global MBA program creatively offered by Columbia and London Business Schools. During those two years of study, alongside my work in the West Bank, I focused on leadership and entrepreneurship with my classmates, who represented over 40 nationalities and 20 cities of residence.

As a self-professed nerd and lifelong learner, I feed my voracious appetite for degrees with supplemental informal education in the form of reading, webinars, and short courses. Reverend angel Kyodo williams, Steven Kotler, Lorna Davis, Ray Dalio, Brené Brown, Michael Neill, Ellen McGirt, Simon Sinek, Krista Tippett, Hitendra Wadhwa, and Adam Grant are among the thinkers I consider teachers.

On the Ground

In terms of my practical work, I created and ran programs related to leadership development for international not-for-profit organizations for 10 years. I worked with youth activists from São Paulo to Freetown, Chicago to Paris, and more than 60 other cities, supporting their campaigns and projects through workshops and coaching. I also helped establish a holistic community center in a Palestinian city to support children, women, and youth in their development as well as that of their community and its refugee camps.

For the last decade, I've been training, coaching, and advising private sector leaders primarily in the US, from MBA students early in their careers to mid-career transitioners (often women looking to reenter the workforce) and folks starting to imagine their encore professions.

I had the privilege of leading about two hundred of these people through a deep 50-to-100-hour fellowship program in which we explored their strengths, interests, and needs and the ways those qualities matched up with the needs of the world around them. With thousands of others, the interaction was briefer: either a workshop or lunch-and-learn to explore the concept of purposeful leadership or a more specific application such as "Having Hard Conversations." Those interactions with such diverse leaders in terms of demography, profession, background, and working styles are what shaped the ideas and tools in this book. I'm very aware that the breadth and depth of input from these participants is what helped distill my ideas and tools into the simple and universal practices they are now.

As my fellow Hartford, Connecticut, native Mark Twain is often credited as saying, "If I had more time, I would have written a shorter letter."[1] After 10 years and a few requisite 10,000-hour stints, I've arrived at an empowering guidebook—not a directive roadmap—to leading and living purposefully. While I've learned not to try to be everything to everyone, I've seen that these tools and approaches are powerful for everyone who's committed to deepening the integration of purpose in their work and life.

On the Record

Most recently, through my *Forbes* Leadership column and in writing this book, I've interviewed about 150 CEOs, founders, chief HR/people officers, and other courageous and wise leaders about their purpose journeys. Their stories exponentially enriched the tools and frameworks I've created from my direct experience, and I've shared their insights throughout this book. Further, their input illustrates the fact that leading purposefully is not restricted to industry, generation, or geography. It can—and I think we'd all agree, should—be done by any human in whatever seat they occupy.

These leaders and their companies represent a wide range of industries, geographies, stages, ages, and sizes. Some are CEOs of Fortune 500 companies and executive directors of regional not-for-profits, as well as repeat founders working on their third brainstorm as a team of one. Others are chief human resources officers (CHROs) of fast-growing tech startups and bootstrapped B Corps. But they all share a commitment to keep becoming their best selves every day so that they can lead their teams and grow their companies in a way that is good for the planet and the people around them.

Check out the full list of interviewees in the Acknowledgments section or on my website at www.inspiringcowgirl.com/goingfirst.

What You're in For

The book includes several frameworks and tools that have emerged from all the study, work, and listening I just mentioned. I've endeavored to describe them theoretically, illustrate them with examples from my own life and the lives of many others, and animate them with reflection questions and activities for you.

Part 1 covers all the reasons why and how to rally or maintain the courage you have to Go First and do things differently—the way you (if I got the first part about why you're here right) want to live, work, and lead.

Part 2 is the big reveal. You'll see what a Purpose Party looks and feels like. This is the section where you'll learn about the Spheres of Impact™ and the Spectrum of Impact™, which combine to make the Impact Dashboard, or Dashboard, as I'll call it throughout the book. You'll also learn the pitfalls of purposeful leadership so that you're better prepared to avoid them and a detailed process to make the party less overwhelming and more effective.

Part 3 is all about diving in and mapping your own Impact Dashboard. You'll go sphere by sphere, thinking about all the ways you already invest in the impact you seek and how you can potentially do more (or less) to get closer to living your purpose. You'll see how your direct actions can have more ramifications on people and the planet in three dimensions: Me, We, and World.

By the end of the journey, you'll be ready to throw your own Purpose Party, making ripples that inspire others to do their version of Going First. That's the upward spiral of purposeful leadership that leads to exponential system change.

A Few Tips Before
We Kick Off the Party

Working and living purposefully is a lifelong journey. This book is designed to meet you where you are, whether you're taking your first step or on your 27th lap. I hope you'll *engage* with this book rather than simply *read* it. I've studied enough neuroscience, behavior change, and pedagogy to know that simply reading the book won't change your life.

My intent in presenting the ideas, frameworks, and tools in this book is for you to reflect, experiment, and change the way you lead and live. You'll find a lot of reflection questions and suggested activities along the way. Learning styles vary widely, so some of them will resonate more for you than others. You might dive deep into some, give some a quick thought as you're waiting for a Zoom call to begin, and save others for later. However you use them is fair game, but please approach this book as an interactive journey to be participated in, not speedread and shelved. I've designed the companion *Going First* Purpose Party Playbook to support that engagement.

When working your way through this book, keep your focus on action, or the impact of the ways in which you invest your time, energy, and attention in your work and life. I take that approach because purpose is rooted in action. By reflecting on the investments you make in each area of your work and life—what I call the Spheres of Impact—you'll see very tangibly the things you're doing that have influence. This process tends to reveal themes among those activities as well as gaps where you might want to have more sway.

The Impact Dashboard is based on what I've seen work for hundreds of leaders in their journeys to becoming more purposeful. Use it! Completing the Dashboard will refine your understanding of your purpose and how you're best positioned to activate it. That said, this book does not include guidance on writing a specific statement of purpose. There are a lot of great resources out there for that, but this book isn't one of them. Check out the Reader Resources section at the end of this book, and/or use Simon Sinek's online content "Start with Why" to guide the process of your purpose discovery.

If you already have a purpose statement, great! And if not, please don't worry. I've seen the process I lay out in this book help people get a lot clearer about what their purpose statement might contain. Particularly for folks who are action-oriented and focused on concrete results, this emergent approach is sometimes more natural, enjoyable, and effective than trying to script the perfect 12-word statement to be etched on your tombstone or memorial.

While self-awareness, quiet time for mindfulness, and independent learning and reflection are critical to purposeful leadership, make no mistake: purpose is a team sport. As you read this book, share what you're learning and thinking with your partner, parent, child, neighbor, yoga buddy . . . at least your dog. As with any new idea or language, it's powerful to proclaim your purpose out loud to hear it outside of your head.

Looking at the World Can Be Difficult

When it's connected to making a positive impact on our and other people's lives and/or the planet, purpose only creates clarity, motivation, and fulfillment. Contributing to that meaningful change requires a deep understanding of the things in this world that make your heart beat faster, tears come to your eyes, or anger well up in your gut. So get comfortable with the discomfort of seeing injustice up close and learning about how and why harm is being done to our planet and people. The only way to find what will be truly motivating to you and is worth the time, energy, and attention that purposeful leadership requires is by seeing what's wrong in the first place.

There are plenty of wrongs in this world that you aren't responsible for but may inspire you to act. You'll also find examples of harm that you do have a role in, even if completely unintentionally. If you want to experience the rewards and deep joy of living and leading with purpose, you need to develop the equanimity and growth mindset to see those wrongs and your role or lack thereof clearly. Only in honestly recognizing past damage based on the experience of those who felt it firsthand can you identify your unique contributions to its repair.

Suffering is there no matter what. But when we choose to endure the temporary discomfort of recognizing it, we open the possibility of healing our relationship to it and being part of the solution.

You might be thinking, *That's all?!* I know. It sounds heavy, but trust me and the hundreds of people who are already Going First in myriad ways when I say that the rewards of living and leading with purpose begin almost immediately and grow from there. And they're worth it.

I'd like to share with you how I learned that.

Your Host's Purpose Story

I found my purpose the day I quit my nonprofit career. If you'd like a little more background on my purpose journey—because it might offer some guidance in reflecting on your own—read on. If you're eager to get to the party, skip ahead to part 1.

For those who are staying, I promise not to regale you with a play-by-play of my path to purpose starting in adolescence, but the starting point is important to the story. My hope is that it will inspire you to look further back than you usually do when thinking about your purpose.

The seeds of our truest selves—what we get excited about, what we're naturally good at, the problems that motivate us to action—are almost always present in some form early in our lives. What began your path to purpose?

My 12-Year-Old Self's Career Vision

When I was 12, I was a sixth grader at Noah Webster Elementary School in Hartford, Connecticut. Noah Webster was the paragon of the great American public school. It was certainly not perfect or immune from the realities of structural racism, but its location drew families that were more representative of our national population than most schools.

I and most of my classmates walked to school. We represented a wide range of racial, religious, and economic backgrounds. Parents were involved with the playground renovation and our annual May Fair. We had art, band, choir, and a "Gifted and Talented" program. Again, these programs were not without bias, and of course I experienced bias through the lens of my own White privilege.

As our sixth-grade graduation loomed, so did a choice. The school I was zoned to attend for seventh grade was a different image of American public schools. It was riven with violence, gangs, drugs, and teenage pregnancy, and as a result, very little energy for learning and growth in the classroom or beyond.

My mom told me either I could enroll in a private school or we could move to a different district. The uniforms and plush campuses I saw on my visits to local private schools looked very expensive. To my

12-year-old understanding of economics, buying a house felt more reasonable, so I cast my vote that we move. My self-employed mom and stepfather pulled together a down payment in order to secure a mortgage, and we found a house on a cul-de-sac with a fenced-in yard. The new house was a mere 700 yards from where I'd grown up, but the boundary between Hartford and West Hartford happened to fall in the middle of those 700 yards.

The Longest 700 Yards

West Hartford was a leafy-green, upwardly mobile suburb where my mother had grown up and my grandparents still lived. It was also relatively diverse, the racial mix being different from Hartford's—more first-generation Asian immigrants than Black and Latino. Rather than being near the top of the economic strata as a middle-class household in Hartford, my family probably came in somewhere in the 40th percentile, just under West Hartford's median household income.

Most relevantly, West Hartford public schools were nationally recognized for holistic excellence. I was trained as a peer mediator within weeks of enrolling in seventh grade. I signed up for Ski Bus and joined 50 classmates for lessons on a nearby ski hill each Wednesday.

In high school, I had my choice of nearly any AP course that existed. After class, only my interests and talent limited how I spent my time, whether in several clubs, JV and varsity sports, a jazz band and dance troupe that toured Europe on spring break, a robust student government with significant budget and authority, a weekly paper and 300-page yearbook, and surely countless others I didn't know existed or don't remember now.

I had a guidance counselor who knew my name from freshman year on and supported me throughout high school with the college admissions process. Her encouragement and intimate letter of recommendation played a not-insignificant role in my landing at Harvard.

The difference between this experience and what my former classmates lived through in Hartford was stark. It showed me, at the age of 12, that while talent is distributed equally, opportunity is not. Knowing those former classmates' talents and passions through our friendships, art shows, band performances, and Mayfair committees, I understood what a shame it was that they didn't get the support, enrichment, and empowerment that I did across the town line. While many of the classmates I still have contact with are thriving, that success looks to be in spite of the weak school system and thanks to their family resources and guidance. It felt obvious that those without such support at home would've had a better shot at making the most of their potential if they had had more robust guidance and resources at school.

As I progressed through the schools in West Hartford, I was also conscious of the fact that most of my classmates had no idea that not all students had access to the resources we enjoyed, even their peers a few hundred yards to the east. They weren't ungrateful; they just never had occasion to see another version of reality like the one I'd known in Hartford. This was an important part of my 12-year-old revelation: people with opportunity usually aren't intentionally hoarding it; they simply don't recognize that they're lucky to have it.

This adolescent experience is the foundation of my resolve to address the unequal distribution of opportunity through my work. I realized it was a real waste of potential for each of us not to support the self-actualization of every person on this planet, and I wanted to do something about it.

Finding My Way

By my senior year of college, I knew three things:

1. I wouldn't join the bulk of my classmates looking for consulting or finance roles.

2. I wanted to live abroad.

3. I would find a role in education.

A combination of curiosity and affection for the path of least resistance led me to teach English in Tokyo. That experience got a 2 out of 10 for professional satisfaction but a 10 out of 10 for cultural and personal exploration.

I'll save the full litany of pivots, disappointments, learnings, and discoveries from the rest of my decade in international development for another book. What matters in the context of my purpose journey is how the satisfaction I took from my not-for-profit work started to wane.

After a few years of teaching English, I found a role managing a community of youth activists, supporting their projects in cities from Rio to Kigali and Hanoi to Quito, all from my employer's office in Rome. That opportunity to build people's capacity as leaders rather than just teach language skills felt like a better fit. Unfortunately, the founder fell ill and stepped back from leadership. As is often the case when founders leave prematurely, the vision fogged, and I lost respect for the way the organization proceeded.

Luckily, I got and seized the opportunity to work more directly for one of that organization's spinoff projects. Its founder had a strong vision and an empowering approach for the local community we wanted to serve. It was to be a community center serving refugee kids and women in Palestine.

After almost a year of research, community outreach, and planning with a local team, the community center started offering early childhood programs designed to improve kids' mental health in age-appropriate ways. And they were working. Within a few years, though, I felt that familiar sense of "So what?" We weren't even making a dent in the millions of refugee children around the world.

Our founder shared my aspiration to grow our reach. Once we worked out our program model and developed ways to measure the effect it was having (from anecdotes as well as data), we were ready to scale—and hit—a wall.

The lack of interest from funders in funding the growth of the model we had proven was a total head-scratcher to me. Wasn't this exactly the model of *scaling what works*, which had become a philanthropic catch phrase? We were a small and very successful organization that could become a medium-sized organization with the right funding. But I was met with blank stares. I specifically remember a program officer from a large international aid agency saying, "But you're a small organization. We couldn't give you that size grant." My reasoning was that with that kind of funding, we'd become a medium-sized organization that would be able to serve more children and women, and wasn't that all of our shared goal?

As my frustration grew, I zoomed out to look at the global system. I didn't have to look far to see Coca-Cola Palestine. They were one of our sponsors, providing juice boxes and bottled water for the children in our programs. (For a number of reasons, Coke wasn't necessarily our first choice for a partner, but they were there in a very difficult place to do business.) Coke's presence and success in the West Bank *and* Gaza against all odds was one of the important seeds of my interest in the private sector. Were there lessons to be taken from their ability to produce, sell, and distribute in these conditions that could inform our ability to "distribute" programming to improve refugees' mental health and resilience?

I wanted to learn more about this private sector. Were there tools or insights I could apply to the work of making lives better? Business school seemed like the best place to answer this question and evolve my approach to the purpose of facilitating the equitable distribution of opportunity. I found the perfect fit: an executive MBA program with a truly global student population that would allow me to continue working for the nonprofit *and* travel between the Middle East and our growing US presence.

Joining 71 classmates for orientation was my first formal interaction with private-sector professionals. My classmates were successful leaders in finance, industry, consulting, and startups around the world. They represented over 40 countries, living in cities from Seattle to Singapore and everywhere in between. There was one other classmate in the not-for-profit sector, but my world was pretty foreign to the other 70. They were fascinated by the direct impact that my work had on refugee mothers, micro entrepreneurs, and youth activists. They shared their various flavors of desire to draw a sense of fulfillment from a day's work and projected it onto my frontline work. For my part, I envied the resources they had access to and the efficiency of the organizations in which they worked. While some of this perception was a "greener grass" phenomenon, the pragmatic, can-do, growth-minded approach of the private sector had real allure.

Another Path to Change

While I had originally found satisfaction in supporting the community members and refugees we served in Palestine, it waned as I saw the power of the global economy and geopolitics limit potential success. Further, spending a decade far from world capitals and power hubs helped me see that the solutions to social and environmental problems must start in these power hubs, not just in the affected communities where I'd been working.

My frustration and insights revealed an opportunity: What if my classmates could find the impact they were seeking without quitting their jobs or moving to a refugee community? What if they could drive change from within the power hubs where they were already established? To have a positive effect, they wouldn't have to take a sabbatical or save up to retire early and start a foundation; they simply needed some guidance to connect the dots between their position and the problems they cared to solve. I could combine my classmates' desire for meaning with the need I saw to effect change higher up the supply chain, closer to the centers of wealth and power that determine so much of the world order and ultimately trickle down to people across the globe who need it. If they could identify the problems they cared about solving and learn about the root causes and best-known solutions, they could identify levers in their current work and lives to contribute in appropriate and effective ways. What an exciting win-win that would be for these purpose-seeking professionals and the populations I'd been serving!

Now I recognize that engaging more motivated, creative professionals is actually a win-win-win that benefits them, their organizations, and the issues they care about. My first company, Inspiring Capital, facilitated exactly these win-win-wins by guiding private-sector professionals to identify two steps: 1) what they cared about contributing to the world, and 2) how to best do that given their skills, needs, and interests.

My Own Purpose Assessment

I've shared the details of my purpose journey to illustrate the twists and turns that purpose journeys almost always take. We often romanticize the term *purpose* to refer to the dramatic, frontline, life-changing work I did in the earlier part of my career. Certainly that *is* critical work, and the people doing it should be better remunerated and supported. However, there's also great impact in structuring mergers in a way that distributes wealth equitably to all stakeholders. Purposeful leaders can accomplish this by taking such actions as training teachers to support students with empathy or growing, cooking, selling, or serving food that nourishes Earth and our bodies.

MY STEP 1

What I want you to take from my story is how I zeroed in on the very specific part of a massive problem that I'm qualified and inspired to solve. Then I found ways to spend my limited time, energy, and attention solving my infinitesimal part of the massive problem I cared to solve: more equitable distribution of opportunity. In other words, I completed the first step—I knew what I wanted to contribute. Now I needed to identify how my unique skills, values, and desires would allow me to best do that. So I took stock.

MY STEP 2

During my 10 years of not-for-profit work, I learned that I'm a starter, not a finisher. I love connecting dots and creating something from nothing, and I get bored when it's time to formalize and refine processes or replicate a partnership or program.

I remembered from those early days at Noah Webster that I'm also a nerd. I love quiet time in the library, exploring ideas and merging diverse wisdom into my own thoughts. I realized that I'm an experience junkie, keen to travel far and wide, eat new foods, try activities, and meet people across the full spectrum of the globe, and that these experiences cost money. So I wanted to earn money and accumulate wealth to satisfy this high experience threshold.

I also recognized that I have both a deep belief in the goodness and potential of every human being and a sense of empathy and curiosity about that potential. I have the perceptive and connective abilities to help people see that potential in themselves and activate it for the good of all around them.

The wider range of people I interacted with, from Nablus to New York and lots of stops in between, the more I saw this aspirational goodness. Very few people wake up wanting to burn more carbon or harm people of other genders, races, religions, or otherwise. Most of us enjoy making the world a little better than we found it and want more of that pleasure. But we've built and become enmeshed in an economic system that is harmful to our planet and most people living on it. I began to see the potential for each of us to Go First by identifying the change we want to catalyze and the ways we're best suited to do it. This opportunity was particularly promising for leaders like my classmates, who held the power and thus the responsibility to contribute courageously and model that approach for others.

Based on these insights about how I work best and what I want to do as that best self, I now guide, develop, and inspire leaders who are committed to putting people first to build better ways of working and living. Specifically, my purpose is to lovingly wrangle people, ideas, and horses to make work fairer, healthier, and more inspiring. I've adopted this purpose based on my belief that fair, healthy, and joyful work is the path to equity and social and environmental justice. When we're connected to our true selves and the change we want to make happen, we do work that's good for people and our shared planet.

Make no mistake, this purposeful approach is hard work. It requires effort, persistence, patience, and a willingness to be challenged and change our ideas and behavior. But I've felt firsthand the payoffs in terms of fulfillment, as well as in my resilience, creativity, effectiveness, and ability to attract and lead incredible colleagues—to say nothing of the impact I've seen in the world around me as a result of my efforts.

Let me share a bit more about this upside, and then you can decide whether it's worth following this process to lead and live more purposefully.

How All This Is Working for Me

Exploring different paths to fulfilling my purpose has been a lot of work. I had to learn several mindfulness practices and build the discipline to maintain them amid the demands of work and life. I haven't made the money I would have by pursuing a more traditional path from Ivy League to consulting or finance. But I've been exposed to and learned to recognize myriad heartbreaking examples of injustice, actively bad behavior, and lazy approaches in our systems and organizations that cause unnecessary harm.

Despite those emotional and financial costs, I'm so grateful I made the choices I did and persevered on the journey to finding work that fits me and my purpose. My passion to shape the future of work keeps me motivated, creative, and focused. I end the day fulfilled far more often than frustrated. I'm physically and mentally healthier, more balanced and grounded, so I'm a better advisor, writer, and colleague. I'm also a better friend, daughter, wife, stepparent, dog mom, and community member.

Finally, I can point to specific ways that people's lives and/or our planet have gotten better because of my work. The impact I have now may seem less dramatic than when mothers used to tell me their children were no longer wetting the bed, having nightmares, or expressing suicidal thoughts thanks to our program. But helping first-time managers realize the critical importance of maintaining their own well-being in order to best serve their direct reports is the necessary foundation for trusting, empathetic, and creative teams to do business in a way that's good for the world. Guiding a CEO/CHRO pair to integrate purpose throughout their fast-growing startup is the best protection for that company's intention to serve all their stakeholders while minimizing harm to people and the planet. Contributing to this more purposeful impact-seeking approach to work is what I've recognized to be the best leverage of my skills toward solving a problem I care about.

Having had the privilege, good fortune, and ability to get to this clarity about my highest and best contribution makes me want to share these insights with every human on this planet who aspires to Go First. It breaks my heart to see people who feel stuck in purposeless roles or who don't see and aren't shown the results of what they do every day. That heartbreak is what led to the ideas in this book and the Purpose Party we're about to kick off.

I'm thrilled you're here. You may be at any point on your purpose journey; this might feel pretty new, or you might recognize parallels between your story and mine. Regardless of where you fall, purpose is a lifelong pursuit. From my study and experience, as well as that of the hundreds of brilliant purposeful leaders whose wisdom I've integrated into this book, I'm confident that you'll find new insights, inspiration, and actionable steps in the pages that follow.

Reflection Questions

Reflection questions are where we take the interactive part of the journey! Fasten your seatbelt and get out your favorite writing utensil. Whether you're using the *Going First* Purpose Party Playbook, a blank notebook, or an electronic file, create a single spot where you'll record your thoughts from this entire book. If you don't have the Playbook, download a free worksheet with these questions (and another for each chapter in the book) at www.inspiringcowgirl.com/goingfirst.

If you speak more freely than you write, use a voice recording tool to capture your thoughts. Then transcribe them with any of several free(ish) transcription apps so you can easily review and search the document later. Just find some way to engage with these questions. If you don't, it's just as well that you save your time and not read the book, because there's no way it can have its desired effect. Let's dive in and practice.

- Why did you buy this book? Why did you start reading it?
- How do you think about purpose right now? Do you have a purpose statement? Even if it's not fully formed, jot some version of it down.
- What's your #1 question about purposeful leadership?
- If you could change *one* thing in your life after reading this book, what would it be?

Part 1

The Invitation

In this part of the book, we'll look at the foundations of a purposeful life. First comes courage, because making any change requires overcoming our fears. Then we'll explore what purpose is and what it isn't, what you need to activate purpose in your life, and the benefits of putting in the effort required to lead and live purposefully.

Finding the courage to Go First is good for us as individuals because setting the example by Going First brings true fulfillment. It's also good for our teams and organizations because it leads to innovation and talent retention. And finally, it's good for the world.

In the early 2020s, we all saw how broken many of our systems were. Whether in healthcare, economics, the political sphere, or the social fabric, we need leaders who are willing to lead by example. We need leaders to model how to choose to do things differently than we have been.

I've had the great pleasure of advising, coaching, and collaborating with hundreds of purposeful leaders across industries, functions, and identities. This invitation comes not only on my behalf but on the behalf of the over 150 purposeful leaders I interviewed specifically for this book: to join us all in the joyful endeavor of leading and living with purpose. Here's how some of them talked about Going First:

"The time and context in which we're living felt to me like a call-up to the A team, even if I wasn't sure I had all the experience or background to build the massive vision we're working toward with AMP. It's time for all of us to 'Go First' in our respective ways."

~Daniel Taylor, cofounder and CEO of AMP

"You have to be *given* the opportunity to Go First. I'm deeply grateful to the people who've come before me, enabling me to be here, Going First in the ways I do."

~Luann Abrams, founder of CEOX

"No one has done it before; there is not a path. That's exciting and it's what draws me to the opportunity of what we're doing with Aspiration."

~Andrei Cherny, cofounder and CEO of Aspiration Bank

"My own goal in Going First is to improve the ecosystem for Black founders. I've gotten a seat at the table with suppliers and customers. For Blk & Bold, the goal is to normalize conscious consumerism and be relevant to people's everyday lives."

~Pernell Cezar Jr., founder and CEO of Blk & Bold

"I guess there are a lot of firsts I can claim. But really, I'm just running my own race. I'm not looking around to see what everyone else is doing; I'm focusing on what I love and how I can do that. I want to normalize credible Black leadership so that no one else has to walk into the room and get asked for coffee."

~Chanel Cathey, founder and CEO of CJC Insights

Chapter 1

Your Invitation to Courage

Have you ever invited an introvert to a party and seen hesitation in their eyes? For some of us, it's a big effort just to show up to a party. For the Purpose Party, that's true for all of us. Joining the Purpose Party can be scary. It may add some work, cause some stress, or build friction into some of your conversations. People might look at you, notice you, talk about you, or question your choices or behavior.

For these and many other reasons, a new type of leader is needed in this moment of massive transition in the way we work and live. Going First and leading purposefully is what retains the most motivated, engaged, healthy, and inspired talent and enables them to innovate in the way required to grow their businesses. Some of the leaders I interviewed realized they had to be willing to get fired before forging ahead in anti-racism, environmental responsibility, lifestyle sustainability, or other areas in which they were choosing to Go First. Nonetheless, they were satisfied by making the choice to do what felt right. Contrary to their fears, most of them didn't get fired. In fact, in a world like today's, the only path to sustainable business success is Going First, so many elements about the way we work are broken.

If you're not Going First, you're certainly not innovating, and you won't survive these tumultuous times. Join the brilliant leaders in this book—and so many more—in Going First as purposeful leaders to inspire action.

The Courage to Lead Purposefully

Our current world is one of chaos, despair, and challenge, whether in terms of political turmoil, global health, disastrous weather, economic uncertainty, inequality, or injustice linked to race, gender, or physical ability.

We need change.

But change by definition requires doing things differently, and that requires courage. People leading a healthier, fairer way of working and doing business will tell you that the courage to diverge from the mainstream came when they found clarity of purpose. John Replogle, for example, is a many-time B Corp CEO and now investor, advisor, and board member of several high-impact organizations. During my interview with him, he explained, "It's about values, not just value. Running companies that are good for the world requires courage, and for that, you need belief. Being clear on your values gives you the foundation to take the leap." When you discover this type of clear vision of the future you want to help shape, you gain connection to your heart. It's not that you lose the fear of getting fired, stared at, or being wrong, but this clear potential outcome leads changemakers to take the courageous steps needed to create the change they want to see, regardless of the risk.

"I was ready to be fired. I knew that my head was on the chopping block," said MassMutual's first chief diversity officer Lorie Valle-Yañez as she told me about her leap in implementing an intense anti-racism program starting with the company's most senior leadership. "Courage is an important part of being successful in this space. It may go really badly, and if it does, it'll be because I misunderstood where they were. I thought, *If they're not ready now, they never will be. If I'm fired, I'll have been doing the best thing for the company."*

Doug Kofoid, CEO at DialogTech, remembered the critical moment he chose courage. As the leader of his company, he was debating whether to say anything about the George Floyd murder. During our interview, he told me that several peers advised him to avoid the topic: "It was uncomfortable. I felt afraid. And when I decided to make a statement to the company, it felt like courage. I got permission from my wife to get fired before doing anything. I'm not sure if I'm less afraid, but I'm definitely growing. And a few other CEOs took the email I used as inspiration for statements they made to their companies."

WHAT IS COURAGE?

Dr. Brené Brown, a professor, researcher, and author, often reminds us that the root of the word "courage" is *cor*: the Latin word for heart. Her interpretation of the original meaning of courage is "to speak one's mind by telling all of one's heart."[2] She takes the word and its meaning in the direction of vulnerability, but what's really significant is that telling all of one's heart requires self-awareness. Speaking one's truth to someone else requires being in touch with what's truly in our hearts. Courage is not the kind of big, heroic act we see in movies. We have this image of swashbuckling bravery that includes jumping off a cliff or in front of a bullet. These references are not only intimidating and unrealistic but also off base. Although it may feel like jumping in front of a bullet, facing our fears with an open heart often reveals what we really care most about.

FINDING CLARITY

Building courage starts with clarity. In order to communicate all of our heart, we have to know what's in there. In this very noisy, competitive, social media-fueled world of perfection, it's often hard to find the quiet to know what our own hearts really want. To find clarity, we have to discover what we care about in the world, what we're well-positioned to contribute to, and what kind of action plan is necessary to implement our ideas.

"You're not aware of values until it's time to test them in a decision with competing values," said Lee Kosmac, who recently pursued her passion for promoting diversity, effective corporate governance, and mentoring as the cofounder and CEO of Left Tackle Capital. Like Kosmac, once you've determined your values you'll gain the confidence to take action, even if it's not a well-trodden path or what your parents or society expects you to do. The change you want to be part of becomes clear, as do the steps required to get there. With clarity, you gain the confidence to make the necessary asks of yourself and the people around you.

Transformational change agent Klay S. Williams, who specializes in courageous conversations, shared with me, "If you're not clear on the intention behind your request, chances are you're unable to have the clarity needed to articulate your ask. Courage to unlock precision asking comes with clarity."

The *confidence* to act and ask comes from *clarity*, and that becomes *courage*. These are the three Cs of our ABCs of purpose, which we'll explore further in chapters 3 and 7.

What We're (Appropriately) Afraid Of

Are you ready to get over your fears and lead others in directly impacting the global community? We've all heard the lectures, read the articles, and watched the news. Now it's time to take action and lead our companies and employees in making ethical decisions regarding our carbon footprints, mental health, and inequalities across gender, race, religion, and other arbitrary identities.

In the early 2020s, people were quitting their jobs at higher rates than ever, so much so that the era was coined the "Great Resignation." One of the many drivers was a lack of understanding how their day-to-day work connected with a larger purpose. Extreme weather and multiple waves of COVID-19 had people rethinking how they were spending their time. In addition to being concerned with their own survival, they were wondering what impression they were having on larger issues and whether they were living their lives to the fullest.

Humans are social beings. We're driven by the need to belong to a group, even those that lead us toward decisions that aren't in our own best interest. Sometimes the purpose we are called to exposes a disconnect between our values and the work we're doing. "There's a fear factor in getting honest about what you care about and what work you want to be part of," said Andrew Glazier, CEO of Defy Ventures. "What if I'm not aligned with [my employer] and now it's out in the open. Where do I go?"

The risks of this purpose discovery are particularly scary for leaders, since their words carry disproportionate weight inside and outside of an organization; they leave a lasting influence on their employees, customers, suppliers, and shareholders. So identifying and aligning with their purpose can be especially terrifying if they're unsure whether their values line up exactly with all of those stakeholders. A few pages back, we heard CEO of Dialog Tech Doug Kofoid share his experience with choosing courage. Let's hear more about the situation in which Doug chose to Go First:

> It was scary to send an email to my whole company commenting on the George Floyd murder. My peer group of other CEOs advised me not to. I got permission from my wife to get fired. But I sent it, and several other CEOs from my peer group used it as inspiration for their own company-wide messages. And that felt good, so I'm glad I got over my fear. Getting over that one fear doesn't mean it's gone; I still felt nervous presenting to our women's ERG. So I

just showed up, explained why I had come, and then shut up and listened. And learned a lot, and walked away not scared.

As Chid Liberty, purpose-leader and many-time social entrepreneur and investor, put it during our interview, sometimes our fears lead to a "Not in my back yard" (NIMBY) sentiment in which we're all for justice until we realize it might change our personal reality. He shared the example of a White male executive who had supported the concept of a racially diverse board for their international import company but then tried to block the appointment of a new (Black) professional to his own role. He was expressing a "NIMBY of people and their power. In other words, 'I am all for distributing power to non-White male leaders, but don't reduce the power I hold and will continue to expand as a White man.'"

There's also the fear of creating unrealistic expectations from doing too much or moving too fast to integrate purpose into our teams. Nick Francis, CEO of Help Scout, put it this way: "It's scary to be at the bleeding edge, building a people-first, purpose-driven company. What is the optimal environment for today's workforce? I don't want our ethos to create unrealistic expectations!"

Courage and Vulnerability

Courage is not the absence of fear, but the willingness to act anyway. In *Atlas of the Heart*, Brené Brown emphasizes her idea that courage comes directly from the heart.[3] We lead best through our own vulnerability, and nothing exposes vulnerability quite like fear. Change will not happen until we gather the courage to face our fears and push through. Purpose-driven leaders can lead only from conviction and can create lasting change only by pushing through even when—especially when—they're afraid. We could ask Brené Brown, but I'm fairly sure she'd call the choice to push through our feelings of fear *vulnerability*.

Without the willingness to discuss and be vulnerable about our fears, how will we ever find the courage to overcome them? And if we don't, we leave a lot of potential impact on the table. "So many of us have the ingredients—the skills, talent, network, experience—to lead purposefully," said Gayle Jennings-O'Byrne, seasoned entrepreneur, purpose-driven investor, and founder and CEO of WOCStar. "But until that moment where we stop being afraid, we don't start being really bold and intentional about how we show up."

Your Path to Courage

As leaders and humans, we all have a different set of fears and different styles to overcoming them. Let's explore three concrete steps you can take to begin working with fear: honoring your own ways of being, talking about your fears, and taking action.

HONOR YOURSELF

In working with fear, it's good to acknowledge and honor your style of thinking and working. Here's a suggestion for how three types of thinkers can do that.

1. Analytical Thinkers:

   For the analytical or science-focused individual, neuroscience holds the answer. The chemicals released in our brains from fear are the same ones that are released from excitement. Scientists recommend that we relabel *fear* as *excitement* and use that energy to better our lives and the lives of the people around us.

   Do this: write down a word or draw an image of what *excitement* means to you and put it on your desk where you'll see it the next time fear threatens to influence your choices.

2. Empaths

If you're motivated more by the feelings of others and describe yourself as an empath, choose one person who would benefit from you overcoming this fear to take action. Only one person. It doesn't have to be someone you've even met before. Give that person a name and a story. Make them real in your mind and think about them in a very real way.

Do this: post a picture of this person, known or not, in a place where you'll see it in those moments of fear.

3. Activists

If you see yourself as a changemaker or an activist, write out your purpose statement.

Do this: Put your purpose statement on your desk, your mirror, your phone background—anywhere you'll see it every time fear creeps in. Then do the things that get you closer to living in line with that purpose statement, even when they feel scary.

TALK ABOUT YOUR FEARS

Whether you're analytical, empathetic, or an activist, it's important that you talk openly about your fears. Don't just share them with your innermost circles or trusted personal friends. Share them openly. Talking about your fears is like turning the light on and realizing the monster you thought was in the corner is just a pile of dirty laundry. It might be a little scary, like adding another to-do for tomorrow, but nothing like the blood-sucking monster you thought it was.

"I'm seeing more and more offline conversations about things we're scared of, which I think is a worrisome trend [because it means we're not talking about what matters in public]," shared Asha Curran, CEO of GivingTuesday and cofounder of the global generosity movement. She goes on to identify why: "As leaders, we are taught to distrust others. And in today's environment, we don't want to be taken in the wrong way. So much communication, especially social media, is so black or white, right or wrong that it can feel dangerous to share our honest thoughts."

Courageous conversations not only serve to reduce our fears to manageable, non-paralyzing size, but also provide a powerful form of learning with other purpose-driven leaders around us. MaryAnne Howland, CEO of Ibis Communications, has been working for decades helping leaders drive performance and avoid lawsuits related to diverse and inclusive communications. She started the Global Diversity Leadership Exchange because she sees having courageous conversations as the main way we can learn from one another: "The best advice I have for current or aspiring leaders who want to be part of catalyzing a more inclusive, anti-racist, and sustainable form of capitalism is to always be learning, and specifically be open to conversation, particularly across differences."

Having the courage to recognize and name your fears drives action both for yourself and for an upward spiral of benefit in the form of inspiration to those around you and learning for everyone involved. In order to lead the world into a healthier, fairer way of working and living, leaders have to make the first move. That's what being a leader is. It's about taking the first step and saying, "Yes, I'm afraid of the unknown as well, but I believe and trust that this is the way forward."

Leaving a worthwhile legacy requires vulnerability and courage in the face of fear. Tomorrow is unknown, and we need purpose-driven leaders like you to help make it a little bit better than today.

Reflection Questions

Remember, these are available as a download at www.inspiringcowgirl. com/goingfirst if you want to get the full benefit of thinking-by-writing.

And for even more fun—and growth—the Going First Purpose Party Playbook *is a deeper dive into the real work of finding this courage for purpose.*

- What are you most afraid of when it comes to Going First? What are your main fears or hesitations about taking on this mission?

- When have you taken courageous action in the past? What helped you get past your fears?

- When did you *not* take an action that would've required courage? What held you back? How do you feel about that choice in retrospect? Is there anything you would've done differently?

- How does your body feel when you're being courageous?

- Do you identify as an analytical thinker, empath, or activist? A blend? Does one of those labels fit better in certain circumstances than others? For example, does one fit better at work versus your personal life or as an employee versus a volunteer?

- According to your primary way of being, what initial action can you adopt to support your Going First choices? What similar or other approaches have you learned about or tried in the past that led you to courage?

Chapter 2

Your Invitation to Purpose

As we just learned, courage comes from the clarity of knowing who you are, what you care about, and how you can help realize that vision. That sounds like a description of purpose, doesn't it? Next, let's put our focus on purpose so you can see how that clarity helps you move beyond your fears into action that transforms your life, your company, and the world. You're here because you're attracted to living purposefully, and I'm guessing this isn't the first time you're realizing that. So we'll start by looking at what purpose means and what it doesn't and then finish this chapter by exploring three steps you can take today that will lead you to the path of purposeful living.

Calling purpose a party might seem like a stretch. It has become alternatively broad and meaningless or a niche-y millennial trend. But I say the term just needs a rebrand, so let's rediscover it.

Purpose is an ancient, even biblical, concept. For most of human history, the reason we did what we did was quite obvious: we contributed to our own and our communities' survival as farmers, parents, shoemakers, or explorers. Unfortunately, the Industrial Revolution divorced us from the purpose of our work, reducing us to cogs in the machinery of extractive capitalism. Technology and globalization meant that basic needs could be met at scale, at least for people who worked in industrialized economies.

Now, in the knowledge economy, or what has been called the "Fourth Industrial Revolution," most of us spend our days working to meet higher-order needs such as faster supply chains or better-performing materials. Given the complexity, abstraction, and exponential change of that work, it's difficult to recognize the influence of our individual contributions. And companies have failed to help us do so. This disconnection from the results of our work has led to stagnant productivity, unprecedented levels of lifestyle diseases that can be directly tied to overwork and burnout, disengagement from work, the highest levels of resignation in recorded history, and a dangerous lack of personal fulfillment. The early 2020s highlighted these problems. Now there is no debate whether we need to change how we work and live, particularly in relation to our jobs.

Reconnecting to purpose addresses the root causes of many of today's most threatening problems, including loneliness and a lack of personal happiness. But before we explore your purpose and how it can change your life, your business, and the world, let's look at what purpose is not.

What Purpose Is Not

Ever since the Industrial Revolution severed our connection to the positive results of our very own hands' work, "purpose" has fallen prey to many skepticisms, including the following:

- "It's a millennial trend."
- "What control could I possibly have toward the major problems I see in the world?"
- "I don't have time to think about my purpose; it's what I'll focus on when I retire."
- "It's just a shallow branding exercise."

- "The problems I care about are too complicated to understand how my contributions matter."
- "I like my life too much to start thinking about the impact it has."
- "I wrote a purpose statement once in a leadership program a few years ago."

Do any of these unhelpful associations live in your understanding of purpose? Allow me to share with you why I don't believe any of them are valid.

PURPOSE IS NOT OVERWHELMING

When you go to a party, you don't have to be the lead dancer, bartender, or wallflower; you only have to play your role. Similarly, your purpose doesn't have to address all the world's problems or even its biggest ones.

Indeed, purpose-driven leaders are clear about which problems they care about solving and what specific solutions they are able to contribute to. During a moment of overwhelm at the scale and complexity of the problems facing his employees and customers, Shawn Riegsecker, founder and CEO of Basis, realized that "Successful people spend their time in a circle of influence, not their circle of concern."

You don't need to work on every issue you're concerned about; you can successfully work on only the issues that are within your influence. Since nearly eight billion people have been invited to this Purpose Party, each of us is free to get exactly that specific about our contributions. As soon as we each understand how to address the $\frac{1}{8}$,000,000,000th (one eight-billionth!) of the world problems that fit into our circle of influence and start taking action, we're on our way to a better world!

PURPOSE IS NOT COMPLICATED

What if we defined purpose as "a reason to get up in the morning"? Actually, the Japanese word for purpose, *ikigai*, translates best to exactly that phrase. And they're not the only ones to have thought about our so-called modern trend of living with purpose. A wide array of thinkers, organizations, and philosophies define purpose as the intersection of our unique strengths and interests with the needs of the world around us. In other words, like a party, purpose is a simple, age-old concept. Purpose is not a modern trend, and it doesn't have to be complicated.

In his 2009 TED talk, which has been viewed 50 million times, Simon Sinek referred to purpose as your *why*. His work has inspired countless people to create a purpose statement using the formula, "TO ____ SO THAT ____."[4] In other words, "What you do so you contribute to some better future."

Particularly in times of fear, loss, and great uncertainty, the mundane framing of purpose as "a reason to get up" can be useful. It's natural to feel inclined to hunker down, focus on survival, and wait for it all to be over before getting back to existential questions or long-term thinking. But what we really need to get through tough times is a reason to persist. If you're not sure that's true, read Viktor Frankl's *Man's Search for Meaning*, which is about how he and fellow concentration camp prisoners were able to survive unthinkable suffering because they had a larger reason to persist, whether it was a music collection, family member, or seed collection to preserve.

In this human framing of purpose, you don't need an expensive coach or marketing consultant to find yours. It's just a matter of understanding the activities, people, and outcomes that inspire you to get up every morning. Further, using this simplified definition, it's not hard to see why purpose is good for team performance as well. Of course employees with purpose are more effective; they get up in the morning to come do their jobs!

YOUR PURPOSE DOES NOT REQUIRE SUFFERING

Living purposefully doesn't require a life of deprivation or suffering. On the contrary, identifying and pursuing your purpose is the way to true, deep satisfaction. Research shows it also extends your life expectancy by seven years, among other significant physical and mental health benefits.[5]

If you've ever hosted a party, you've likely experienced the tension between working to make sure your guests have a good time and enjoying the party yourself. Similarly, purposeful leaders must balance their commitment to the outcome they want to make—which could always be more—and protect their own wellbeing. Ultimately, the most impactful people are those who learn to balance their own needs (physical, intellectual, financial, emotional, and spiritual) with their work so that they can perform to their highest capacity for the longest time.

During our interview, Asha Curran gave credit for her deep sense of purpose to her "deeply unconventional parentage."

> My mother was a poor, single woman in New York City in the '70s, living through homelessness and poverty. She had great courage, living in line with her own integrity, not what made it easier to fit in. I saw how many of her decisions made it harder for her—having me out of wedlock, giving up financial security—but were best aligned with her values. I was inspired by her, but also very conscious that I don't want to be a martyr to my values. My upbringing has made me feel very strongly that people shouldn't suffer in terms of their salary or quality of life to work in the social sector or otherwise pursue their purpose.

While there are often trade-offs in the journey to living purposefully, which we'll discuss in detail later on, experience and research show unanimously that it's the only path to true and deep fulfillment.

YOUR PURPOSE IS NO ONE ELSE'S

Going First doesn't mean you can't learn from others, be coached, or follow a mentor or role model. You can. We must! But remember the nearly eight billion purpose statements that are floating around globally. To activate your own purpose, you cannot follow the choices and behaviors of others; you must identify a purpose that fits your unique blend of skills, needs, and passions. Your purpose is yours and no one else's, and *you* have never existed before.

Biotech entrepreneur Nina Tandon pointed out to me that "No one's actually the 'first'; we live in a community of several billion people. And yet every moment is new. The dots that can be connected at a given space-time moment are always new." This is an important qualification of "first": your purpose may have echoes of things others have done or aspired to do, but it's showing up uniquely in this time and space as *you*.

YOUR PURPOSE IS NOT A ONE-AND-DONE

As you evolve, your purpose will too. Finding your purpose is not a one-time exercise that you accomplish upon graduating college or changing jobs. A lot of the underlying themes, values, and areas of interest may persist throughout life, but the way we understand the problems we care about solving, and the ways we choose to contribute, will evolve significantly. Thus the importance of developing a practice of leading and living purposefully, using tools such as the Impact Dashboard I share later in this book.

Purpose Done Right

Now that we know what purpose isn't, let's take a look at what it *is* so that we can recognize it when we feel it or see it in others. Once you know what to look for, you may find it more frequently than you think.

ACTION BEATS OVERWHELM

Your purpose doesn't have to address all problems, remember? Starting somewhere with a small but concrete action that gives you some sense of fulfillment is the way to go. You don't need to go through a six-month, six-figure process run by a branding department or certified coach to figure out what to start with. If you're early in your purpose journey, look for the micro satisfactions of someone smiling at something you did or sighing with relief because of you. Or perhaps you simply recognize an internal sense of pride. Any of those are enough of an indicator to start with.

The specific actions that serve purpose often aren't particularly dramatic or magical. Purpose is found in making meaning of those actions and the results they have. So fret less about what you're going to do to help your direct report find balance, reduce the carbon in your supply chain, or help your son navigate middle school, and just do something that feels right. Then examine the impact you see it have and consider how to ladder that up to your desired change (see figure 1).

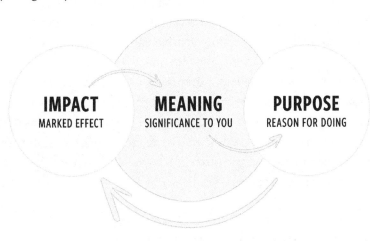

IMPACT
MARKED EFFECT

MEANING
SIGNIFICANCE TO YOU

PURPOSE
REASON FOR DOING

Figure 1. The cycle of leading and living purposefully.

We do things all day long that have impact. In fact, *everything* we do has impact; it just may not be our desired impact if we're not purposeful about what we do! So leading and living with purpose may not be about doing things totally differently so much as noticing their effect and understanding the larger implications for the people and planet around us.

I don't mean to undervalue the complexity or action required to solve many important problems. I just don't find it productive to get buried by the magnitude of it.

Start somewhere. Then notice what you do that has consequences you find meaningful. Better yet, track them. Patterns will emerge that start to look and feel like a reason for getting up. You'll start seeing even more ways to elicit those smiles and sighs of relief. How's that for a simple, action-oriented approach to purposeful living?

IT'S ONLY HUMAN

The phrase "a reason to get up in the morning" makes it easy to see that this approach to purposeful living is not a trend or a matter of taste. Purpose is a universal human drive. All of us, regardless of race, geography, age, generation, or profession, are neurologically wired to contribute something larger than our own survival. We all need a reason to get up in the morning, and when we're in touch with our best selves, we have one. This humanness of purpose also means that it's accessible to all. It isn't reserved for people of a certain stature or wealth. Purpose can be, and often is, felt even more vividly by those with less financial wealth and/or pressure.

HEALING WITHOUT GETTING SICK

Asha is in good company in her commitment to not being a martyr in order to live purposefully. I share that sentiment, and I hope you will too after reading this book, if you don't already. But I'm not here to protect you from the effort of leading and living purposefully—or the discomfort it might provoke along the way. On the contrary. I've told you transparently that this takes effort. If you don't feel uncomfortable at certain points, you're not having optimal impact.

The power of purpose comes from looking beyond our immediate needs and desires to the greater good. We get fulfillment from contributing to others' well-being. Understanding what will improve their well-being means closely examining their suffering, but it does not require *us* to suffer. Many families have been through a very practical version of this. When one parent got sick with COVID-19, they self-quarantined to avoid infecting the entire household. The other partner would do everything possible to care for them without getting sick themselves, which would've endangered the well-being of the other household members.

Purposeful leaders do come face-to-face with injustice, violence, poverty, environmental degradation, and plenty of other versions of suffering. But in order to persevere in the work of reducing that suffering, we have to find ways to buffer ourselves from getting "sick" from that exposure. Learning to heal the problems we care about without getting sick is what enables all the benefits of purposeful living that I'll share in chapter 4.

FOR YOU, BY YOU

Remember that your purpose is one of the nearly eight billion valid and inspiring purpose statements up for grabs. And only one. If we each find, refine, and live out our own purpose, everything gets done. That's the beautiful thing about the diversity of this planet—if we make the conditions to cultivate and engage with it, that is. Just like the actions that make up your purposeful leadership, the process to refine that approach is your own. No one can identify your unique purpose for you. You might seek guidance, examples, or inspiration from others—such as the leaders in this book—but the decision to dedicate the time, energy, and attention to living on purpose is yours alone.

Alexa Teare is a deeply purpose-aligned person and professional (more from her on that alignment in chapter 4), as is appropriate for her role as chief people and coaching officer at Lingo Live. During our interview, she explained the launch of her purpose journey: "It was really me stepping into my own power and voice. That came from the work that I was doing internally, the work that I was doing to understand myself and grow. It was nothing external."

A WORK IN PROGRESS

Both the decision to lead and live purposefully and the realization of that commitment are lifelong journeys. From everything I've heard and seen, it never becomes effortless, particularly given some of the pitfalls we'll explore in part 2 of this book. That can be good news or bad news, depending on how you take it. I choose to see it as a comforting lifelong pursuit that reduces the pressure. I don't have to get it right if I'm still going to be working on it next year, no matter how "right" or "wrong" I get it now.

In other words, as you'll hear me remind you many times throughout this book, *perfect is the enemy of good*. But it can be good to have some notion of your purpose to inform the actions you're going to take. I hope this pragmatic, action-oriented, and human description of purpose will help you plunge in and draft a purpose statement. I know I said that purpose discovery is not the focus of this book. And it's not. But having a loose, nonbinding draft is a helpful premise for what *is* our focus: integrating purpose into all we do. And if you follow along through the next section, you'll have done just that before the end of this chapter!

A Down and Dirty Purpose Statement

You could throw a party without telling people why. They'd appreciate the reason to dress up, enjoy some great food and drink, and laugh with new or old friends. Similarly, you could proceed through this book without a purpose statement. But isn't it a bit easier to get excited for a party when you know why it's happening?

Exactly. So here are three simple steps to painlessly drafting a purpose statement—just as a backdrop for what's next, not as a binding statement about your next 40 years.

1. Think about all the problems that are affecting the people you care about. What news stories make your heart beat faster? What frustrates or angers you most? What innovations or solutions inspire you? (Remember that you can look at these issues up close without suffering directly.) Based on this quick brainstorm, pick one problem or perhaps an overarching one that includes a few you thought of. What exactly is the change you want to contribute to that will address some element of that problem?

2. Think about who (or what) you aim to serve by solving the problem you identified. Please remove judgment at this stage. If you picture serving colleagues on your team, your family members, or your neighborhood, those are the right audiences for this version of your purpose statement. Remember that your actions don't have to be dramatic or lifesaving to be worthy pursuits. Indeed, it's often most realistic—and thus impactful—to focus your efforts on those close to you, within your circle of influence.

3. Think about how you're going to contribute to driving this change for these people. Again, I recognize that there are entire books and development programs dedicated to identifying your strengths. This is a shorthand version. What is it you do when you're at your best?

And just like that, you've got the components for a purpose statement that follows this formula:

> I want to change [what you want to see]
>
> for [who you want to serve]
>
> by [the unique way you can contribute].

These words won't be etched on your tombstone or published on your LinkedIn headline, so avoid analysis paralysis and give yourself room to play. Live with this draft for a few weeks at least. Read it out loud to see if it feels authentic. Can you connect it to your daily agenda? If not, is that because the statement isn't right or because your daily agenda needs to change?

If you're on a roll and want a next step, ask others about their purpose. Once you've drafted your own purpose statement, it becomes easier to ask friends, family, social media, and coworkers about the problems they care about, the people they're here to serve, and the ways they want to contribute. I promise you'll end up in some fascinating conversations that will lead to deeper relationships.

According to Marc Spencer, CEO of Summer Search, it's never too early to ask for someone's purpose statement: "We can't underestimate the importance of being asked what our purpose is. It should happen at elementary school, through higher education, and in the workplace. And then, as leaders, we have to hold space for the reflection that people need to zero in on their purpose over time."

I hope you've refined your own definition of purpose as you've worked through this chapter. Next up, we'll take a look at the qualities to bring to this purpose potluck and how to be yourself all the way through.

Reflection Questions

These are really foundational! I highly encourage you to download this worksheet at www.inspiringcowgirl.com/goingfirst for the full benefit of actually writing down your thoughts about purpose. And of course, don't forget the Going First Purpose Party Playbook for a deeper dive companion.

- What's your current feeling or thinking about purpose?

- What's the reason you are most eager to get up in the morning, or at least, what was it today?

- In this chapter, I wrote, "We get fulfillment from contributing to others' well-being. Understanding what would improve their well-being means closely examining their suffering, but it does not require *us* to suffer." What's your response to this thought?

Chapter 3

What to Bring to the Party

If this notion of purpose as a party seems like it might be what you need to reboot your own work or your team's, you're invited! And by "you," I mean your whole, best, dynamic self. In this chapter, we consider the traits you need to bring with you on your path of purposeful living, including your authenticity, self-acceptance, self-awareness, willingness to change, tenacity, and purpose. We'll also consider the one practice that is universal among purposeful people.

Authenticity

It's easy to look around and think there's a certain way of looking, thinking, or behaving that makes a good leader. But actually, the complexity of the problems we're facing means that they'll only be solved if every single one of us contributes in our unique ways to our respective work and lives.

Recall that being purposeful does not require us to solve all the world's problems, only the one eight-billionth that fit our skills, interests, and realms of influence. Delivering on that fair share requires great specificity! We must lean deeply into our unique profiles and get clear about what we want to do and where, when, and with whom we want to do it. If we all come to the Purpose Party clear on our best way to contribute and ready to collaborate with others who have complementary pieces of the solution, our Purpose Party will have the greatest impact possible.

Jeff Le, a public policy expert who speaks out against hate crimes from his own experience as an Asian American, put it this way during our interview: "People need to be empowered to embrace who they are. You start with yourself and then move into a bigger circle. Actions have chain reactions."

SELF-ACCEPTANCE: THE POWER OF DIFFERENCE

Purposeful leaders find ways to make their unique profiles create positive outcomes even when people or systems around them don't see that uniqueness as a strength. Ward Vuillemot, people-centric technologist and CPrO/CTO of Real Self, has been on a long journey of self-discovery after prestigious but frustrating and unhealthy roles earlier in his career. After years of mistakes, reflection, experimentation, and an adult autism diagnosis, he finds that "It's actually freeing to be wholly myself, including my insecurity, the autism, and everything, really."

Tanya Perkins, a startup COO and venture capital investor, recalls trying to find her way in finance at the beginning of her career.

> Trying to emulate the people around me came off as inauthentic, first of all. Secondly, even if I could do a particular task to the 99th percentile of excellence, people didn't assess my work in the 99th percentile. Because that was not what made me unique. Trying to play the part also took a huge emotional toll on me. My leadership evolved when I started to lean into my own style, bringing my unique perspectives. And colleagues responded well. That was an aha moment for me, realizing when we're true to ourselves, we are often more successful.

Nuno Guerreiro is a chief diversity and impact officer in training who grew up in Portugal and has worked in New York, San Francisco, São Paulo, and Dublin. Like Tanya, he found the strength of his uniqueness, which might be commonly seen as a challenge to overcome: English is not his first—or even second—language.

> It's funny being in leadership roles for American companies when English is not my native language. Often, where I add tons of value is translating what different parties want, need, and are scared of. It's not that I'm a perfect English speaker: I have an accent, and my grammar is not perfect. But it's exactly because I'm not a native speaker that I have gotten really good at really trying to understand what people are trying to achieve. I can hear fears and frustrations and goals, even if they're not explicitly stated. Having that diverse state of mind allows me to bridge what might seem like conflicting perspectives or even challenge more traditional thoughts on either side of the conversation.

Put another way, Sylvana Sinha, founder and CEO of Praava Health, realized that when she resigned from positions before she founded Praava, "They found other people to do my jobs pretty quickly." She's clear that now she's in the right spot: "I am uniquely positioned to build Praava as a Bangladeshi woman who has had an international upbringing and education. My ability to bridge the global and local is why Praava is innovating at the front edge of healthcare."

Taking the time to identify and refine exactly the ways we can contribute most powerfully will optimize the influence we have on the people and planet around us. It will also make us more essential and harder to fire!

YOUR RIPPLE EFFECT

The power of embracing your unique profile doesn't stop with benefit to your own performance and comfort in the workplace. It ripples immediately and powerfully out to those around you, setting an example for them to embrace their own uniqueness. Of course, this in turn benefits your team, unlocking the most unique strengths possible to achieve your goals.

For example, Ward's teams benefited from his efforts toward self-acceptance and the approach to leadership that resulted. Scott Burkhalter, who worked with Ward for several years, recounted his experience with Ward as a leader: "Ward would use the word *love* in group chats, team chats, and even global chats. That heart emoji confused me for a while, as I had never encountered that supportive, celebrating, non-conflict culture in an engineering team. Working with Ward changed my unconscious daily anxiety level and allowed me to grow, learn, rock, and then lead and continue growing with confidence and pride."

Much as Ward hoped would be the case, Scott no longer works with Ward. He has a new role as head of engineering for Bansho, an e-Learning platform, where he uses his own version of the purposeful leadership that Ward modeled. Ward's willingness to first learn his own unique way of working and then lead in a way that fit him best was not only freeing for him but also powerful for the people he was leading. Ultimately, that's creating a diaspora of purposeful leaders who have that same effect on the people they are now leading.

How to Show Up for the Purpose Party

Wear whatever you want to the Purpose Party—ideally, that outfit that makes you feel most uniquely you. And comfortable shoes.

But there are some important things that everyone needs for a Purpose Party. Think of it as a sort of potluck. In this section, we'll cover four things to bring: self-awareness, willingness to change, tenacity, and of course, your (ever-evolving) purpose as you understand it today.

SELF-AWARENESS

The foundational requirement for Purpose Party guests is self-awareness. To work or live purposefully, you must be committed to and already in the process of getting to know yourself.

Ward Vuillemot pointed out that "Self-awareness is the path to self-actualization, by helping us understand what actions to take." What are the mental and physical routines, key skills, working styles, frustrations, and skill gaps that are necessary to do *your* best work?

It can be helpful to look back to your childhood. Often the activities or topics that most enlivened us as kids persist in some way throughout our lives. That's certainly the case for Kari Warberg Block, CEO and founder of EarthKind. She shared, "I knew my purpose when I was five. I wanted to know where 'away' was when you throw things away."

If you look carefully, you may see at least hints of your approach to purpose early in life, if not quite that early. Doug Kofoid, CEO of DialogTech, found an approach for discernment as an undergraduate and carried it forward. When deciding which extracurricular activities to join, "I used to ask myself, *Why would that club be better because I was a member?*"

Our childhood experiences shape the ways we contribute and the issues we care most about. As I shared earlier, I was 12 years old when I learned that while talent is distributed equally throughout the human population, opportunity is not. I knew at that moment that my life's work would somehow contribute to a solution to this massive, complex problem. It has taken decades of study, experience, frustration, learning, and work with mentors to refine my purpose. I'm still learning my best ways to contribute; I have to be, since they change as my experience grows and my needs evolve. But that early experience provided a durable foundation and clarifying focus for my pursuit of purpose.

Kirsten Dunlop, CEO of KIC Climate, Europe's leading climate innovation initiative, shared her experience: "Moving countries every six months as the child of expats gave me privileged access to seeing things. I developed an avid curiosity for relationships between things. As a result, I fought my university to take an interdisciplinary approach to my post-graduate studies. I thought across disciplines and trained myself to connect ideas from divergent fields. This element of my upbringing informs my approach to climate innovation."

Similarly, Ron Gonen, CEO of Closed Loop Partners, recalls growing up among "lots of different people and situations. It helped me evaluate what's important: I saw poor people with great integrity and rich kids who were sad and lonely, and everything in between."

Being willing to explore and accept your unique makeup is a prerequisite for identifying and activating your purpose, but it's not something we're widely taught or supported to do.

WILLINGNESS TO CHANGE

Once you're clear about and comfortable with self-awareness as part of the purpose journey, make sure you're ready to engage with new ideas and people. Purposeful living is not yet the norm, but that doesn't mean it's not natural. It just requires an approach that's open to change.

For most of us, reawakening our natural connection to purpose requires doing new things, meeting new people, or engaging with the same people in new ways. You may know how you react to new people or ideas already. If it's not obvious, think about your approach at (non-purpose) parties. Do you run to the middle of the dance floor seeking out new friends, or do you find an old friend and stay by their side all night?

When you start becoming more self-aware, you'll likely have to change some habits, resist tradition, question assumptions, and relearn a lot. Those activities lead to a deeply rewarding and flowing existence, but they require great effort and patience. The wise poet Rumi wrote, "Yesterday I was clever, so I wanted to change the world. Today I am wise, so I am changing myself."[6] That quote was manifested in my interview with Scott Shute, who had spent more than two decades as a customer-facing executive in the tech world when he decided to bring his meditation practice to work. He led weekly sessions for his colleagues at LinkedIn for years, attracting a few participants initially and eventually reaching hundreds. That level of interest led to an official new role as the head of mindfulness and compassion programs at LinkedIn and then his bestselling book *Full Body Yes*. Scott's purpose is to change work from the inside out. He explained, "I believe the most important thing we can do as humans is work on our own development. If we focus on our own development, then everything else gets better. We become better at relationships, better at leading, more aware of our customers, of our employees as leaders. We're a way better version of ourselves."

Rachel Gutter Hogdon has always known that we "have to be willing to wander and find our unique path—even when it terrifies our parents. We maintain that special sauce as we grow, which is why I am doubling down on my self-reflection and work with coaches so I can evolve and model that evolution to my team." Rachel's willingness to explore and evolve has revealed her purpose, which is to help resolve one of the world's many sufferings at a global scale. Steve Jobs's mandate to "Put a dent in the universe"[7] resonates with Rachel, but she isn't attached to a single issue like climate change or racial equity. For now, as CEO of the International WELL Building Institute, she's focused on making physical spaces that drive health and equity.

You may also find that your purpose is more or less issue-specific and may have more to do with how you contribute rather than exactly what problem you help solve. Like Scott and Rachel, leaders can set a powerful example of this willingness to change for their people.

Shawn Riegsecker demonstrates the power of modeling and also of concretely supporting his team's evolution. He's been recognized many times over for his approach to company culture. These accolades are based on his understanding that we need to change to collaborate effectively: "Without intentional effort, we haven't evolved enough to do the work of working together in a healthy way, which requires that we have conflict, be candid, transparent, and vulnerable." Shawn's appreciation for the complexity and challenge of human interaction informs the talent strategy at Basis. "We invest a lot in training and have always had continuing education budgets for our employees," he explains. This tangible support of their employees' growth led to Crain naming Basis the #1 Place to Work in Chicago for three years in a row.

Of course, organizations never change effectively or efficiently if their people, from top to bottom, aren't willing and supported to change first. So channel your favorite Hypercolor shirt or mood ring and give a thought to when and how you navigate change best.

Now that you know something you'd like to change and some reasons you might struggle to do so, try linking the change to your purpose by crafting a motivating statement like this one:

> I want to be/do more [desired change]
>
> so that [desired outcome for the world].

Might that reminder help you overcome the obstacles you foresee?

TENACITY

Working with purpose is a marathon, not a sprint. Specifically, it's a journey that lasts until the day you leave your physical body and move on to whatever is next. Jimmy Etheredge, CEO of Accenture North America, described the nature of transformation to purposeful leadership simply: "We're sprinting a marathon." And that's not a sustainable approach. So manage your energy. Learn what drains you and what replenishes you. Working and living in alignment with purpose is the most frictionless, and therefore most efficient, way to live. But getting there, particularly in a world that's not yet set up to support the journey, has its demands.

Kristin Hull, founder, CEO, and CIO of NIA Impact Capital, has been Going First for a long time in the slow-to-change world of investing. She told me, "Following our inner guide is important. And it's hard when we're swimming upstream. I didn't mean to be as far ahead of the mainstream as I find myself, and it can be lonely. But it's worth it to me because I want to make sure the road is paved with beautiful bamboo stepstones!"

Purpose is a powerful motivator and contributes to the tenacity it requires, as Kristin explained. But having a purpose hidden in your journal or annual plan is not enough. Katie Hunt-Morr has worked for famously purposeful organizations such as Etsy and Virgin Unite and most recently as managing director of the NationSwell Council. In her words, "Be brave, have a vision, and beat that [purpose] drum all the time. Be so strong in your conviction that other people will eventually buy into it or get tired of arguing about it!"

PURPOSE

The final thing you need to bring to the Purpose Party is, of course, your purpose: the contribution you want to make to the greater good of the people and planet around you.

"But I don't know what my purpose is yet. I'm still discovering it. I have a draft, but I'm not ready to say it out loud or commit to myself." I know. I've heard these and millions of other reasons why you're not ready, which is perhaps why I'm such a fan of the mantra, "Perfect is the enemy of good."

Purpose doesn't have to be that complex, remember? It's just that reason you get out of bed, and it's rooted in action. It's the things that have always brought you energy and that you still find great joy in doing. It's that simple.

That said, I know that purpose pressure is real. So over the last 10 years of working with thousands of professionals, I created a simple, universal framework for the areas in our work and lives that makes purpose very concrete and actionable. And you're going to get your hands on it very shortly in part 2. But for now, I want to illustrate the point that purpose can be simple and mundane and still be powerfully motivating.

Consider a friend we'll call Jeff. Jeff's wife, kids, and doctor were desperate to get him to the gym, or at least on daily walks, after years of inactivity following knee surgery. He understood the science, heard his family's and doctor's pleas, and admitted that he felt better when he was more active. Still, he couldn't get back into an exercise routine . . . .

Until the day his wife hosted his daughter's baby shower. The décor, games, and baby paraphernalia strewn around their living room were a visceral reminder of how much he wanted to be a part of this new life for as much quality and quantity time as possible! Jeff finally felt a reason to do what he knew he should. Exercise was now connected to a larger purpose. His daily 45-minute walks started the next day, and now they often include the upper-body challenge of a stroller.

Your Purpose as You Understand It Today

It took Jeff over six decades to have the experience that clarified his why, at least when it came to staying in shape. These purpose-revealing moments happen in different ways at different times in our lives. Our purpose usually retains a core of the things we're good at and care about, but it evolves with the different stages of our lives and careers.

Vanessa Barboni Hallik crossed the US and then the Atlantic to complete her undergraduate studies. She was a finance professional for over a decade before she left to be a human rights lawyer. But then she became fascinated by the complexity and (negative) ramifications of the fashion industry. After five university enrollments and two and a half careers, she founded Another Tomorrow, a certified B Corp providing modern sustainable luxury while also building community and being an activist in the industry. Vanessa explains her purpose journey in this way: "I have tons of interests, so it's easy to have 'shiny-object syndrome.' I tortured myself for years trying to identify what unique approach I bring to the table. How can I meet the needs of the time, and how can I be of most service? I have landed in a place where I feel deeply aligned with my purpose to realign human behavior with nature and dignity by staying flexible. The needs of the time change. We're in a very dynamic world."

Lee Kosmac, an elementary school teacher turned investor, had a similar journey to and through her purpose: "I've been opportunistic in how I pursue my purpose. Because of my deep curiosity and empathy, I have a lot of conversations and ask a lot of questions, and opportunities for impact just appear. Then it's up to me to decide whether I want to move forward or not with each one."

It's also important to acknowledge that there are more problems in the world than we can solve ourselves. We might support others in addressing some issues, but we have to get specific about how to direct our own best contribution. And this choice is essentially one of preference; there's no right or wrong.

Stuart Landesberg has experienced how that preference can change. He started his career investing in consumer product goods companies, and he deeply valued what he learned from that work. But then his preferences changed after he saw the environmental costs of the industry he was supporting. So he founded Grove Collaborative in line with his belief that "It is urgent that we use business to solve environmental problems." He recognizes that there are other important challenges in this world: "Eliminating plastic in consumer-packaged goods is certainly not the only problem we're facing. But it's the one I feel most personally drawn to."

Defining a purpose beyond our own well-being or performance is motivating in a sustainable way. As we'll see in the next chapter, it's good for our physical and mental health as well as our performance and the teams to which we contribute. But these benefits do not require our purpose to be to save every whale, eliminate systemic racism, or address all the problems we care about. Our responsibility in being purposeful is just to identify the way we are each uniquely positioned to serve someone or something greater than ourselves, and then take action to do it.

The ABCs of Purposeful Leadership

To be a successful leader in the 21st century, whether that's as an individual contributor, CEO, or something in between, you've got to evolve your leadership. And you've got to start today.

You don't have to finish the work tomorrow, or anytime soon, for that matter. Being the kind of purposeful leader who will succeed in the 21st century is an ongoing journey—lifelong, actually. All you have to do is begin. Start with something small, simple, and local, and then repeat it every day.

I don't think that any of us are where we want to be in terms of our empathy, our ability to stay present amid chaos, or our ability to be unbiased and anti-racist. I certainly am not. But if you set the intent, ask smart questions, take small, repeated actions, and set up honest checks on your impact along the way, you're doing the best you can. And that's all we can possibly ask of ourselves or anyone else.

Over 20 years of studying purposeful leadership and helping leaders incorporate it, I've observed five steps of this ongoing journey. It's helpful to know these steps so you can understand where you are and what comes next. They are the "ABCs of Purposeful Leadership."

Mauricio Gutierrez, CEO of NRG, the leading integrated power company in the US, lived the process as CEO in his work to make NRG Energy a more diverse and inclusive company. He values awareness—the A in the ABCs—as "an open line of communication, not just with employees but [with] all the other stakeholders. We all have to recognize that having a more diverse workforce is good for all of us. We also all have to own that there are things ingrained in our brain—beliefs that need to change to create that more diverse workforce." Mauricio continued on to describe the B, C, D, and E of our process: "Then we can worry about getting the numbers and reporting [to get clarity], and ultimately continue our journey, which is not just education [building confidence and courage], but also learning what we can do differently [dive in and evolve]."

A IS FOR AWARENESS

Purposeful leadership starts with awareness. Be aware that it *is* possible to lead in a way that is empathetic and still effective. You can be powerful and still be humane to the people around you. This approach to leadership results in increased team performance, innovation, and loyalty.

B IS FOR BELIEF

This step is simply a decision—a decision only you can make for yourself—to believe in the power of leading and living purposefully.

All the research is there, the anecdotes are many, and the evidence of people who lead in a human way and succeed is ample. But you have to believe—not just think, but truly believe—that leading purposefully with a human-first perspective will lead you and your team to sustainable success.

C IS FOR CLARITY, CONFIDENCE, AND COURAGE

Being purposeful means having clarity about who you want to be; what you can best add to the challenges that you, your team, and your company are facing; and what your priorities are among those challenges. Working on your own and with your team to get that clarity is what gives you the confidence to act, even amid ongoing and significant uncertainty.

There are at least 134 things you could be doing with any given moment of your day. The same goes for all the people you work with. But when you have clarity about why you do what you do, what value you're trying to add, and the priority of the challenges you need to overcome, you have the courage to act. Success requires change, so start getting clear on how you want to change yourself, your team, and the world around you.

D IS FOR DIVE IN

The next step is to dive in—get started and do something. Impact comes from action. And while it's important to be thoughtful about all the stakeholders affected by any given decision, it's also important not to get stuck in analysis paralysis. In a moment as urgent as today in terms of the business risks we're facing, as well as the larger existential threats to our environment and communities, we each have a responsibility to move forward and act.

Often, diving in is a simple matter of having a conversation, even if it feels like a difficult one. Anna Goranson, head of people at fast-growing logistics expert Airspace, advised her team, "Have the conversation even if you don't have the answer!" In fact, "It's often better not to have the answer; you'll listen to [your colleague], not for [what you're expecting to hear]."

Britney Pierini, head of people experience at the powerful SaaS automation tool Torii, echoed Britney's notion: "You just start talking about whatever's the challenge of the day! And then you'll get a sense of what's really going on. People will talk about it if you do! But no one will talk if you don't Go First."

E IS FOR EVOLVE AND EVALUATE

Leading with purpose requires evolution and evaluation. You need to have honest checks and balances by gathering qualitative and quantitative information about the effects of your actions so you can assess whether they're creating the change you want to be part of. Then, in the spirit of continuous improvement, you can make smart adjustments to what you're doing or how you're doing it. You're never done, as Gayle Jennings-O'Byrne revealed: "I've grown into my purpose. I'm practicing, and I know that I'm coming into my voice still."

Although all the information and knowledge we need to lead purposefully exists, it hasn't yet penetrated our training, cultures, and practices of leadership. Mark Atkinson, a deeply purpose-driven tech entrepreneur who built Mursion, an AI-powered tool for leadership development, believes in his company's manager-development resources for that reason: "Technology has commoditized learning, but the world is not populated with autodidacts. We have to practice to really change!"

What's more, we learn more about the influence we want to have over time. Elissa Sangster is CEO of Forte Foundation, which is doing important work to equal the playing field for all genders in the work-force. She told me, "Purpose shifts. In fact, it's constantly evolving. In our situation, we can't do the same thing next year as an organization or as individual leaders. The context is changing too fast around us."

Once you know you're on the right track (at least in the current context), you can evaluate what you're doing to ensure you're covering more areas of your work or including more people on your team. Alexa Teare, chief people and coaching officer at Lingo Live, is deeply conscientious that "What got us here won't get us there. I think that in our space [of purposeful leadership], the risk is always hubris."

Once you've evolved and evaluated some aspect of your leadership, you circle back to the beginning of the process. You and the people around you become more aware and believe more strongly in the power of purposeful leadership. This return to A and B expands the foundation from which you can get clear about what's required to approach the next challenge or deepen this one, and so forth through the five steps.

But today, all you need to do is start somewhere.

And here's a hint: that first step might be just having compassion for yourself. If you're a little bit behind on something or not performing the way you'd like to, perhaps you can give yourself a pep talk, reassure yourself that it's going to be okay, and tell yourself that maybe the best next thing to do is rest and come back to that deadline next week.

Cutting Down the Noise

Self-awareness, willingness to change, tenacity, and purpose are four elements of your ticket to the Purpose Party and are relatively straightforward. This is probably not the first time someone has suggested that you "know thyself" or "remember your why."

But straightforward doesn't mean easy. It's not easy to get clear about who we really are amid the noise of modern life. With the algorithms giving us so much reinforcement that our current thinking is right, it's not easy to be open to changing our ideas or behavior. In a world where our reality seems to change on an hourly basis, it's not easy to persevere. And the world presents lots of whys—a bigger bank account, fancier title, better body, or younger skin—few of which link to the betterment of people and the planet.

All that noise can be deafening. So developing some sort of mindfulness practice to access this level of reflection is actually step zero of living purposefully. (And don't worry if you're not a meditator! There are other options.)

THE NEUROSCIENCE OF MINDFULNESS

The ancient practice of mindfulness meditation has been put under the modern microscope in the last few decades, revealing valuable insights about how it improves our physical and mental health as well as our cognitive performance.[8] This is relevant to the topic of purpose because our education system, media, and workplaces do not support the self-awareness required to identify, much less practice, our unique way of contributing. Indeed, these external forces have very clear ideas—informed by a specific, extractive form of capitalism—about what we should be doing with our time, talents, and treasures.

I haven't met a single leader who self-identifies as purposeful (or whose team recognizes them as such) who doesn't have some regular mindfulness practice. Longtime social entrepreneur and purposeful leader Marc Spencer, CEO of the life-changing nonprofit Summer Search, put it this way: "To demonstrate your moral and ethical self requires vulnerability and attention to the discovery and presentation of your authentic self. As a purposeful leader, I know I am constantly challenged to bring that forward and amplify it. To meet that challenge, it's important that I spend time in self-reflection, thinking about who I am as a leader and how I show up to model for my team how my values connect to our work."

As well as this day-in-day-out application Marc cited, mindfulness is also important for the ongoing process of recognizing or clarifying your purpose. Chanel Cathey was on a break after a fast-moving and successful career in communications, rising quickly through corporate and agency roles, when she "took some time to reflect. I was in a hotel lobby during a business trip, and all the business books in their little library were about White men. I didn't see myself or my fabulous clients there, and I wanted to change that." Based on Chanel's identities as a Black woman, the daughter of an educator and nurse who grew up in the Jim Crow South, and the granddaughter of a woman who lived in such profound racist segregation that she was never able to even shop in a department store, this observation catalyzed a change: "I realized that it's one thing to be a critic and another to be a critic and have the skills to change that. I wanted to work with more diverse clients, so I founded CJC Insights repping Women and BIPOC Founders from Harlem."

These daily and periodic breaks to check in with the change we really care about and how we might be able to help make it happen are essential to purposeful living. Without the pause for intentional reflection, we are carried by the powerful currents of what the present-day system wants us to do.

EIGHT BILLION FLAVORS OF MINDFULNESS

While the importance of a mindfulness practice is a consensus among purposeful leaders, the form that practice takes is not. There may be as many forms of mindfulness as there are purpose statements: one for every human on this planet. Again, the secret to finding yours is starting somewhere and experimenting. There are myriad tools (free and paid, digital and real life) for meditation, and each one comes in hundreds of flavors, from music to words and from movement to stillness.

I know plenty of deeply purposeful leaders who don't meditate, and their performance doesn't suffer. Perhaps running, cooking, dancing, walking in nature, or simply staring at the sky or ocean is your path to mindfulness. There is some science about all these activities being ways to achieve the neuroscientific, emotional, and cognitive benefits of mindfulness, and there are hundreds, if not thousands, of books written on the topic. So I ask you to commit to mindfulness as the key to leading and living purposefully only in the way(s) that you find works for you.

Reflection Questions

This is critical preparation for a successful Purpose Party. Download these questions as a worksheet at www.inspiringcowgirl.com/goingfirst if you're serious about leading and living more purposefully. The Going First Purpose Party takes you even deeper, if you like the idea of really integrating this approach into your work and life.

- What is one element of your unique approach that you might've seen as a weakness or challenge that you could actually use to your advantage, as Ward, Tanya, Nuno, and Sylvana have?

- What experiences from early in your life might influence the ways you are best positioned to contribute? What activities have you always enjoyed? What issues have you always cared about?

- What changes have you made successfully in the past? Why were they successful? What motivations, strategies, and/or tactics worked for you?

- Are there any changes you'd like to make now but struggle with? What do you think the obstacles are? Is it a matter of time, effort, skill, fear, or other logistical constraints or emotions?

- What habits or values have you managed to maintain despite pressure from family, friends, colleagues, or media? How have you held onto them?

- What habit or value are you struggling to maintain right now? How could you connect that value more closely to your purpose to motivate yourself to keep it up?

- What topics make your heart race or induce you to read all the way to the end of an article?

- What kind of a world do you picture for your grandchildren, real or imagined?

- What would you like to see change before you leave this earth?

- What do you consider your responsibility is in being purposeful?

Chapter 4

Results, or Why You Want to Accept This Invitation

We've addressed many prerequisites to purposeful living: courage, clarity, self-awareness, willingness to change, mindfulness practices, authenticity, and vulnerability. All these demands may have you plotting the most credible reason to politely decline my invitation.

But wait! The reason you picked up this book probably hasn't disappeared, and as usual, the rewards for those willing to work the prerequisites are well worth it. Let's shift our focus to the benefits of leading and living with purpose. Before we plunge into my framework for supporting your purpose journey, which is coming up in part 2, it's worth taking the time to clearly identify your motivation.

One of the things I hated most about working in the not-for-profit sector was the comments I'd get along the lines of, "Wow. Good for you!" or "You're such a good person. I'm not sure I could do it." My favorite was, "How was it to give up the career and salary you could've had in New York?" Each of these comments was accompanied with a literal or imagined pat on the head for being such a "good girl" (and, by the way, fantasies about the size of my trust fund—which, for the record, has never existed).

I didn't go into the not-for-profit sector because I'm a do-gooder or was chasing a ticket to heaven or some other luxurious afterlife. I chose my work to solve a problem. I couldn't stomach the inequitable distribution of opportunity I experienced when I was 12 that was robbing us all of so much talent. I hated that my sixth-grade classmates didn't get the support and resources I did to help them grow into their best. Even more than the unfairness, I hated the cost to the rest of us of these people not becoming fully realized.

Did I change some lives during my decade of not-for-profit work? Yes, several that I know of, and hopefully lots of my ripples changed lives in ways I'll never know. But the people I worked with and the experiences I had in that decade changed my life too. They gave me a great deal of joy and satisfaction as well as volumes of learning that inform my current efforts and are still directed at my original aspiration to bring out the best in as many humans on this planet as possible.

Now I want to help you see the potential benefits of identifying the activities that *you're* good at, enjoy, and drive the change you want to see in the world. Doing those activities is where you'll be at your best and create the most positive results for yourself, your teams, and the world around you. In other words, it's a win-win-win, which is a more sustainable arrangement than doing something out of guilt or obligation.

If you're feeling some skepticism, you're in good company. We have deep-rooted beliefs that we cannot possibly be doing good if we're enjoying ourselves! Let's address that misconception head-on.

Taking a Long-Term, Interconnected, Holistic View of Success

"No pain, no gain."

"There are winners and there are losers."

"There's no such thing as a free lunch."

These commonplace sayings reflect our conflicted relationships with effort and enjoyment. But what if activities that make us feel good were also good for the world around us?

The good news is that this is exactly true. When we take a long-term, interconnected, holistic view of our well-being and act accordingly, we do things and make choices that serve the greater good.

The bad news is that we've been socialized, educated, trained, and rewarded to take a short-term, in-group-focused, financial-success-only view of our actions.

But the world has changed around us and that short-term, in-group-focused, financial-only view has expired. John Replogle, seasoned B Corp CEO and investor, put it this way during our interview: "The 20th-century model is broken. The end is in sight for the zero-summers. There's been an awakening to what our long-term well-being really calls for, as well as our global interconnectedness. Consumers have more power than ever, and employees are voting with their values." The people and companies who thrive in this new context will reset their beliefs to line up with a long-term, interconnected, holistic view of success and align their behavior and choices to optimize well-being in those dimensions. In short, they will lead—and live—purposefully.

The Benefits of Leading with Purpose

Connecting to purpose has dramatic, scientifically documented effects on performance. It's good for your physical,[9] mental,[10] and cognitive[11] well-being; your team's levels of trust, innovation, cohesion, and productivity, particularly during crisis and transformation;[12] and your organization's financial performance.[13]

So is purposeful leadership the ultimate life hack, a self-promotion tool, or a branding exercise for people and organizations? Yes! But those powerful benefits do not negate the positive social and environmental effects of working and living purposefully, as long as we act within the new rules of the game: long-term, interconnected, and holistic. And when we make this shift, it's powerful! Magnetic, even, as it attracts others to us, expands our opportunities and influence, and inspires people around us.

Gayle Jennings-O'Byrne has seen this power in her own life as well as for the entrepreneurs in whom she invests: "So many of us have the ingredients—the skills, talent, network, experience—but they're not working for us until that moment where we stop being afraid. Then we start being really bold and intentional about how we show up. It's beautiful to see people living in that space. You can feel they're on their purpose journey because they have an energy and authenticity to them."

Alexa Teare, chief people and coaching officer of Lingo Live, is certainly enjoying the benefits of her purpose journey. She explains, "My values and my purpose are aligned professionally and personally. The fact that the way I show up personally is the same way that I show up professionally has allowed me to unlock potential in myself that I didn't realize was there."

This powerful connection to purpose is what today's ever-changing, increasingly complex market demands. Christie Smith knows something about that market. As the global lead of Talent & Organization/ Human Potential for Accenture, she and her team advise three-quarters of the Fortune Global 500. On the imperative for purposeful leadership, Christie explained, "In the '80s and '90s, saying 'I want to make a difference when I get up every morning' got a nice pat on the head. Now purpose has been elevated with the recognition of the power it has to drive performance."

As founder and CEO of Grove Collaborative, Stuart Landesberg is glad to have been early to this realization, even if it still makes him a contrarian in many circles.

From my experience in the public markets, I saw that people who are most successful long-term felt conventional wisdom is often wrong. And personally, I often bet on conventional wisdom and lost! I saw that these outlier trends do go mainstream, and when they do, they create big value. So now I am aligning two things that have often been positioned as incompatible: business results—capital, focus, engineering—versus social and environmental impact. This approach gives us a sustainable competitive advantage because we solve an important problem for consumers of keeping their houses and households clean without risking the health of their families or natural environment.

This still-contrarian-but-growing movement of purposeful leadership needs you. In the interest of generating sustainable motivation to get you there, here's a spoiler about the research-backed results that come from leading purposefully: you'll be more resilient to stress, live longer, and make more money.

Three Dimensions of Output:
Me, We, and World

Parties have outcomes. Have you ever woken up after a great party with an afterglow of warm feelings? (Distinct from, though sometimes alongside, the feelings of a hangover; that's another kind of outcome.) You recall why you've always felt like you belong in that friend group. You chuckle to yourself at the story a new friend shared. You wake up with a happier outlook for your day than you've had in a few weeks.

Attending the Purpose Party has similar results. From satisfaction with your life to your business's bottom line to the state of the world, things look better when we understand why we're here. We'll explore these results in three dimensions: Me, We, and World.

ME

The first dimension of impact is on yourself. This refers to

- your holistic wellbeing, which includes your physical, mental, intellectual, emotional, and spiritual self;

- the ripples that affect other "Me's" around you, such as your family, colleagues, neighbors, friends, and community members; and

- your influence in helping other individuals connect to purpose more often and/or more directly.

Your Health and Happiness. Aligning with your unique purpose delivers physical and mental well-being. Those of us with a reason to get up in the morning live longer. Having a sense of purpose has been shown to improve cognition, memory, and executive functioning throughout adulthood.[14] Controlling for other health and genetic factors, those with purpose have shown 30 percent less risk of dementia than others.[15] Finally, a longitudinal study published by the American Medical Association showed that people over 50 who have a strong sense of purpose are less likely to die prematurely than those who don't.[16]

In terms of our mental health, living with purpose in service to others leads to a deep, sustainable version of happiness. Purposeful experiences of happiness affect our biology, improving our resilience to negative events in a way that the self-centered happiness of a promotion or an ice cream cone do not.[17] So if you want a mood booster, don't reach for another cookie; call a friend and ask how you can help.

In addition, professionals with a stronger sense of purpose find more enjoyment in their work (even if they self-report as workaholics!) and have less conflict about their work–life balance.[18] In the intensity of the 21st-century workplace, having a holistic sense of purpose to mitigate the risk of burnout is powerful.

Your Performance. Research and leadership theory from top academic and practitioner references have reached a consensus: employees are more motivated[19] and stay longer[20] when they have a sense of purpose. And purposeful leaders build more trusting, inclusive, resilient teams.[21]

Purposeful leaders exemplify these findings loud and clear. Clay Adams, CEO of Mascoma Bank, put it simply: "I can live as myself a lot better when I'm leading a business that supports my values and commitment." He has found that alignment at Mascoma, a mutually owned B Corp-certified bank.

Even in the not-for-profit space, getting to true purpose is a journey. Andrew Glazier was brought in as CEO of Defy Ventures at a difficult moment for the organization. Defy's work is helping incarcerated and formerly incarcerated people learn entrepreneurship and build economic independence after incarceration. Even after years of doing this work, which could look obviously purposeful from the outside, Andrew was really overwhelmed during the turnaround, sometimes questioning his ability or even desire to see it through. One day, he had an epiphany and realized that he hadn't been connecting the work to his purpose. Once he did make that connection, his energy for the work shifted.

> When I felt morally and ethically bound to do this work, it was much more soul-crushing than connecting to purpose. Approaching it as an obligation. I didn't have agency. I continued because I didn't want to lose. When I realized I am *choosing* to be here and do this hard work, it created an overnight shift. My new purpose-driven approach was catalyzing to others too. As long as I am working with purpose, it's okay if something doesn't work. It was still a grind, but [it] shifted

from failure to succeeding—not just why I'm working here, but why everyone else is too.

This description resonates exactly with my experience in the not-for-profit sector. Doing "good work" as a moral obligation isn't sustainable, much less energizing. But when we do "good" (and often hard) work because it aligns with our skills, interests, and needs—when it connects to our purpose—it's empowering for us and those around us. Purpose granddaddy Viktor Frankl often paraphrases Nietzsche: "Those who have a 'why' to live, can bear with almost any 'how.'"[22]

Clarity. Another benefit of purpose is the clarity it provides. In a world that needs so much and presents so many problems to be solved, it's easy to feel overwhelmed and even paralyzed.

Gayle Jennings-O'Byrne could certainly succumb to that overwhelm in her work choosing women and BIPOC-led companies to invest in. Luckily, as shared earlier, she is deeply connected to her purpose: "My life purpose is a great BS filter! It provides so much clarity in what I get up to do, who I do it for, and how I do it. It helps with how I organize my day. Who I choose to spend my day with, what I do—will that amplify my purpose? And if not, does it deserve space on the schedule?"

The clarity you get from purpose can also help inspire others to find theirs. Trevor Crane, founder and CEO of Epic Publishing, explains that he took a step on his purpose journey after meeting an entrepreneur whose purpose was to "make disease optional." Trevor realized, "I was tired of not knowing what my thing is. I also want a clear statement of what I believe in that I can share with others, along with a clear path of what I'm doing to make it happen."

This clarifying function of purpose comes up over and over at the individual, team, and organizational levels. When you know what you're here to do and how you're best positioned to do it, it becomes a lot clearer how to spend your time, effort, and other resources.

WE

The second dimension of the impact we have by leading purposefully is on the formal and informal teams to which we belong. This refers to

- the performance and profitability of your immediate team and organization,
- your family's holistic well-being, and
- the sharing of skills in mutual support, collaboration, and resilience with the communities to which you belong.

Team's Performance. Purpose-aligned employees deliver benefits to their teams that are similar to the individual benefits of purpose. After all, teams are a conglomeration of individuals. People who are healthy, happy, motivated, and clear compose teams with those same features. These outcomes of leading and living purposefully translate into all kinds of positive outcomes for the organization's bottom-line costs as well as their top-line revenue growth and nonfinancial performance.

Purpose drives financial performance thanks to employee engagement and retention, customer loyalty, cost of capital, and innovation. Crucially, it's not the mere statement of purpose but an employee's clarity about that purpose that drives this outsized performance.[23] This value-creation opportunity for purpose-driven companies has increased since the onset of the 2020 COVID-19 pandemic.

When Søren Andersen was brought in as CEO to turn around weather intelligence leader StormGeo, he "suspected that connecting our people to purpose would unlock potential. Indeed, over the last 18 months we've seen 40 percent growth in earnings before interest, taxes, depreciation, and amortization. There are several tactical elements to the changes we've made, but I primarily credit the way we've been able to remind people the impact our work has on the shipping industry globally."

Mid-level employees support this sentiment. Hunter Davis, director of engineering at RealSelf, shared, "Because I am crystal clear about the impact of the work we do and how it connects to my own purpose, there's no negative in my heart about making more money for this place."

Indeed, purpose-driven investor Matt Greenfield, partner of Rethink Education, has shown that purpose-driven companies "are more likely to succeed because they solve real problems. When the going gets tough, which it always does, they and their teams are motivated to persist because they care about the solution more than purely commercial ventures do."

This dynamic is the reason that Matt and other investors, including Gayle Jennings-O'Byrne, John Replogle, and others I interviewed for this book, invest in purposeful entrepreneurs and business models. They know that purpose is a key driver of success and profitability rather than a threat to either.

No Profit, No Purpose. Purpose and the results it generates do not come at the cost of profitability; purpose-driven leaders know well that profit and purpose can and must go hand-in-hand.

Cecilia Saez, chief people officer of Aspiration—one of the first Public Benefit Corporations and B Corp-certified banks to go public—explains their approach: "No money, no mission! At Aspiration, every customer is a tree we plant."

Similarly, Eric Hudson, founder and CEO of B Corp Preserve, reminds purpose-driven entrepreneurs, "No profits, no purpose! You have to remain a profitable company or you're not going to have any impact at all."

Luckily, purpose drives profit in many ways. Ben Cohen, cofounder of longtime B Corp Ben & Jerry's, knows this from experience: "We discovered if you actually do the work—serve the community, work to promote justice, equality, fairness—you form a bond with customers based on shared values. That is the deepest bond you can form with a person, and it pays off in customer loyalty."

In some cases, the focus on purpose isn't baked in from day zero but becomes a critical strategy for growth or even survival. Mauricio Gutierrez has had that latter experience. He explains, "In the energy sector, we've had no choice but to transform. We have a sense of urgency that other industries don't have yet. They will, but for us the disruption came early. I embraced it, and now we're charting a new path that will allow us to create tremendous value over the long run and have a positive impact on our employees, communities, environment, and suppliers."

Like Mauricio, our self-aware and human-centered technologist Ward Vuillemot recognizes that this approach is simply good business: "Say we put aside the moral and ethical reasons to run your business [purposefully] and care only about extracting value. Well, the data and anecdotal evidence are both clear: if you treat people with dignity and provide psychological safety, you'll have the highest chance of providing the highest amount of value." Supporting people to realize their own purpose—their truest selves—is the surest path to that dignity and psychological safety.

After Hours. The benefits of purpose also accrue in our non-work "We's," whether family or community. Families who share values and a sense of how and why they're united enjoy deeper and more resilient relationships than those who get together on the holidays because that's what's done.

I've certainly been part of community groups, formal and informal, that flounder and fade for a lack of clear and shared purpose. I'm also grateful to have had the pleasure of membership in purpose-driven groups that work efficiently and effectively to realize shared goals.

Purpose is not a professional mandate. It's a path to well-being, performance, and clarity for any set of individuals hoping to achieve something, whether that be unconditionally loving relationships or school reform in their community.

WORLD

Our final dimension of impact is the world: the outcomes we have on people and the planet beyond the confines of direct relationships. Perhaps this is a good time for another reminder that we don't have to take on all the world's problems, just our unique one eight-billionth.

We do have to do at least that much, though, because today's social and environmental problems threaten our collective long-term success in terms of health, prosperity, and environmental safety. The nature of those problems means that we risk a "tragedy of the commons," the economic phenomenon in which people exploit resources held in common. Ensuring that we're pursuing a purpose with consequences greater than our own well-being—some benefit to the commons—is the way to mitigate that risk.

Doing our part isn't an unnatural responsibility to take on. It may have become unusual in some cultures and organizations, but that doesn't make it contrary to our instincts. We are evolutionarily disposed to leave the world a better place for our progeny. We don't wake up in the morning wanting to burn more carbon than necessary or hold people back from being their best selves because of their gender or race. But we live in a complex and interconnected world, one that an extractive form of capitalism has strongly shaped. To achieve the natural human drive to make the world just a little bit better, we need to learn how our default actions may unintentionally cause harm. Then we can change our habits so that our actions cause less harm and perhaps even improve the lives of people and the planet.

Remember Jeff from chapter 3? Jeff's purpose was simply to stay healthy so he could share in and support his granddaughter's thriving. She needs him to take an interest in eliminating the gender wealth gap so she can earn a fair living, provide safe and affordable healthcare so she can stay healthy, and steward natural resources so she can breathe well and enjoy walks with her own grandchildren one day.

Business leaders are well-positioned to advance some of those long-term solutions by how they run their companies. Ben Cohen recalls that when he and Jerry Greenfield founded Ben & Jerry's with the intent to use the business as a force for good, their business advisors said, "It's not possible to worry about these social problems. You'll go broke!"

"Regardless," Ben said, "we decided to resist the knee-jerk reaction that if it's not exclusively focused on increasing short-term profits, there's no interest. And Ben & Jerry's hasn't gone broke. It's not about giving away money, it's about choosing to do your business operations differently, in a way that is sustainable and scalable. And good for the world!"

But how can customers, employees, or investors know which other business leaders think this way? One option is presented by B Lab, a not-for-profit that certifies businesses that are "good for the world" based on their audited performance in five domains: environment, customers, workers, community, and governance. The resulting certification, B Corp, is the most holistic and rigorous measure of how businesses are contributing to solving global problems, whether by reducing their harm or creating positive outcomes. For the former CEO of B Lab Anthea Kelsick, "Rethinking how we work and live and why it matters is an invaluable part of the challenging task of moving toward a more inclusive and sustainable economic system."

B Corp is not perfect, and B Lab doesn't claim to be. Certifying as a B Corp doesn't ensure a company is doing no harm or having the most positive influence it could. But for now, B Corp certification is the highest and most universal standard to evaluate a company's impact. Two important drawbacks of the B Corp certification are that it's costly (of time more than money; the certification fee is prorated to a company's revenue) and less known than it will become, which makes it inaccessible to many historically under-resourced and marginalized leaders and their companies.

B Lab is working to address this inequity. In the meantime, over 10,000 companies have certified and are building high-impact business models. For example, longtime Ben & Jerry's partner Greyston Bakery (whom you may already know if you've sampled Ben & Jerry's Chocolate Fudge Brownie or Half Baked) "bakes brownies to hire people," not the other way around. There are lots of other B Corps, Conscious Capitalism members, Public Benefit Corporations, and other unaffiliated but like-minded businesses that bake sustainability into the very fabric of how they do business.

> *Businesses Giving Back.* Charitable giving by businesses has been fairly critiqued as "lipstick on a pig," in the words of particularly vocal critic Anand Giridharadas.[24] He suggests that business leaders could simply take less the first time around, so they don't have to give back after the fact. This perspective is valid. It's important to keep in mind how much we're taking as we rebalance our system to reflect today's mandate of long-term, interconnected, and holistic practices. But in the meantime, too much has already been taken, so corporate giving done well can be a powerful way to support communities and engage employees in the effort of change.

Bryan de Lottinville, founder and chair of Benevity, a corporate-giving software platform, shared the incredible win-win-win that can result from strategic giving programs: "Corporate charitable giving programs help employees activate their unique purpose at work. Organizations have seen 60 percent reduced churn! This is very important for their bottom line, as well as top-line growth, particularly in this talent market."

These paths to social and environmental impact through business strategy, operation, and/or giving are not intended to overwhelm, intimidate, or shame any Purpose Party guests. Leading purposefully is not about denying ourselves joy or privilege. Your invitation is to use that joy to fuel your work toward the greater good in the ways you're uniquely positioned to do and to extend or leverage your privilege to advance the well-being of others without it.

Different Kinds of Happiness. Before we all run off in search of good feelings in the form of a path to sustainable change-making, it's important to note the type of good feelings that will get us there. For that distinction, we'll look to the ancient Greeks.

A civilization that was familiar with pleasure as well as inequity, the Greeks had separate words for different kinds of happiness. One is the kind that comes from eating an ice cream cone from the Good Humor truck at the beach. The other comes from eating ice cream that you know was made by formerly incarcerated folks who would've struggled to find work if you hadn't bought Ben & Jerry's ice cream enhanced with Greyston Bakery brownies. The former is what the Greeks called *hedonia*, or happiness as pleasure. There's no doubt that your seaside ice cream is tasty and refreshing on a sweltering day. The Ben & Jerry's cone, though, could provide *eudaimonia*, or happiness as fulfillment. And that comes from the satisfaction of contributing to a solution larger than your sweet tooth. This latter category of good feelings is what aligns us with purpose.

On the path to eudaimonia, there will be moments that are less happy. Mark Griffin of PurposeFused called these "hill sprints": the hard tasks you may not enjoy in the moment but find rewarding because of what they enable you to do in pursuit of your purpose. We unlock eudaimonia when we're purposeful about creating impact in the World dimension, despite the challenges along the way of looking at suffering head-on, challenging our own biases, or accepting certain constraints on what we buy or use.

How Purpose Leads to Justice. I care about purposeful leadership because it's the only way I see us getting to the equitable, just, and joyful world that I believe is possible. I'll repeat my belief that most humans don't want to burn more carbon or discriminate against people of other races or religions, which is backed by the evolutionary biology that tells us we're encoded to leave the world better off for our offspring.

That said, making the world a better place means looking closely at where it's not a great place. Who's being treated unfairly and why? Which resources are we overusing unnecessarily or ill-advisedly? Where are we misaligning incentives for individuals or organizations given their long-term impact on other people or the planet? Initially, those questions can be uncomfortable, sad, and even heartbreaking to answer. But while looking the other way may allow us to experience hedonia, it will not lead to eudaimonia and true satisfaction. Nor will avoiding these hard truths enable us to shape a healthier, fairer, more joyful world to leave behind for our children, whether those children are biologically ours or more generally of our community.

Racial discrimination at work robs us of the full range of human talent that we need to thrive amid current challenges. Wage gaps lead to wealth gaps, which lead to social unrest. Gender bias reduces your kids' or your neighbors' kids' ability to reach their full potential. Air pollution causes asthma and increases sick days for the workers who keep our economy running. Again, we don't have to solve *all* these problems or even wholly solve any of them. But we do have to recognize that our well-being is tied up with that of others around us, and we must find the ways within our circle of influence that we're equipped to contribute to solutions.

We live in a complex world of invisible interconnections, exponential rates of change, and apparently competing interests. It's essential to continuously learn about the actual repercussions our actions have on the people around us and the planet. Only from that awareness can we choose to take positive action and find balance, satisfaction, and wellness.

The Impact Dashboard

The Impact Dashboard that I introduce in the next section of this book is a critical part of purposeful leadership because it connects our day-to-day actions to our desired outcomes. By definition, your purpose is a lofty statement about how you want your work and life to matter. But what changes the world is when we *activate* purpose.

Activating purpose requires that we translate a lofty statement about the future we want to contribute to into *what* we can do today and *how* we might do it to get closer to our desired impact. It's in those tangible actions that we see the ways we're contributing (or not) to the betterment of people and the planet. So, we'll dedicate the next two parts of the book to understanding and then using the Impact Dashboard. It's in this specificity about the actions we take that we can hold ourselves accountable for having the influence we seek, track the learning when we get it right, and see when we need to course correct.

It's Party Time!

By now, you must be hungry for an ice cream cone. Don't worry, Purpose Parties have great snacks. I also hope you've begun to reconcile the idea that you can and should pursue eudaimonia, not only because it improves your well-being and performance, but because it's good for the world.

Reflection Questions

Rewards are critical for any change! Be sure you've got your eyes on the prize to keep yourself motivated—download these questions as a worksheet at www.inspiringcowgirl.com/goingfirst. And if you're ready to really treat yourself, The Going First Purpose Party Playbook is an inspiring and action-oriented tool to guide your work.

- How have you felt the power of purpose improve your mental or physical state, motivate you, enhance your performance in a personal pursuit or at work, or clarify your choices?

- How have you seen your team harness the power of purpose to get clear, aligned, and motivated? What was the purpose? How did it affect business outcomes? How about the team's well-being?

- How have you seen purpose at work in another team or company, at home, or in a community setting? Identify the motivating purpose and outcomes for that group.

- Does your business intentionally make choices that are good for people and the planet? If not, where do you see opportunities in which different choices can result in better results?

- If you've been part of a charitable giving program at your company or the recipient of corporate gifts at a not-for-profit, what was great about it? What downsides or conflicts did you see or feel?

Part 2

Leading Purposefully

Congratulations! You've summoned the courage to continue your journey to lead and live more purposefully. Thanks for accepting the invitation.

Here in part 2, we'll begin digging deep into a simple and universal framework that will help you organize all the ways you already generate purposeful results. From there, we'll be able to identify ways you'd like to have more impact through your work and life and the obstacles that might be in the way of that. This action-oriented approach is a powerful and sustainable way to lead purposefully starting now, regardless of your training, role, seniority, politics, or otherwise.

The structure we use—the party game, if you will—goes back to the ABCs we explored in chapter 3: an ongoing process from awareness and belief to clarity, confidence, and courage, to diving in and then evaluating and evolving.

Throughout part 3, you'll build your own Impact Dashboard. As the name suggests, this is a control panel that tracks your efforts to lead and live with purpose so you can see the choices you're making (and not making). It tracks two overlapping frameworks: the Spectrum of Impact™ (chapters 5–8) and the Spheres of Impact™ (chapters 9–14).

First, though, in the next three chapters, I'll lay out the components of the Dashboard as well as the common pitfalls that leaders encounter along their purpose journeys. These chapters in part 2 are designed to set you up for success once you get to the Dashboard in part 3.

Let's introduce you to the Spectrum of Impact, the Spheres of Impact, the Impact Dashboard, and an example of how they work.

The Spectrum of Impact™

The Spectrum of Impact (see figure 2) describes the full array of organizations that can—and should—create positive social and environmental impact. This includes four types of organizations, all of which offer ways for you to have sway as an employee, customer, or investor:

- the traditional for-profit private sector,
- the rapidly growing world of social enterprise, or "Business for Good" (for-profit companies that are committed to minimizing their harm and optimizing their social and environmental sustainability),
- not-for-profit, and
- government.

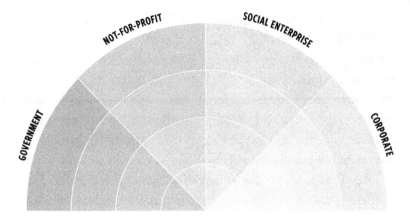

Figure 2. The Spectrum of Impact™.

The Spheres of Impact™

The Spheres of Impact (see figure 3) describes the six areas in our lives and work in which we can all lead and live purposefully to have the impact we desire: self, family, job, workplace, community, and money.

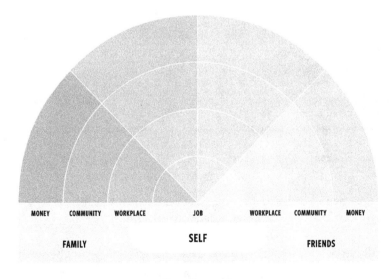

Figure 3. The Spheres of Impact™.

The Spheres are a simple tool to map what you're already doing and what you'd like to do more of, and perhaps even what you're doing that you'd like to stop doing. Mapping your activity in this way reveals your current and potential influence so you can see where you're on track toward the purpose you want to have and where you're not. The Spheres of Impact provide a comprehensive way to map our fears as well as our desires, ensure there's nothing lurking behind the surface that might hold us back, and help us see what we're already accomplishing. Together, they are a chart to and an ongoing reality check for aligning your work and life with your purpose and desired impact.

The Impact Dashboard (see figure 4) combines the Spheres of Impact and the Spectrum of Impact. It's a comprehensive way to map all the activities in your life and work that do—or could—contribute to the effect you want to have.

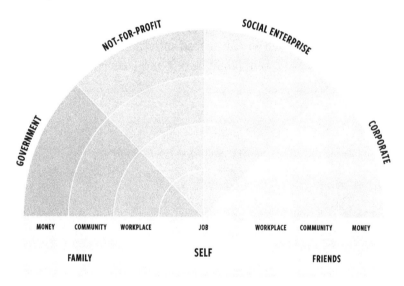

Figure 4. Combining the Spectrum of Impact and Spheres of Impact to create the Impact Dashboard.

Working with the Dashboard helps us optimize our impact by getting and staying clear on how closely our activities align with our purpose.

You can use it, review it, and revise it to inform your journey toward working and living more purposefully, ultimately reaching the level of performance, satisfaction, and outcome you want to have. And don't worry, you'll get a very hands-on walk-through of how to do that in part 3. For now, the idea is just to start getting a feel for the Dashboard and how it can serve you.

A Case Study

Here's one broad example of how your Dashboard can help you troubleshoot and find insight on what's going on in your life. This story goes under the "If only I had known then what I know now" heading.

As I shared earlier, when I worked in the not-for-profit sector, my Dashboard was full of positive contributions. The organization I worked for provided life-changing personal and economic development programs. We helped moms learn about nutrition and physical activity and then start or grow their own microenterprises to support their families. We trained teachers to deliver early childhood education classes like art, music, and sports, but through a lens of mental health. When they taught a song, they were actually teaching empathy, comfort expressing emotions, and resilience. And yet I wasn't energized by this work. I struggled with understanding why I felt so depleted when I was doing so much good.

In retrospect, I can understand exactly why. What I now recognize as my Dashboard was severely imbalanced. Those major impacts I was having were all crowded into my Job and Workplace Spheres. But for more than three hundred days a year, I was more than three thousand miles away from my (now ex-) husband. I also didn't have regular chances to be with other friends or family. I had no community to engage with other than my colleagues and professional partners. We did buy a treadmill for our center since we couldn't walk or run outside, and our food was de facto organic and local. But I hadn't yet evolved the self-care routines that I now know keep me humming. In other words, I was severely underinvesting in my Self, Family, and Community Spheres.

There was also an alignment problem: I wasn't playing at the point of the Spectrum where I was best positioned or most inspired to contribute. We'll talk about that alignment in greater detail in part 3. For now, let's focus on the first step of using the Dashboard: mapping your effects across the Spectrum of Impact.

Chapter 5

The Spectrum of Impact

The Spectrum of Impact is a framework that describes all the organizations that we might interact with throughout the economy. On the Dashboard, it's represented by four words outside the colored spheres and four differently colored "slices" under each word (review figure 2). (The Spectrum doesn't apply to the Self or Family and Friends Spheres; more on those in chapters 9 and 10.)

The primary reason I started highlighting the Spectrum of Impact and integrated it into the Dashboard is the misconception that doing good and making money are mutually exclusive. After my decade of not-for-profit work, it became clear to me that the problems we're trying to solve require far more than what can be done by philanthropic efforts. Not-for-profits don't have a monopoly on influence, nor is government the only sector that serves the public. The breadth and depth of change we need to achieve a healthy and equitable world for all of our grandchildren requires all hands on deck across the breadth and width of the deck. Each sector has a different but critical role to play in this change. Although this all-hands-on-deck approach presents a challenge to traditional commercial organizations that consider their impact more deeply, it's also an opportunity to get involved in the motivating and rewarding work of doing business that's good for the world.

I intentionally labeled this framework as a Spectrum because, as you can see from the representative logos and narrative in figure 5, the delineations between government, not-for-profit, Business for Good, and corporations are not rigid.

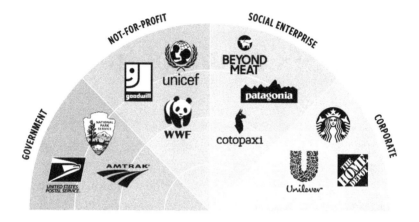

Figure 5. The Spectrum of Impact with representative logos for each type of organization.

Increasingly more private and public partnerships are taking the form of quasi-public not-for-profit entities. Many small, locally owned businesses wouldn't consider themselves "Businesses for Good," but ultimately the choices they make and influences they have on their stakeholders are far more positive than those made by a complex global company. Nonetheless, to evaluate the way a given organization is best positioned to have impact and what it's supporting, it's valuable to understand where it is on the Spectrum.

Government

Purportedly, the public sector is charged exclusively with serving the public. From the federal level to the local, government agencies exist to provide necessary services for the people who make up their communities.

Of course, this is an idealized and simplified description. Different governments and regimes have their own definitions of "necessary services" and which people are entitled to them. However, those nuances are for a different book. For now, what's relevant is to recognize that we each can bring about results by interacting with government agencies in any of the six Spheres of Impact.

Not-for-Profits

Not-for-profits, by which we mean those officially recognized by their government as a charitable (and in the US, tax-exempt) organization, are charged with delivering some public good or service. There are 1.3 million not-for-profit organizations in the US alone, and they range widely in their size, geographic range, and area of work.[25] Not-for-profits include everything from religious institutions to colleges, hospitals, local pet shelters, and global healthcare innovators. The vast majority are small: 88 percent have annual budgets of less than $500,000.[26]

Because they are many in number but mini in budget, not-for-profits make up only 5.6 percent of the US's GDP.[27] Anyone who hopes for not-for-profits to save our ship in terms of education, health, or environmental conversation will be sobered by this number. There's no chance that we can rest all our hopes for a healthier, fairer future on the not-for-profit sector.

As we think about our involvement with not-for-profits, it's also valuable to get clear about their business model. We often imagine not-for-profits as being reliant on charitable giving by individuals, corporate donations, or foundations. However, nearly half of not-for-profit revenue comes from private individuals or entities as fees for services, and another 32 percent comes from government contracts and grants for services. Less than 15 percent of not-for-profit revenue is actually donated.[28] Because of the common label "nonprofit," this might be counterintuitive, but not-for-profits can indeed charge fees, sell things, and make money. They just can't pay out that revenue as dividends to shareholders like a for-profit company does.

In terms of the Dashboard and the journey to purposeful leadership, it's valuable to know these realities about the not-for-profit sector. That way, we can properly design our interactions with not-for-profits in terms of how they might be part of our impact strategy.

Business for Good

Businesses can make and sell products in a way that's good for people and the planet, from suppliers, employees, and customers to the individuals, animals, and environments who are touched all along the company's supply chain. For shorthand I'll refer to this approach as "Business for Good," although I realize it's another oversimplification (like the notion that government bodies exist to serve their communities).

Indeed, some Businesses for Good, such as Patagonia, are clear that their very existence does inevitably do some harm to the planet and even people whom it touches. They work toward a goal of minimizing that harm. Accepting these important caveats, the concept of Business for Good is an important outlet for purposeful leaders, and it isn't new. In the early 1800s, Robert Owen's New Lanark Cotton Mills paid fair wages and advocated for social reform.[29] The Rochdale Society of Equitable Pioneers was a cooperative that provided healthy meals for factory workers in the 1840s (and still exists today as the International Cooperative Alliance).[30] Florence Nightingale's nursing school was another early Business for Good in the 1860s.[31]

Now, as the concept becomes more mainstream, it's going through all the growing pains of any movement, most notably in the debate about stakeholder capitalism. There's skepticism about whether Business for Good works and how genuine its leaders are in their quest for justice. Ultimately, many are asking, "Can we really reform capitalism to be good for the world, or do we have to tear it down and build a new system?" The founders of B Lab, the not-for-profit certifying Businesses for Good that we met in chapter 4, certainly believe the former. They've designed an incredibly thoughtful and rigorous framework to measure and audit the "goodness" of companies.

As a proponent of evolution, not revolution, as well as a founder of, advisor to, and proud customer of B Corps, I believe that businesses can and must be a force for good. This doesn't mean that we've figured out the perfect balance between impact and growth, or that certified B Corps are above scrutiny or critique. But supporting companies that are striving to do well by doing good is a powerful way to expand your influence as a leader who works, gets paid, buys things, and invests.

Corporate

The corporate realm is a broad category of more traditional for-profit companies, whether large and corporate or small and local. Small businesses often lean toward the Business for Good part of the Spectrum, given their tendency to create jobs, distribute opportunities and wealth to women and non-White owners, and remain accountable to their communities—because of proximity and transparency, if nothing else.[32]

For-profit businesses are best positioned to create goods and/or services and distribute them to customers. *What* they do can certainly have positive impact. For example, some companies make software to teach reading and others create and distribute medicine to heal diseases. Of course, there are also many private companies in the modern economy that deliver products that some would argue have primarily or exclusively negative impact, such as cigarettes or weapons.

How companies create and distribute their wares also shapes a company's influence in a major way. Even the healthiest food could be sourced from distant farms, rely on transport that generates huge carbon emissions, be packaged by underpaid workers in dismal conditions, or be distributed in wasteful and non-recyclable plastic containers. Similarly, a value-neutral product like outerwear can be designed using minimally impactful materials with a circular supply chain that generates no waste; sold by employees who are paid living wages, provided with ample medical coverage and family leave, and empowered to grow; and repaired or collected at the end of its life for another use.

Purposeful leaders get clear about the companies they work for, invest in, and buy from in terms of what they do in the world and how they do it. Expanding our view to include both elements of a business significantly increases our leverage for impact. After all, as leaders who work and live in modern society, it's nearly inevitable that we'll interact with for-profit companies and at least some global corporations. Our power comes from considering both elements—what those companies do and how they choose to do it—and adjusting our relationships with them accordingly.

Reflection Questions

The Spheres of Impact are a powerful tool to make sense of all your efforts toward the impact you want to have. Download these questions as a worksheet at www.inspiringcowgirl.com/goingfirst as a helpful ongoing tracker of where you're spending your time, energy, and attention. Of course, the best ongoing accountability tool is the Going First Purpose Party Playbook!

GOVERNMENT

- How do you most often interact with the public sector? By voting? Donating to candidates? Serving on a local board or committee? Working for a government agency?

- How would you like to interact more with government institutions or find ways to achieve your desired outcomes that involve working with the public sector in some way?

NOT-FOR-PROFIT

- How do you currently interact with not-for-profits? By donating money or supplies? Volunteering your time? Serving on a board? Working at a job with a not-for-profit?

- How would you like to interact more with not-for-profits or achieve your desired impact that involve working with not-for-profits in some way?

BUSINESS FOR GOOD

- How do you think or feel about the notion "business as a force for good"? What are some B Corp-certified companies or public benefit corporations you've heard about or had experience with?

- How do you currently interact with Businesses for Good? By buying their products? Referring them to colleagues, friends, and family? Investing in them through the public markets or privately?

- How would you like to interact more with Businesses for Good or achieve your desired impact that involve working with them in some way?

CORPORATE

- How do you currently interact with private sector companies? Global corporations? Do you buy from them? Hold their stock?

Are you in the 50 percent of the US workforce that has a job with a large (over 500 employees) for-profit company?

- How would you like to interact more or engage less with companies and corporations or achieve your desired outcomes that involve working with corporations in some way?

Chapter 6

Getting to Know the Impact Dashboard

Mapping your efforts—current and/or desired—on your Impact Dashboard (which we'll refer to simply as the Dashboard going forward) helps you recognize the influence you're already having and where you can do more to reach the purpose you seek. The Dashboard isn't about getting to a perfect 10 in all six spheres or perfectly covering every sphere across the whole Spectrum of Impact. The point is rather to understand

- how you're allocating time, energy, and attention across the entire Dashboard;

- what outputs those efforts provide in the Me, We, and World dimensions; and

- the pitfalls that might undermine your impact.

In this chapter, we consider tactical suggestions for using the Dashboard. To bring it to life, in the next chapter I'll share some real-life Dashboards from my own experience and those of a few fellow Purpose Seekers. These case studies are designed to help you see the insights you'll gain from using the Dashboard on an ongoing basis. In part 3, we'll do a deep dive into each of the six spheres, including more specific examples and reflections. That's where you'll really interact with the Dashboard. For now, we're just getting really familiar with it to set you up for success!

A Practical Approach to Tracking Your Impact

Remember that purpose "done right" in this context is universal. It isn't something you earn at a certain age, wealth, or position in an organization's hierarchy. We activate our purpose by choosing how we spend our resources of time, energy, and attention. Let's look at some practical ways you can bring those choices to life.

THE DASHBOARD IS A LIVING DOCUMENT

I chose the party metaphor intentionally! I invite you to see the Dashboard as more of a party game than a tool. A purposeful life is a joyful life, and yes, we're contemplating heavy topics such as climate change, institutionalized racism, misogyny, and other wrongs we'd like to help right. But what keeps us going is focusing our smaller day-to-day wins toward remedying those major issues in the medium term.

I've already shared many times that purposeful leadership is a lifelong journey, and one that evolves. The Dashboard, then, is not a one-and-done, frame-your-finished-product-and-hang-it-next-to-your-diplomas type tool. It's a lifelong guide intended to be drafted, revisited, revised, and even restarted many times throughout your life. It can and should shift over time, increasing the emphasis on some spheres over others, or some activities within a certain sphere. What you write down in the next few weeks as you proceed through the next chapters doesn't have to stick forever. So play with the Dashboard! Remove the seriousness and explore what investments feel engaging, exciting, or even joyful. Then try them out—and if they don't work, change something up.

IT'S A REGULAR PRACTICE

Since the Dashboard is a document in flux, it's important to revisit it regularly so you can witness and shape that evolution. As a one-time exercise, it provides a helpful organizing system for you to think about your impact. When used regularly over time, however, its real power is as an accountability and planning tool.

I suggest the following tempo to fully integrate your Dashboard into your life and work, but the most important feature of how you use it is that it works for *you*:

> *Daily.* Checking in daily is a must when it comes to purposeful living. Daily check-ins can be extremely brief and simple—just find some way to interact with your Dashboard on a daily basis so it becomes integrated into your everyday choices and behaviors. This daily practice can be as simple as putting a sticky note on your mirror or adding a background image on your phone or laptop that reminds you of the sphere of focus for the quarter. It could be asking yourself what you'll do today in that sphere while you brush your teeth or taking a quick inventory of all six spheres as you look at your calendar for the day.
>
> Just as perfect is the enemy of good, complexity is the enemy of regularity. Choose a simple daily action and try it out. Momentum Habit Tracker is a simple but powerful app to help you track your progress on any daily practice, and Day One is a customizable journaling tool that works well if your daily practice requires more than just Yes/No tracking. Links to both are listed in the Reader Resources at the end of the book.
>
> *Monthly/Weekly.* It's helpful to have a higher level regular check-in with the Dashboard too. Pair it with something that already happens. Do you have a weekly team meeting you can tack 10 minutes onto to review your Dashboard? A monthly bill-paying session

you can reward yourself for by spending 20 or 30 minutes with your Dashboard? Again, the most important element of your Dashboard is that it fits your life and your style of working and learning.

Quarterly. Pick one sphere to focus on each quarter. Three months is a reasonable amount of time to build a new habit, complete a project, or explore a new partnership or collaboration. Set a tentative schedule of which spheres you'll focus on in which quarters during your yearly Dashboard review. Revisit that plan each quarter to ensure that the sphere you're focusing on is the most timely for the point where you're at.

Yearly. Whether you choose the first week of January, on your birthday, or at the end of the year, set aside an hour or so to review your Dashboard from the last year and envision what you want it to look like in the year to come. You can use my Annual Planning Template available at www.inspiringcowgirl.com/goingfirst to review what went well, what you missed, and what you learned in the past year. Those answers can inform any changes you want to make in terms of starting or stopping activities as well as what you want to keep doing.

IT'S STRONGER IN COMMUNITY

The Dashboard is most enjoyable and effective when you use it with other people. Whether you share the tool with friends, colleagues, or your social media audience, merely talking about your impact out loud reinforces your actions.

Further, with the Dashboard you can model purposeful leadership for the people around you, giving them permission and even inspiration to reflect on their own investments of time and energy. Because the Dashboard is so intuitive, they don't have to have read this book or have done any other work to understand what you're talking about. Of course, the conversations can get even richer if they do have that background!

Finally, by working with the Dashboard in the Community Sphere, you can create accountability partners for yourself. When people around you hear you talk about your focus on the Self Sphere for this quarter and then see you looking a bit frazzled, they're more likely to ask about that commitment you had shared than comment on your stress out of the blue.

IT REQUIRES BOTH CARE AND CHALLENGE

Working with the Dashboard requires a balance of care and challenge. If you've ever been the recipient of tough love done well, you've felt that potent combination of support and truth-telling. Kelly Wendorf's "Kanyini Care" concept (figure 6) is the best reference for applying care with challenge. It builds on the Radical Candor model that balances care and challenge and integrates an indigenous worldview. Wendorf writes, "Care leverages the authority to challenge others. Without care, challenge is destructive, yet without challenge, care is poweress."[33]

A particularly profound example of Kanyini Care in my life was a relationship with a dear and trusted colleague whom we moved into a more sales-focused role than the program delivery she had previously done. We were a small team, so she was willing to try the shift, and I could see her potential in this new role. She had shadowed very talented salespeople in the past and had the natural inclination to empathy and curiosity that drives our relational approach to sales. But our ideal customer profile, sales timeline, and pipeline status proved to be bigger obstacles than her attributes were strengths. We weren't closing deals with her in this new role, so there was nothing for her to deliver—or get paid for. Over a few months, we had many deeply

CARE
CONNECT

Caretaking
We care about others
but we stay silent and
don't challenge in order
to protect their feelings.

**Unconditional Love &
Care With Responsibility**
We care for the whole
and are direct, clear,
and freely challenge.

DON'T
CHALLENGE

CHALLENGE

Self Protection
In an unbalanced
care for own welfare,
we withhold challenge.

**Careless &
Confronting**
We challenge
aggressively.

DON'T CARE
DISCONNECT

Figure 6. Balancing care and challenge with Kelly Wendorf's "Kanyini Care" diagram
(Used with permission.)

caring but honestly challenging conversations about her involvement.
She ended up finding a perfectly suited role in her new hometown
that put her back into her (several!) zones of genius.

We maintain a friendship and mentorship and would both gladly
work together in the future should an opportunity arise. But we'll be
exponentially smarter about the conditions required to make that
a win-win for us and a win-win-win for our organizations and the
people around us!

Kanyini Care for the Dashboard

Just as in the process with my colleague, it's important to have grace, compassion, and understanding as we complete and evolve our Dashboards. The Dashboard is most effective when applied with this blend of empathy and love alongside a spirit of curiosity and continuous improvement. For starters, we can't always do as much as we want, so it's important to recognize what we *are* doing to expand our impact across the spheres. This grace needs to be balanced by a willingness to ask provocative questions and challenge ourselves about whether we're avoiding certain forms of influence because of discomfort, outdated habits, or other common pitfalls. Purposeful leadership gets us to equity and justice only if we look at the hard things we want to change.

I, for one, have not achieved the precise balance of knowing I'm doing the best I can in any given moment and striving to keep learning so that I can do better in the next. I do know that my best chance of reaching that balance comes from a place of love and curiosity, paired with active and eager listening to the people and planet I'm hoping to serve. The same blend of care and challenge is equally important when we begin to have conversations with other people about their Dashboards, whether that's with our kids, friends, colleagues, or clients.

It's about Aligning Activities, Not Adding Them

We all have the same amount of time; what we control is how we allocate it. My intent is not for you to cram dozens more activities into your days and weeks to be more impactful. By being intentional about the investments we want to make in each sphere, we can use our time purposefully and, just as importantly, protect our time from other activities that don't serve our highest priorities.

Energy and attention are also limited resources. But as with time, if we get clear and intentional about what brings us energy and how we spend our attention, we can dramatically increase the resources we allocate to living and leading with purpose.

You now have a very good sense of how to use this Impact Dashboard as a dynamic, interactive, best-in-groups tool to map the investments you're making in leading and living purposefully. You're welcome.

Reflection Questions

The Impact Dashboard is the foundation for the rest of our work. So it's worth getting to know by spending some time with these questions! Download them as a worksheet at www.inspiringcowgirl.com/goingfirst. And if you like coloring—or just want more support in learning to live purposefully by your Dashboard—check out the Going First Purpose Party Playbook.

- What's your impression of the Impact Dashboard? Does it remind you of anything else?

- What's a good tempo for fully integrating your Dashboard into your life and work? How often and when do you plan to revisit it?

- How might your time and effort working with your Dashboard pay off?

- What's your reaction to Kelly Wendorf's Kanyini Care model? Have you experienced this kind of relationship in the past? Have you used its concepts with others?

- How can you balance care and challenge in your purpose work? Do you need to practice more? Start enlisting accountability partners? Better align your activities?

- What activities are you doing now that don't connect to the impact you want to have or represent your highest priorities, whether in the Me, We, or World dimension? Why do you do them? What would happen if you stopped doing them?

- How could you free up your time, energy, attention, or money to do the things that are most aligned with the impact you want to have?

Chapter 7

Diving in to Using the Dashboard

Enough already, I hear you thinking, *how does it work?* Great question! It's time!

This chapter provides a description of the process you'll use for working with each Sphere of Impact in your Dashboard. As we move into the subsequent individual sphere chapters, we'll apply the process specifically to each sphere. For now, this is a general introduction and practice.

Do yourself a favor and don't skip this part. My stories and the examples from hundreds of other leaders in this book are worth nothing if you're not playing with what the spheres look like in your own life and how you might want to change that.

My choice to invest so much of my time in creating this process and asking you to take the time to do it too is based on my background in adult learning. Many pedagogists have talked about the importance of learning by doing, including John Dewey, an American philosopher and psychologist who significantly influenced educational reform.[34] The sentiment was captured far earlier in *Xunzi*, a set of 32 books of Chinese philosophy that quotes Xun Kuang as saying, "Tell me and I forget, teach me and I remember, involve me and I learn."[35]

So please dig in and do the process described here and as you read each sphere chapter—if you want to learn, that is! I promise that what I'm asking you to do is

- painless, though not without the healthy challenge of growth;
- proven, but demands adaptation to your unique situation in this moment; and
- powerful, regardless of how simple it may seem in the moment.

A Baseline Assessment

Since this is the first time you're getting your hands dirty in the Dashboard, we'll start with a simple brainstorm of how you've been spending your time in general before we zero in sphere by sphere. It's an important precursor to all the work we'll do for each of the six spheres. You can follow along with the process here or, if you have the playbook, it's presented there.

First off (ideally after some mini-mindfulness practice like a moment of deep breathing or just eyes-closed stillness), get into true brainstorm mode—no judgment. All answers that come to mind are valid and get written down. For this brainstorm, you'll be writing down what you spend your time doing. You can do this in any form that appeals to you: a blank piece of paper, the margin of the book, or my "Impact Dashboard Excel Worksheet" that you can download from my website. It *is* nice to have it in an Excel spreadsheet because that allows you to easily sort and analyze your answers later.

1. Start with what you did today or yesterday. Pull out your calendar, if that's helpful, and go back through the last week, just jotting down a word or phrase to describe the things you spent your time doing. After you've covered this week, review the list and add any important activities that are missing—maybe things that are less regular, such a vacation, monthly massage, or quarterly catch-up with a mentor.

   Ta-da! Step one, done! See? Painless.

For those of you thinking, *Okay, this is too painless to be powerful,* bear with me. We're getting to the analysis, and there you can go as deep as you want. As Kalyn Wilson, coach, advisor, and people professional with a PhD in organizational psychology, says about integrating purpose into your work and life, "This stuff is not sexy! It's about tracking the small stuff to get data about how you're doing on having the impact you want to have."

2. Estimate how many hours a week you spend on each activity. If you love this kind of stuff, go ahead and get really detailed about it (there's space in the Excel template and the playbook if you're using one or both of those). And if counting hours gives you chills, don't worry: this is really just a quick, top-of-mind estimate.

    For those less-than-weekly activities, include what they break down to on a weekly basis. There are 168 hours in a week (10,080 minutes, if that's the unit you use). So, for example, if your monthly hike with friends is a four-hour event door-to-door, put down one hour a week. If you spend 90 minutes with your mentor each quarter, it's about 0.1 hour a week. The idea isn't to count your time to a thousandth-of-a-second accuracy but just to get an indication of how much time you're spending on which activities. Do a quick check of how exhaustive your list is by adding up your time (after you thank me for the Excel template). Don't forget to add sleep, a critical activity in the Self Sphere.

    Okay! Congratulations, especially to those of you who have some level of allergy to numbers and/or Excel. Two down, just one fun one to go.

3. Assign each activity you listed to a sphere. It's okay if you don't yet know the specifics about each sphere; if you're uncertain about which sphere to put an activity in, trust your instinct and move on. This is just an initial brain dump. You can always recategorize or add activities as you continue learning more about each sphere.

And just like that, you're done with this important, foundational part of mapping your Dashboard: your Baseline Assessment. Nice work! Save this list in whatever form you wrote it, because you've now already done the first step of the work in each chapter to come.

Zeroing In on Each Sphere

This section walks you through the process you'll follow in chapters 9–14, one for each sphere. No need to do any work now; just get familiar with the steps.

This is a five-step process that follows the ABCs of Purposeful Leadership to examine your investments in each sphere. I designed it based on over 10,000 hours of work I've done with hundreds of purpose-driven leaders as well as my study of human development, adult learning, motivation, and behavior-change science. Here's a reminder of those ABCs and a breakdown of the five-step model you'll follow for each sphere:

1. *Awareness.* How are you doing in terms of your investments in this sphere? Get a rough estimate.

2. *Belief.* Do you believe that making some change in your investments in this sphere will increase your well-being, performance, or fulfillment?

3. *Clarity, Confidence, and Courage.* What ONE activity do you want to add to your activities in this sphere for the next month?

4. *Diving In.* What's going to keep you from building that new habit? How can you avoid that risk?

5. *Evaluate and Evolve.* How's it going? Are you seeing and/or feeling your desired impact? Is the new habit energizing or a drag? What do you want to change?

I encourage you to trust the process and follow along as I've laid it out. As you grow familiar with it, feel free to adapt the format, question, or order of operations if another way makes more sense to you or sticks better. But at least for this first time, let yourself follow along and then revise as needed later. That advice goes for the handy Excel tool I've provided too. It's evolved from a lot of Dashboard-mapping sessions I've done! But if you prefer pen and paper—or crayon and posterboard—by all means, do you.

To give you an idea on time, you can do these five steps in 20–30 minutes for each sphere. If you're keen to dig deep and reflect on your past experience or do research as you look forward, that could certainly absorb hours. My advice is to do a minimum viable product first. Do a "quick and dirty" version to get familiar with the process and build some momentum as you move through all six spheres. Then, the framework, ideas, and tools are yours to spend as much time with as you'd like going forward.

Remember, revisiting the Dashboard on a regular basis is necessary to leverage its power for your more purposeful approach to work and life. It's a marathon, not a sprint, so don't overwork yourself at this stage. Keep it light and keep it moving.

STEP 1. GETTING A BASELINE: AWARENESS

The process starts with a few numerical ratings. On a scale of 1–10, 1 being "Not at all" and 10 being "As much as possible," you'll rate yourself on a few simple statements in three categories for each sphere: present, past, and future. Below is an example of one of the statements:

I invest time, energy, and attention in this sphere.

NOT AT ALL · AS MUCH AS POSSIBLE

1 2 3 4 5 6 7 8 9 10

After you've rated yourself for how true that is right now, you'll answer the same question for how you felt about each statement a year ago. I don't have a time machine to go with the worksheet, so you'll have to do that part yourself. For now, take a minute or two to close your eyes, picture that date, and think about where you were personally and professionally. What was happening in the world? At work? In your family or friend group? In your own physical, mental, and spiritual well-being? Integrate all that data into a simple rating:

Last year, I was investing time, energy, and attention in this sphere.

Finally, rate the three statements again for what rating you want to have a year from now. And resist any good-student urge to put perfect 10s in all categories. Remember, there are six spheres, and you're probably already using your limited time, energy, and attention pretty fully. So think about the right balance between where you want to be and where you can realistically get in a year.

Next year, I'll invest time, energy, and attention in this sphere.

We'll revisit all of your goals in a final exercise, and you'll have the chance to prioritize the spheres. In other words, you don't need a final answer at this point, but do give it more thought than simply aspiring to perfect 10s across the board.

STEP 2. WHAT YOU NEED FOR THIS SPHERE: BELIEF

The next step is to arrive at a belief about what you need to do in the sphere to improve your well-being, performance, and/or fulfillment and thus get closer to your desired impact. It's important to spend the time here in each sphere so you truly *believe* that these changes will make a real difference. If you don't believe it, the rest of the process is worthless; your intended changes will be blown away like a leaf by the wind of competing priorities.

Based on your 1-to-10 ratings above—particularly the one about where you want to be in a year—you'll examine what change is needed to your investments in this sphere. Do you need and want to maintain the activities you're doing? Change what you're doing? Do more? Do less? You'll write you answers to these questions in the Excel sheet, playbook, or wherever you're doing the work. If you're using my handy Excel sheet, you'll see that the tab for each sphere will auto-populate with the activities from your initial brainstorm. Then you'll add anything you didn't include in the first few blank lines, along with an estimate of how many hours you spent doing them each week.

Ultimately, you'll draft a simple, clear, and measurable belief statement about what you want to change in that sphere. The belief statement won't include exactly *how* you'll achieve the goal you're setting; you'll just identify *what* you're going to do and *why* it matters.

STEP 3. WHAT'S NEXT: CLARITY, CONFIDENCE, COURAGE

This stage has just one step. Yup, you can achieve all three Cs with just one step, even though it's a big one. That's how purposeful leadership works: by identifying the activities that really move the needle; in other words, those that have outsized payoffs that extend beyond yourself and impact the people and planet around you. So, this step is about choosing one—and only one—new activity that you're going to try in the sphere.

Once you've chosen your One Thing in each the sphere, you'll start getting really specific in determining exactly what it's going to look like, at least to start; you can revise the details as you learn. During this step, you'll be asking yourself questions like when and where you're going to do it and for how long, what items you might need to track it, and how you're going to hold yourself accountable and reward yourself. Addressing these details of your new activity goes a long way in setting you up for success. (Read *Atomic Habits* by James Clear or *The Power of Habit* by Charles Duhigg if you want to understand why I'm torturing you with this level of commitment.) That said, even this level of planning doesn't mitigate all the reasons you might not adopt this new investment in your sphere, so next we look at how to build in some support.

STEP 4. SETTING YOURSELF UP FOR SUCCESS: DIVING IN

You know you best, and I'm quite certain that this book isn't your first attempt at general self-improvement or the specific goal of working and living with more purpose. So you'll start with what you know. What obstacles have prevented you from making the changes you wanted to make in the past? Maybe it's not making time or that the people you spend the most time with aren't aligned with your desired change. Or maybe you're just not wholly convinced that it would make a difference to anyone else if you were, for instance, more rested or better nourished.

In the next chapter, we'll look at the most common pitfalls to making change, along with specific ways that I and other purposeful leaders counter them. But step 4 is about creating a support system for One Thing you want to try, despite the obstacles you know will arise.

After all of this reflection, you'll write a plan. Like your belief statement, it will be a simple, clear, and measurable behavioral plan to keep you on track. Here are a few examples:

- When I'm tempted to give the dogs a chew toy instead of taking them on a walk, I'll look at my pedometer for the day and see if I've hit my target steps.

- Whenever I think there's not enough time to start a meeting with a personal check-in, I'll remember that awful meeting when my direct report didn't even celebrate their promotion because they were so distracted due to their father being in surgery that day.

- Every time I'm tempted to buy a new outfit, I'll spend five minutes in my closet making sure there's nothing there that would work just as well.

STEP 5. CONTINUOUS IMPROVEMENT: EVALUATE AND EVOLVE

Given the rate at which the world is changing around us and we're changing within it, it's critical to approach the purpose journey with a growth mindset. So you'll want to find ways to evaluate what you're doing and make changes accordingly along the way. This, too, can be lighter and more fun than it sounds; in fact, you're more likely to stick with it if you don't let it become too heavy or serious.

Tracking habits is an essential element of making change. When you get to this step, you'll consider how it has worked for you to track new habits in the past, as well as what hasn't worked. You'll take the time to experiment and choose a method that works for you, whether that's a habit tracker app, an accountability buddy at work or home, a highly visible checklist, or gold stars.

When tracking your purpose journey, it's important to capture not only this type of quantitative data (how often did I do the thing) but also qualitative information (how did it make me feel and what effect did it have) about your new purposeful habit(s). This can be in the form of journaling, quarterly updates with yourself, or a quiet reflection session. In taking this step, you might notice that you haven't been doing the new habit as often as you thought. Or it might be just the opposite (you tend to only miss Sundays, for instance). Maybe you'll notice that you're doing the thing as just another task, without much thought to this new habit or its impact. Or maybe when you journal, you'll realize a few outcomes of your new habit even though you hadn't realized until then what had been causing them. Perhaps this new habit doesn't feel quite right but has made you realize what you *do* want to start doing.

Whatever the observations, the important thing about evaluating your investments in each sphere is to capture what you've been doing and then start recognizing the results they're causing (or not) in the Me, We, and World dimensions. This will lead you toward your desired outcomes.

Case Studies: Some Sample Dashboards

To make the Dashboard come alive, I want to share a few samples. I'll introduce our Purpose Seekers now, and we'll follow them throughout the next six chapters. My hope is that these examples give you a practical sense of how the Dashboard can track and inform your investments toward living and leading with purpose. Each Purpose Seeker summarized their initial learnings in three areas: 1) What I'm Doing, 2) What I'm Not Doing, and 3) Am I Doing Me? (These "characters" represent composites of the hundreds of people with whom I've used the Dashboard over time, not any specific person.)

GABRIELA

Gabriela moved with her family from Panama to Texas when she was 11 years old. She's now 43, lives in Ohio with her husband and two kids, and works in marketing for a large, privately held consumer product company. She was recently promoted and now has six people reporting to her. The company has been through a lot of change in the last few years but is now doing quite well. Gabriela imagines this could be her last employer if she continues to advance to other roles throughout the organization.

After an experience with postpartum depression and a stress-related ulcer, Gabriela has refined a self-care routine that keeps her going. She's committed to these practices, including her healthy diet, midday walks, seven hours of sleep, and guided meditations each morning. Importantly, Gabriela has also brought her family and colleagues along on this journey, and they understand and encourage these practices to support her well-being.

Gabriela is a volunteer for her church's Sunday school, though now that her kids are in middle school, it provides less of the family time she valued so dearly when they were younger. She sits on the board of a local not-for-profit that supports maternal health, with a particular focus on immigrant mothers and families. Knowing how much need there is among families in the area, she would like to give more generously to this organization and others.

Since her promotion, Gabriela has been working on getting to know her new direct reports better. She's conscientious of the fact that they are overworked and not yet comfortable with the organization's new direction or hybrid work arrangements. She overheard two of her younger colleagues talking about their efforts to use less plastic at home and their conflicted feelings about helping to sell more plastic.

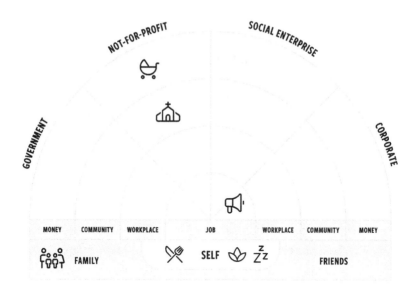

Figure 7. Purpose Seeker Gabriela's Impact Dashboard.
(She chooses to draw icons where she participates in
each Spectrum of Impact and sphere.)

We'll explore Gabriela's profile in greater detail in the chapters to come, but let's look at her initial takeaways from her Dashboard.

What I'm Doing. Despite always wanting to do better, I really am proud of the balance I've achieved in my non-professional (Job and Workplace) spheres, particularly having built a regime of self-investments that turned my physical and mental well-being around. I had no choice, but honestly I'm grateful for that wakeup call that got me taking better care of myself.

Seeing the Dashboard also showed me the extent to which I've been able to land a challenging and rewarding position at a company I really do feel aligned with, even if we're not necessarily saving lives or whales. We're not officially a Business for Good, but there's a lot we do that puts us closer to that side of the corporate section of the Spectrum of Impact.

And it's gratifying to me to see my commitment to our family come alive on the Dashboard. I take that seriously, but I don't always give myself full credit that this is a real investment that has consequences on me and the people I love most.

What I'm Not Doing. I notice several places on the Dashboard where I'd like to expand my efforts. At work, I'd like to focus on helping my direct reports manage their overwhelm, adapt to the new reality at the firm, and explore outlets for their environmental concern. Perhaps this can be done through lessons learned or partnerships with Businesses for Good in similar industries that have reduced the environmental harm of their packaging and supply chain.

In terms of finances, it occurs to me that I could probably better direct our family spending and investments in a way that supports women's health, moving beyond the not-for-profit part of the Spectrum. We're only able to donate so much to not-for-profits, but perhaps I could find more impact by engaging with Businesses for Good or corporates in our investment portfolio.

There's a stark gap in the government sector on the Spectrum of Impact. I really haven't engaged with public policy or elected officials, and I wonder how I might do that going forward.

In an intersection of the Family and Community Spheres, now that the kids don't attend Sunday school, it might be time to realign my volunteer activities as the kids' interests and activities change. That might mean volunteering with another not-for-profit organization or perhaps participating in a government-related activity per the last observation.

Am I Doing Me? I can honestly say that at this point, my Dashboard does represent my best self well. That said, it also reinforces the feeling I've been having for some time that I'm on the verge of a new phase in my career and life. I want my Dashboard to evolve to authentically guide and/or mirror that evolution.

Specifically, I see an opportunity to pay forward my learnings about self-care to my team by modeling tactics for avoiding burn-out and giving them permission to discover their own cocktail for well-being.

My kids have expressed an interest in policy and activism, particularly related to immigrants like their mom and grandparents. This seems like a way I can support family activity in the public sector, filling in a part of the Spectrum I haven't previously been active in.

DAVID

David is a Black man who grew up in the Bronx. He's 31 and has worked in finance since college. He's been a top performer in a few different roles, and after business school he began his current role as a vice president at a medium-sized private equity firm in Chicago. He expects to propose to his partner in the next year, so he's thinking about the next phase of his life in terms of lifestyle, financial stability, and building a legacy.

David learned to meditate through a program at his high school and has continued that practice almost daily ever since, recognizing how it helps him manage a busy and stressful career. He has always made time for basketball with friends and got into golf with a mentor earlier in his career.

He joined the junior board of a not-for-profit through his company before business school, but he didn't find it particularly satisfying and hasn't had time to explore anything similar since starting this new role. He worries about prospects for his future children in terms of racism in the workplace and American society more broadly, as well as the way climate change is affecting their health and living conditions.

Figure 8. Purpose Seeker David's Impact Dashboard.

We'll explore David's profile in greater detail in the chapters to come, but let's look at his initial takeaways from his Dashboard.

> *What I'm Doing.* I'm proud of my career success and the wealth I've been able to accumulate pretty early in my career. My family provided what I needed, but in college I saw a different level of wealth. It became important to me to earn a generous salary so I can treat my parents to trips and provide an abundant lifestyle for my future kids.
>
> There's no doubt I've been pretty singularly focused on my career in the corporate sector for that reason, which has squeezed out investments I could've made in other spheres and at other points on the Spectrum. I'm eager to find ways to rebalance how I'm spending my time in this next phase of my life, particularly as I look forward to marriage and having kids.

That said, I'm so grateful for the meditation I learned early in life. I know it's been a critical element of my Self Sphere to protect my well-being as I navigate a competitive career in finance, particularly as a gay Black man.

What I'm Not Doing. Several gaps occur to me when I look at the Dashboard and think where I'd like to be in terms of the impact I'm investing in.

In the Family Sphere, there's an opportunity to deepen the conversation with my partner about our shared values and how we want to pursue marriage and childrearing.

In the Community Sphere, I have a desire to find ways of engaging more deeply with my neighborhood now that we've settled down in a place where I can envision raising children. I've always respected small businesses; our neighbor ran the local grocery store where I used to help out after school. I'd love to find opportunities to support the businesses around us in ways other than just buying from them.

Financially, I want to revisit my charitable contributions as well as our investment portfolio. I'm eager to learn more about ways to align our income and wealth with the future I want to shape for our children. Perhaps this could also tie into the local business support.

Am I Doing Me? My Dashboard feels quite authentic and appropriate for where I'm at now. I was intentional about focusing on my career, and it's worked. That said, other than my desire for financial abundance and professional recognition, my efforts haven't been particularly reflective of my own identity or interests.

This moment feels like a natural time for me to consider ways to rebalance my investments across the spheres in a way that connects more specifically to my background. I'd like to integrate some of the elements of my identity, including my gender and family background, into the investments I make across my Dashboard.

I'm also realizing that there are powerful levers for the change I want to see in the government, not-for-profit, and Business for Good sectors, so the next chapter of my life will include more engagement in those areas.

LISA

Lisa is a partner in a midsized consulting firm. Her family moved from Korea to Southern California when she was a teenager. She's now 58, divorced, and living in Boston, and her daughter will graduate from college this year.

After eight years at a Top 4 global firm, Lisa went to work for a different firm because of its culture and focus on client projects with some dimension of social and environmental influence. Her choice of firm, as well as her top performance, has enabled her to choose high-impact projects in the private, public, and not-for-profit sectors across the Spectrum of Impact. Lisa takes great satisfaction in the positive changes she has contributed to, ranging from diversity in hiring strategies, affordable housing partnerships, and not-for-profit outcome-measurement tools.

Now, thanks in part to a pre-retirement program her firm offers for partners beginning to contemplate their next phase, Lisa has realized that it's time to see herself as the client. She's burned out from long hours and the constant outward orientation that client service requires. She knows she has a lot more energy and wisdom to contribute, but she wants it to align more closely with her own interests and needs.

Figure 9. Purpose Seeker Lisa's Impact Dashboard.

We'll explore Lisa's profile in greater detail in the chapters to come, but let's look at her initial takeaways from her Dashboard.

What I'm Doing. I'm proud of what I've achieved in my career. I've navigated a challenging and very White-male-dominated field to excel in a wide variety of client settings. And what's more, over time I've gotten increasingly more adept at helping clients integrate all stakeholders into our solutions so that they become win-win-wins. Now I can say that most of my client work contributes to real change with social and environmental impact as well as commercial benefits.

I also feel great about what I've invested in my family. My ex-husband and I navigated our divorce well and coparent relatively effectively, though I've always been the dominant parent. My daughter is maturing into a young woman whom I respect and have a great time with. I've also been able to spend the time and money to give my parents a very dignified old age, which was always important to me culturally and personally.

I guess I do the basics of self-care. I eat well, run a few days a week, and have gotten into yoga. I'm sure I could sleep more, but there's just not time.

What I'm Not Doing. I've never put myself first, and that's the most striking realization when I look at my Dashboard.

My Family Sphere dominates the lower half of my Dashboard. Between my cultural sense of duty to my parents, a career in client service, and being a single parent for most of my life, I've always had a full plate of others to whom I felt responsible that has eclipsed my investment in myself.

At work, I've started to see how my failure to understand, much less serve, my own needs and interests is holding me back. I haven't been able to be an inspiring leader or a creative problem-solver for clients in my Workplace Sphere.

My Community Sphere is also quite empty. Given that I'm not interested in retirement of the grandkids-and-golf variety, I wonder how investments in that area might come into play. I love the intellectual stimulation of my work and want to extend that as far into my life as I'm able, whether in formal employment or other activities. Perhaps the Business for Good sector would be a good space for this.

Am I Doing Me? My life to this point does represent a lot of the core values I recognize as being authentically me. But I'm also conscientious that they come as much from my cultural background and the profession I chose as they do from any sense of my unique self. I'm not sure what I would find if or when I do the reflection to uncover that true self, and it's a little scary to think that it might lead me to change how I spend my time or even regret what I've done for the last 40 years. But I think I've reached a point of curiosity combined with frustration that outweighs the fear, so I'm ready to discover what it is that I really want and need for the next phase in my life and make changes accordingly.

The Evolution of a Dashboard

You're probably clear by now that purposeful leadership is an evolving lifelong journey. You may find that exciting, overwhelming, or some of both. But I've yet to meet or learn of someone who has their purpose "figured out" for good. That's why I emphasize the importance of the ABCs of living and leading with purpose as a cyclical process. To illustrate this evolution, I'll share my own Dashboards for three decades of my adulthood to demonstrate how they can change and evolve.

THE 20S: EXPLORATION

As I've shared, when I graduated from college, I knew I wanted to help right the inequitable distribution of opportunity. Based on my understanding and cultural bias at the time, that meant to me that I would work in the not-for-profit sector. I was flexible in terms of the specific populations I'd work with.

As with David and many 20-somethings, my time, attention, and energy were predominantly focused in my Job and Workplace Spheres. I was making those investments in the not-for-profit sector on the Spectrum of Impact. Specifically, I focused on advancing human development and distributing opportunities to those who didn't have easy access.

In terms of my Family and Friends Sphere, I lived abroad, far from family and longtime friends, making expat communities linked to my jobs and local alumni clubs the center of my personal life. I met my first husband in my early 20s. We married when I was 26, though we both traveled extensively for work and didn't share many elements of traditional domestic life.

In my Self Sphere, I wasn't investing much at all in my physical or mental health, much less my personal growth or spirituality. It didn't feel like an act of rebellion at the time, but in retrospect I see that I ventured pretty far from the holistic approach to wellness, mindfulness, and spirituality that my mom modeled for me.

On an international development salary and with a lot of travel on my doorstep, I lived paycheck to paycheck, with very little attention or intention invested in my Money Sphere other than making minimum student loan payments and saving up for my next trip.

Figure 10. My Impact Dashboard for my 20s.

THE 30S: CONSOLIDATION

The beginning of my next professional decade was marked by business school, which I attended in a global executive program while working full time at the not-for-profit I had helped start in the Middle East.

In terms of my Job and Workplace Spheres, the MBA marked my move into the private sector, though at the Business for Good part of the Spectrum. It also propelled my formal shift to entrepreneurship. I always tended to be involved at the conception, something-to-nothing phase of projects, whether it was my party planning spinoff from my babysitting business at 12 or the projects and organizations I helped to start in my 20s. The MBA provided the vocabulary, strategic perspectives, and mentorship that still ground my identity as a founder.

Specifically, I started Inspiring Capital, a certified B Corp that developed tools, experiences, and connections to help people align their skills, needs, and interests with the needs of the world. My professional investments were focused on making work healthier, fairer, and more joyful for all of us, which was the focus of my Workplace Sphere throughout the decade. The specific activities I did in my Job Sphere evolved over many of Inspiring Capital's pivots.

At 32, I moved back to the US for the first time since college, which enabled more time with family members and longtime friends. In my home country, it was easier to make friendships based on common interests and values rather than driven by links in the expat community.

In other family and friends activities, this decade dawned with the demise of my first marriage and then was enlivened by meeting, falling in love with, and marrying my second husband and building our family.

My efforts within the Self Sphere also made an entrance in this decade. After the grueling and heartbreaking work with refugee women and children in Palestine and the physical and mental exertion of a global executive graduate program, I was burned out. I credit my mom's early modeling for my ability to develop mindfulness practices at this point, and my second husband for the physical fitness I began to value and prioritize more.

My Community Sphere investments were indistinguishable from my work. I was building a community of purpose-driven professionals as the customers and partners for my business, so I spent all my time on that form of community. These activities certainly aligned with my purpose and remained quite diverse given our cross-sector approach, but they offered neither diversification in terms of industry, relationships, or task categories, nor the truly extracurricular form of service that can be so rewarding about community investments that are unrelated to our work.

Figure 11. My Impact Dashboard for my 30s.

Finally, living in New York and entering my 30s increased my focus on the Money Sphere. I became aware of the B Corp movement and grew more conscientious about what I bought and from whom. I made more of a commitment to add monthly to the stock market portfolio my dad had started with me in college, even if in small amounts. I also started making small recurring donations to not-for-profits working on issues close to me and with a sense of urgency. I began to include political campaigns and grassroots organizing groups in my donation portfolio as well. Most of my financial investments, though, were in the equity of my company and my own professional profile, with my salary as a social entrepreneur still far below that of my peers.

THE 40S: EXPANSION

Now that I'm in my 40s, my Self Sphere investments have taken their proper place as the foundation of my impact. After years of exploring and consolidating that learning, I have a clear sense of what I need to feel and function at my best. As new tools and technologies for wellbeing cross my radar, I experiment eagerly, both to refine my own "wellness cocktail" (more on the "Cowgirl Chiller" in chapter 9) and to pay it forward as part of my work in guiding purposeful leaders. I've never felt more balanced, stronger, or better nourished, and I've never enjoyed more emotional resilience and equanimity.

I'm proud to have developed strong relationships with my stepkids, who've become an intimate and deeply rewarding part of my Family and Friends Sphere and are supported by the reflective and always-deepening marriage I share with my husband. I'm also closer to my mom than I was while living abroad or in the throes of entrepreneurship and dating in New York City, a relationship that I value deeply.

My friend groups continue to evolve based on geographic and logistical realities, as well as my own evolving priorities. My role as dog mom has also firmly implanted itself as a joyful investment in this sphere.

In terms of my Job and Workplace Spheres, a lot of learning, failure, and reflection have informed my shift from startup founder and CEO to the "Inspiring Cowgirl" (my LinkedIn title) who is wrangling a portfolio career and still focused on the outcome of distributing opportunity more equitably.

One important lesson came in my 20s when I was solely focused on one role in one organization: my expectations of the pace of work and change were unrealistic, which was causing frustration and stress for my team (and me) and ultimately resulted in inferior services for the refugee women and children we aimed to serve. Now I recognize that my best way of contributing is as a dot-connector ("wrangling ideas and people," per my purpose statement) to several organizations at once in more of an advisor or thought-partner role. The investments I make in my Job Sphere include designing and delivering leadership development programs, creating frameworks and tools for purposeful leadership, and advising and coaching leaders. I've learned to engage partners, employees, contractors, and technology to ensure that my job activities take the form of my ideal forms of contribution as often as possible.

In my Workplace Sphere, I've realized how important it is to me to reflect my own values and the nature of our work in the policies and practices of the organizations with which I'm involved, whether as founder, partner, or faculty. I've designed meeting agendas that include mindfulness and well-being as well as a team anti-racism practice accordingly. This portfolio approach has enabled me to build in more community activities that are truly external to my work. I've taken on advisor and board roles for purpose-driven startups and not-for-profits, and I participate in industry groups that promote Business for Good.

Thanks to a move out of the city, I've been able to ride horses a few times a week, a childhood habit that I've missed for decades and a beloved hobby that greatly enriches my Community Sphere. As goes the magic of community activities, this hobby has now blended with my professional interests, leading to another community activity of becoming an EQUUS faculty member, where I'm inspired by facilitating equine-assisted learning with the formidable Kelly Wendorf, whose Kanyini Care model appeared earlier in this chapter.

I find the most fulfillment from volunteering my time to advise, connect, and inspire entrepreneurs in the not-for-profit and Business for Good sectors. I also offer my time informally to my extended network and in mentor roles with not-for-profit entrepreneur networks, university programs, and events I attend locally and online.

In terms of money, I continue my efforts to be a conscientious consumer, donate to not-for-profits doing effective work to solve problems I care about, and invest in impact-conscious and purpose-driven companies. My main focus in this sphere is wealth creation, using the expertise and intellectual property I developed during the last decade of consolidation to expand my financial resources. I look forward to being able to pay forward the investments that others made in me to other purpose-driven entrepreneurs and thinkers.

Figure 12. My Impact Dashboard for my 40s.

I hope that in sharing this evolution of my own Dashboard you can appreciate the dynamics of the ways we live and lead purposefully and see the value of this tool as a guide for making that evolution intentional and impactful.

The next chapter is all about the obstacles that purposeful leaders bump into when trying to better align their work and lives with their desired outcomes. Because let's be honest, this all sounds great, so why aren't we already living deeply on purpose? Well, there are plenty of reasons, and none of us is exempt from their effects. I suggest examining them up close so you're best prepared to avoid or overcome them when they do come up.

Reflection Questions

Now we're really getting into the actionable portion of the book. If this is what you're here for, you can't miss out on the Going First Purpose Party Playbook. Get it at www.inspiringcowgirl.com/playbook.

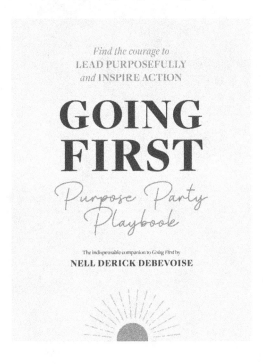

Or, for a taste of what that interactive work is like, download these questions as a free worksheet at www.inspiringcowgirl.com/goingfirst.

- What did your Baseline Assessment tell you at a glance? How do you feel about it?

- What has worked for you to track new habits in the past? What hasn't worked?

- What are your first and second choices to try: a habit tracker app, an accountability buddy at work or home, a highly visible checklist, or gold stars?

- What will you need on hand when you get to this point in each of the spheres? A downloaded app? A checklist? Gold stars?

- How will you record both quantitative and qualitative information? A journal? Quarterly updates with yourself? Quiet reflection sessions?

Chapter 8

Perilous Pitfalls to Leading Purposefully and How to Overcome Them

The main obstacles we encounter in leading and living with purpose fall into the same three dimensions as the action we inspire by leading purposefully: Me, We, and World. And I'm guessing all three of the upcoming pitfalls will sound pretty familiar. You've probably bumped into them before, whether in trying to lead and live more purposefully or in another change you were trying to make.

In the individual dimension, Me, we are plagued by inaction. We simply don't do what we want or need to do to improve our own well-being or that of other people and our planet.

In the shared, or We dimension of teams, organizations, and informal groups, we're swayed by "shoulding" and a drive to keep up with the neighbors. This shoulding comes in many forms, including policies, rules, incentive structures, and implicit norms.

And finally, in a more meta dimension, our World resists any changes to the status quo, or what I'll be calling "orthodoxy." The physical, biological, and social drivers for this resistance are perhaps the most critical pitfalls to overcome in our collective journey toward a healthier and fairer way of working. Going First is a powerful antidote to orthodoxy.

For each of these three pitfalls, we'll review why we fall into that particular pit, what happens when we do, and what to do instead. Then, in the chapters dealing with each sphere, we'll explore how each pitfall manifests in that sphere, help you identify how each one manifests for you, and provide specific tactics you can use to avoid them.

For now, let's explore these obstacles. After all, acknowledging a problem is the first step to overcoming it!

Pitfall #1: Inaction

The #1 pitfall in purposeful living is simply not doing it. We just don't spend the time, energy, or attention on the things we know would improve some element of our well-being, help a family member or colleague, or be good for the planet and the people around us.

A saying often attributed to a Chinese proverb goes, "The best time to plant a tree was 20 years ago. The second-best time is now."[36] That sentiment is likely not new to you, and we can say the same about Going First to lead purposefully. Most of us recognize our inaction in the moment—or shortly thereafter—at least sometimes. And yet we remain frozen. What drives this inaction despite our best intentions?

It's important to note that this pitfall resides squarely in the Me dimension. Whether we do something or not is in our control and our control alone. Of course, there are external factors that influence the likelihood of us taking action, and we'll get to those. But first, let's recognize that inaction is a problem we cause ourselves and can therefore be fixed by us.

WHY WE FALL INTO THE PITFALL
OF INACTION

We've all been there: sitting on the couch after a long day at work, thinking, *I really should go for a run. Or just a walk. Or at least get down on the floor and stretch* . . . and then proceeding to not move a muscle other than the remote finger. We recognize the signs of inaction: seeing burnout spreading through our team from behind the Zoom screen; becoming increasingly more concerned about the way we're paying our suppliers, having seen several of the smaller ones go bankrupt; or hearing a comment referencing the habits of a religious group that doesn't sit right. And then we proceed to not do anything about any of it.

Why, why, why do we sabotage ourselves through inaction throughout our work and lives? I see five main states that nudge us into the pitfall of inaction: inertia, apathy, fear of failure, trade-offs, and inconvenient truths.

Inertia. The first driver of inaction is a universal law of physics. Isaac Newton's First Law of Motion states that "A body at rest will remain at rest, and a body in motion will remain in motion unless it is acted upon by an external force."[37] So we tend to keep doing whatever we're doing in any of the spheres. And that tends to not be purposeful, because most of us are living in an extractive version of industrial capitalism that's contaminated by financial-only metrics, institutionalized racism, and devaluation of productive human traits such as empathy and collaboration.

To avoid confusion or conflict with ourselves, our families and friends, our colleagues, or our fellow community members, it's "easiest" to keep doing things like we always have. Particularly in an age of overwhelm, the status quo is the path of least resistance. And therein lies the success of inertia in preventing us from taking action.

Apathy. Another reason we don't take action is apathy. This lack of caring often originates in one of two extremes: hopelessness and pride.

"It's too late. I can't change the world."

This is the sense of hopelessness that comes from some combination of the sentiments that our lives are too difficult, the issues too complex, and the outcomes too constrained by external forces. We lapse into believing there's nothing we can do to substantially improve our own well-being or that of other people or the planet.

"I'm doing pretty well relative to so many people in the world. Do I really need to do anything more?"

Self-affirmation run amok can encourage us to rest on our laurels. In my interview with her, Chid Liberty shared the example of people interested in becoming anti-racist: "They think they're already in the Promised Land because they haven't said the N word in five years." This apathy is dangerous, particularly in a time of rapid change.

Fear of Failure. How many things would you like to try but don't? Fear of failure is a common reason for inaction. It's easy to think, *I'll never be able to maintain a daily meditation practice*, or *None of the other managers have mentioned their team's need for more flexibility; why should I bring it up?* It's also easy to write those thoughts off as silly when reading them here on the page—but they have more power over our choices than we'd like to think.

Another psychological phenomenon that makes fear of failure so powerful is loss aversion. We're more motivated by what we stand to lose in making a certain choice than we are in the upside of what we could gain. "What if the client hates that I mention our reduced environmental footprint in the pitch?"

is less likely to inspire action than "Who would the client be excited to tell about our reduced environmental footprint if I mention it in the pitch?"

Trade-Offs. As we've explored, our time, energy, and attention are limited, and most of us are using them for something already. So the inaction we're talking about is usually not doing something *differently* as opposed to not doing anything *at all*. Action, then, requires trade-offs. To invest our time, attention, and energy toward a more purposeful approach, we have to stop doing something else. As Ward Vuillemot explains, "You have to recognize you can't have everything. When you recognize the one thing you want, you become willing to sacrifice others. Let go of external motivators and look to yourself for your own justification for a certain behavior."

To make those trade-offs (which can look to our brains like an example of attention-catching loss), it's important to have a real understanding of your own desired impact and what is needed to achieve it, including that trade-off you're about to make. For example, maybe you know that a bigger or fresher breakfast will fuel your brain better for the day ahead, but it would mean reducing your Sunday night reading time to make egg muffins or overnight oats. In order to accept that trade-off, you have to be really convinced that the change will improve your well-being, performance, or fulfillment.

Similarly, you might want to invest in suppliers owned by women or another historically under-resourced population. But statistically those are smaller businesses, so you know it will take some time for your team to get onboarded to your procurement system, and it's a really busy season. You have to believe strongly enough in the potential ramifications to willingly choose the trade-off of your team's time.

Inconvenient Truths. A final fear that can lead to inaction is particularly insidious: We worry that if we reflect on the way we're spending our time and energy, we'll discover something in one or more of the spheres that isn't compatible with our current identity. We worry what inconvenient truth might pop up if we examine reality too closely, so we choose to do nothing at all.

The 2020 COVID-19 pandemic provoked massive change for many reasons, but one of the most commonly cited experiences was being forced to slow down, which made time for reflection. A lot of us didn't like what we saw about our pre-pandemic lives. We didn't like who we were with our life partners after exhausting days of commuting, working, and after-work drinks. We didn't like how we were managing our teams or relating (or not relating) to clients or suppliers. We didn't like how we were treating our own bodies and minds. And we didn't like that we stopped donating to a mental health organization after those first knee-jerk responses to a friend's post about her struggle with depression.

We have the choice to make time for reflection, even in the absence of a global pandemic. Are we willing to see what might emerge?

WHAT HAPPENS WHEN WE FALL INTO INACTION

The siren call of "business as usual" reverberates through all the spheres. Let's look at how succumbing to the lure of the proverbial couch of inaction plays out in the macro, team, and individual dimensions.

World. Inaction toward a healthier and fairer way of working is not okay for our collective well-being. The Climate Change 2022 Report issued by the UN's Intergovernmental Panel on Climate

Change stated, "Adaptation is urgent to the extent that soft adaptation limits are currently being approached or exceeded and that achieving levels of adaptation adequate to address these soft limits requires action at a speed and scale faster than that represented by current trends."[38] In other words, we must change our behavior now (in every sphere) if we want to preserve a livable planet.

The same is true for human well-being. Mental health is at a global all-time low in terms of incidences of anxiety, depression, and suicide among several demographic groups. We simply cannot carry on with our Industrial Era lifestyles in terms of pace, diet, and mental health practices.

Finally, inequity among races, religions, genders, ethnic groups, forms of ability, and other elements of identity is causing great harm that will grow if we don't take action. Lives are being lost as a result of racially motivated violence, international political unrest, and domestic abuse, among other equity-related issues. And the economic cost of this inequity is massive as well: $22.9 trillion just in the US in the last 30 years.[39]

The well-being—indeed, the very survival—of humankind relies on each of us making significant changes, starting today.

Here's how Swedish climate change activist Greta Thunberg, direct as always, talked about this during her speech at the Extinction Rebellion protest in London: "Humanity is now standing at a crossroads. We must now decide which path we want to take. How do we want the future living conditions for all living species to be like?"[40]

We. Simply put, with inaction we and our organizations crumble. This has always been true; it was about 100 years ago that Will Rogers said, "Even if you're on the right track, you'll get run over if you just sit there."[41]

These days, the specific form of inaction that's fatal for companies is to not recognize the demands from consumers, investors, and—perhaps most potently—employees to align our work with our values. In 2021, McKinsey published a report titled *Help Your Employees Find Purpose or Watch Them Leave*. Their threat presaged the Great Resignation, including a month during which more people left their jobs since the US Bureau of Labor Statistics started tracking this data.[42] Similarly, customers are switching away from brands that don't embody and communicate their values (interestingly, whether they match perfectly with the customers' values or not), and investors are divesting from companies that aren't addressing their holistic impact on all stakeholders.

Granted, this is all happening at a slower rate than many of us would like to see, but like most change, it's likely to continue accelerating. The average tenure of companies on the Fortune 500 list is shrinking—from 33 years in 1965 to 18 in 2012—a trend that's projected to continue.[43] For 21st-century organizations, the central question is "Evolve or die?" And the specific direction of evolution must be toward a healthier and fairer way of working that achieves justice and equity for all.

It's worth repeating that one reason to accept this invitation is our very existence as teams and organizations. Remember John Replogle's death sentence for zero-summers, who will lose if they don't change their approach to fit today's interconnected world.

Me. "Evolve or die" holds true for us as individuals too. As human beings, we're up against physics and the force of entropy. Without intentionality about how we invest our limited time, energy, and attention, we decline toward a state of disorder.

Further, that disorder will be in line with status quo norms, processes, and rules of the broken 20th-century model. The cost to individuals who don't learn a purposeful approach to their work and life will be professional irrelevance, to say nothing of isolation, depression, and an increased risk of heart disease, dementia, and premature death.

In other words, if we don't take action to shift our way of working and living in all of the spheres, we will not survive the rapid change, uncertainty, and increasing interdependence of the 21st century. Change is a mandate to individual thriving in this dynamic, interconnected era as much as it is for organizations and communities.

WHAT TO DO IN THE FACE OF INACTION

Now that we know why we tend toward inaction and what happens when we do, let's look for antidotes. No matter where you are on your purpose journey, you can be sure that you'll be confronted with inaction at some point. I want to highlight four approaches to overcome it: start somewhere, start with why, find opportunity in crisis, and reward yourself.

Start Somewhere. We blamed inaction on Newton's First Law of Motion, but it also states that "an object in motion stays in motion." So the first critical antidote to inaction is to start somewhere and make that law work for you by staying in motion once you begin.

Okay, but where to start? How do I know if I'm starting in the right place? I'm so glad you asked, because it brings us to my corollary to Newton's law: perfect is the enemy of good.

A commitment to continuous improvement, not perfection, is the enabler of action. We'll dig deeper in the chapters to come, but first—because trust me, you can do this!—pick a sphere you want to focus on and start there with one small but tangible action. It could be learning, interacting, doing, or changing something that will better align your impact with your desired outcomes. And if you haven't totally wrapped your head around the spheres yet (don't worry, we'll get there), I'm sure there's some action or habit you've been wanting to start. Pick that!

Your one action doesn't have to be brilliant, huge, or the thing you're now going to do daily for the next decade. Just try doing something and then see how it feels. Modern Western culture has devalued emotion and intuition as soft or touchy-feely, but ultimately our feelings are data. How ironic that in today's data-worshipping culture we're choosing to throw out these freely available forms of data!

Give yourself the advantage of having access to a richer data set: pay attention to your gut reaction when you try a new workout, a new meeting format designed to build more trust with your team, or any action you choose.

Start with Your Why. Still stymied as you try to gain traction on inaction? In the bestselling words of author and speaker on purpose Simon Sinek, "Start with why." Connect to what you care about. Remember Jeff and how his new granddaughter got him to the gym after 60 years? Or Lisa's commitment to providing clients with solutions that are both good for them and their employees, suppliers, and communities? They were motivated to act by staying in touch with their values.

Raj Thakkar, CEO of social ventures Charter School Business Management and Foresight, connects to his values to overcome apathy and loss aversion. He explains the tactic that helps him step out of his comfort zone across all the spheres: "Curiosity is a core value for me! I've always enjoyed exploring new ideas and experiences. Part of that exploration is reading. I borrow library books not only to minimize my purchases, but also so I have a deadline to read them by. Reflection is important to me, which I get at by meditating regularly and peer learning through groups like Entrepreneurs' Organization and Young Presidents' Organization."

What value or purpose is driving you now? Maybe you're motivated by growth, equity, joy, watching your granddaughter thrive, or creating win-win-wins for your team, your clients, and the environment. If you're still stuck, the next six chapters will help you take inventory of where you're already investing in working and living the way you want to—which inevitably also reveals some gaps.

Find Opportunity in Crisis. Another approach is offered by Purpose cofounder and CEO Jeremy Heimans: "How to overcome inertia? Take advantage of crisis! In the multiple crises of the 2020s, we're seeing a mix of old-power and new-power surges. Turn those surges into new-power structures, which are open, participatory, and peer driven."

Indeed, COVID-19 and simultaneous human and environmental crises drove many leaders to embrace purpose more publicly and/or translate it into action more boldly than they had before. Activist and public policy expert Dia Bryant agrees that we have a great opportunity to transmute these crises "from a moment into a movement, with sustainable changes in why, when, and how we take action."

What crises are you facing in your life, whether personal, in your team, or more macro situations that weigh on your reality? They need not be catastrophic to provide the opportunity to change; sometimes they're simply big transitions, such as being promoted, having a grandchild, or being ill. They're often catalyzing because they provide a higher-level reason for change. Gayle Jennings-O'Byrne described these opportunities as a "moment where we stop being afraid."

Reward Yourself. There's one more way to make science work for us in overcoming inaction: operant conditioning. Just like Skinner's rats in the lab, we respond to rewards. And we respond best to rewards that are internal (feeling good about ourselves) rather than external (a gold star, extra dessert, or praise). The outcomes of purpose are exactly the internal drivers that motivate us in a sustainable way.

So as you try these new, small, imperfect actions to live and lead more purposefully, make sure you observe the upsides, whether it's a simple warm fuzzy feeling, longer periods of concentration, or smoother collaboration with a colleague. Then tie that outcome to what you did and write it down in a simple affirmation or quick journal entry like this one: "When I open the team meeting with a quick personal check-in, I feel more connected to the team, and we have more productive problem-solving conversations."

Pitfall #2: Shoulding

The second major pitfall on the path to leading and living with more purpose is doing what we think we "should" do. This "shoulding" may be based on what our colleagues, neighbors, or family members do or on what they told us, directly or indirectly, that we should do.

Shoulding is often heavily influenced by mass media. And we see plenty: ads are the form of media most closely tracked, and the average number of ads we see a day is rising exponentially, from about 500 in the 1970s[44] to as many as 10,000 in the early 2020s,[45] with no slowing in sight. Some ads directly tell us what advertisers think we should do. Others include professionally developed fictional and real-life stories that may be less obvious but are very effective at influencing our choices about how we invest in each of our spheres. Just think about the images of "family" depicted in advertisements for coffee, pasta sauce, or minivans or the images of a "professional" in laptop or broadband ads. I'm guessing that the people, activities, and/or values reflected don't necessarily match your image of your best self.

The brilliant writer Margaret Atwood advises, "*Should* is a futile word. It's about what didn't happen. It belongs in a parallel universe. It belongs in another dimension of space."[46] Until we manage to banish *should* to another dimension, we can at least get better at recognizing shoulding and building strategies to avoid its grip.

Shoulding is a We-dimension issue. The notion of something we *should* do can arise only from groups. Sometimes the group presents the notion of what we should do; sometimes it's just our imagination or interpretation of group norms. A lot of good comes from being part of and identifying with groups, whether a neighborhood, work or sports team, religious association, horoscope network, or otherwise. But the downside to any of these group affiliations is a narrowing of what we see as possible or desirable. Indeed, "groupthink" is a recognized psychological phenomenon by which groups accept suboptimal decisions simply to maintain harmony. The group-based origin of shoulding is important to recognize as we prepare ourselves to resist it when it counters our purpose-aligned behavior.

WHY WE FALL INTO SHOULDING

Let's consider why these group-generated ideas of what to do can have such sway over our choices. Hint: it's no accident!

Organizations are designed primarily to align action by a group of people, and alignment is easiest to maintain when there aren't changes or discord in pace or direction. So organizations tend to encourage, reward, and even demand that we do nothing different from what we did yesterday or what our colleagues are doing. You might recognize this as "Because we've always done it that way" syndrome. Different organizations certainly suffer from (or enjoy) different strains of this ailment, but even the most innovative and fast-moving must have some norms to shape their members' behavior.

Purposeful "unconsultant" Meighan Newhouse, CEO and cofounder of Inspirant Group, recalls working with a client on a transformation project. As always, they had started with the process at hand and were reviewing the team's steps in a certain business activity. One particular step jumped out as cumbersome, so Meighan asked why it was done that way. The client team was quiet, and then one person said, "[A former colleague] told us to do it that way."

Before Meighan could ask more, another member of the client team exclaimed, "[That former colleague] hasn't worked here for five years!"

This type of shoulding is incredibly pervasive once you start looking for it. And not surprisingly, shoulds are often incredibly unhelpful! Try to identify and undo them whenever you can, and as quickly as possible.

A particularly explicit form of shoulding comes in performance metrics, such as sales targets, output expectations, or quality standards. But it also shows up outside the workday in the form of our phones telling us to walk more, our spouses pushing for a spending limit in our households, or a volunteer board requiring us to raise a certain amount of money. There are also explicit but less measurable expectations we've integrated from childhood, such as "work hard" and "be generous." These expectations not only constrain the way we invest our time, energy, and attention (often without our awareness) but also account for a narrow range of outcomes, which can lead to overemphasis on certain quantitative elements of our inputs and results.

Responsible-luxury fashion entrepreneur Vanessa Barboni Hallik feels the pressure of these shoulds, saying, "It's hard because collectively we still measure results in a narrow way. I'm conscious that my team's well-being, suppliers' living wages, and customers' delight at our products have very direct bearing on our survival and profitability. But the vast majority of investors merely want to see a downward trend in unit cost and accelerating progress toward profitability."

These bottom-line measures are important, to be sure, and purpose-driven leaders are clear that the shoulding that aligns with their desired impact is more nuanced than the black-and-white financial indicators we tend to focus on. There are also sociological, evolutionary, and psychological reasons we're subject to shoulding.

Tribal Shaming. As well as explicit and implicit forms of shoulding from organizational forces, our peers also work to keep us "in line"—often unknowingly. Clinical neuropsychologist Dr. Mario Martinez leads the thinking about *tribal shaming.* This concept is basically the idea that people use shoulding to protect a shared group by maintaining its norms and discouraging deviance.

In practice, tribal shaming shows up in the comments from friends, colleagues, or the devil-in-an-angel-costume on your shoulder when you take action to lead purposefully. Your spouse remarks, "You seem so tired since you started getting up to meditate. Are you sure you're getting enough sleep?" A colleague comments, "Congratulations on that new hire. Good for you for finding someone qualified who didn't go to an Ivy League school!" These observations are rarely intended to be mean or devalue your investment in positive change, but their effect in discouraging your courage is undeniable. Your new behavior doesn't fit the established group norms, and that creates discomfort for people in the group who haven't yet changed.

Humans Tend to Conform. Before moving on to the risks of shoulding, let's recognize our role in these group-driven pressures. Shoulding comes from groups, and as social beings we're inherently susceptible to it. If we are to survive as a collaborative species, we must have some interest in meeting the expectations of the various groups to which we belong.

Research has shown that we learn from our peers to like or fear things even without having direct experience with them ourselves. Whether it's our preference for bananas or apples or the way we run a meeting, we follow what we see others doing rather than experimenting and coming to our own conclusions. This social learning is the root cause of "Because we've always done it that way" syndrome. It's very helpful in building and maintaining culture, but it conflicts directly with change, including the change required for purposeful leadership to become the norm.

Further, most humans (not all, allowing for neurodiversity) have an innate desire to please, be liked, and perform well. We want to meet the expectations that our groups set out for us, even when they aren't in line with our desired impact.

Particularly in fast-paced, high-stress, and hybrid or remote organizational settings that elicit and reward continuity, all of this means that we're unlikely to make the choice to do something new or different.

Shoulding Ourselves. Beyond the formal and informal shoulding put forth by our various groups, we also create our own from images in the media, examples set by our parents or other mentors, and other abstract inputs we encounter beyond the confines of any specific group. These can often be the most dangerous forms of shoulding, because we make them up ourselves and they are thus difficult to trace or uproot.

Shoulding sometimes reveals itself easily by the presence of the word *should* in a thought or statement. But it can also hide in the form of what we accept as consensus reality, or simply "how I do things." I'm a perfect example. It took me 10 years to undo the belief that I *should* spend my career in the not-for-profit sector if I wanted to have an influence on the way opportunity is distributed. No career counselor or measurement tool told me this; I just absorbed it from my cultural surroundings, which say (particularly loudly, in the 20th century) that not-for-profit is the place to do work that's good for the world.

As she approaches her fifth decade of work, our Purpose Seeker Lisa is just beginning to see how accepting that she *should* put her family and clients first limits her potential as a mom and strategic partner. And David spent the first decade of his career following the shoulds of what to wear, how to speak, and where to live as a finance professional. Now he's opening up to the learnings shared by Tanya Perkins and Nuno Guerreiro in chapter 3 about the ways our unique features can be strengths.

Like Lisa and David, hone your ability to recognize illusory, outdated, or counterproductive ideas about what you should do or how you should be doing it, particularly as the world moves so quickly around us. Eventually, by following the ABCs of Purposeful Leadership and using the tools in this book, you'll be able to turn up the volume on the only worthy form of shoulding: the type that comes from your true, purpose-aligned self.

WHAT HAPPENS WHEN WE FALL INTO SHOULDING

Shoulding is dangerous. In such a fast-changing era as the 21st century, external shoulds don't make a lot of sense. In fact, established ideas of what we *should* do have become counterproductive or even risky. If we are to live and lead in line with our purpose and have the impact we want to have on this world, we'll have to overcome shoulding and update our behavior to reflect current realities and available knowledge.

Think about dietary advice over the last 20 years. Eggs were a deadly vector of cholesterol; now they're the best breakfast you can start with. Cholesterol itself was the public enemy #1, to be avoided like the plague, until we learned the difference between its good and bad versions. Butter, carbs, and fat have each ridden their own version of this rollercoaster.

"Best" practices have also changed dramatically. From an era of "Six Sigma" error-free uniformity to the "Agile" approach to software or management that uses self-organized teams and real-time process changes, we build things differently than we used to. In addition, the five-day workweek was all but buried during the 2020 COVID-19 pandemic.

Surely other "best" practices will emerge with time, yet the outdated guidelines about how things should be done still exert a lot of control over our behavior and choices. To live purposefully and contribute to a fairer and healthier world, we need to escape this We-level shoulding.

WHAT TO DO IN THE FACE OF SHOULDING

The ultimate antidote to shoulding is independence of thought. This could be seen as complete neutrality or enlightenment. When asked about the source of her courage to Go First and lead purposefully, for example, Chanel Cathey explained, "I may have achieved many firsts, but I'm not even aware. I'm just running my own race, not looking around to see what everyone else is doing. I get clearer and clearer about what I love and work at how I can do that."

Other leaders I've worked with and interviewed shared a similar perspective, but I'm conscious that this ability to avoid the shoulding we encounter at work and in life is a high bar. If you're crossing it even sometimes, congratulations! If you're not, you're just not there yet. Keep that growth mindset and feel good that you'll get there eventually. In the meantime, hopefully by now you've come to believe me when I say that I'm a pragmatist. So I'll offer a practical approach to freeing yourself from shoulding:

Surround Yourself with Purposeful Leaders. Rather than trying to break free of shoulds, leverage your biology and neurology as a social animal. Shoulding can be positive, but only if and when it aligns with your own desired impact. Change the shoulds you're exposed to by surrounding yourself with others who model and support purposeful leadership.

If you haven't yet found purposeful people in your daily life, you can make them part of your reality in other ways. Read their books (Congrats! You're here, aren't you?!), listen to their podcasts, and follow their social media feeds or newsletters. As you make decisions, ask yourself, "What would Gabriela (or Nell or David or Lisa or any of the other purposeful people in this book) do?"

Since non-purpose-aligned shoulds are hard to completely eliminate, there's another powerful method you can use in tandem with surrounding yourself with purposeful leaders. Since shoulding falls into the We dimension, so does one of its primary antidotes: conversation. Talking about the shoulds you feel trapped by and the shoulding you'd like to replace them with helps gather accountability and momentum for your desired change.

Longtime purpose-driven multihyphenate MaryAnne Howland recommends having courageous conversations to learn from one another: "It's why we created Leadership Exchange. So that [Purpose Seekers] can have experiences together, immersing ourselves in a purposeful approach to our work, and learn that new language."

Likewise, visionary community-builder and investor Vicki Saunders, founder and CEO of Coralus (formerly SheEO), learned from her parents' barn-raising parties that "Engaging people in your dreams gets them engaged in your dreams." Sharing your new shoulds as you learn and practice them has the same effect.

So have a conversation and share your desire to align with your purpose, the questions it's raising for you, and the ways it's making you think about how you *should* behave. Therein lies the power of Going First. By sharing your interest in aligning with a larger purpose, you start to normalize it and make it safe—and eventually a default for those around you to do the same.

Here's the upside of our social nature: we're disposed to mimic the behavior of those around us. There are cells in our brains (mirror neurons) dedicated to this purpose, whether it's smiling back at a smile or adopting our conversation partner's speech pattern.

The tides are with us as Purpose Seekers in the 21st century. The interconnectedness, existential crises, and technological advances of our time are moving us toward a reality in which shoulding is about prioritizing purpose as a guiding force in our work and lives. And it's happening fast. So even if you'd swear that your manager (or Aunt Judy) doesn't feel any sense that she should (!) be thinking more about the impact she has on a day-to-day basis, why not ask a simple question to feel it out? You might be surprised how she responds to the simple one-two: "What are you excited about these days? Why does that matter to you?"

For those of you who haven't yet uncovered this Purpose-Seeker shoulding, do keep looking. Purpose Seekers are often hiding in plain sight, and they're becoming more common and more visible every day!

Replacing Our Shoulds. Eventually, when enough of us are Going First, asking Aunt Judy what matters to her and why and running our meetings and family dinners accordingly, we will change the shoulding to line up with a healthier, fairer, more joyful way of working. The professional and personal groups to which we belong will change their norms about what behavior and outcomes are valued. We do this first by changing processes, structures, and performance metrics, which is already happening.

At Accenture, Christie Smith advises the majority of the Fortune 500 on their people and culture strategies—their formal shoulding. She pointed out, "Leaders are now being measured on how they are investing in their team's overall well-being and being held to account for their engagement with employees."

The same organizational tools for the status quo shoulding that led to rampant burnout, stagnant productivity, and gender and racial bias and inequity in our companies and society can be replaced with training, rules, and incentives that elicit the healthier, fairer way we want people to lead and live. Purposeful leaders recognize this and are doing something about it. Tech sector people leader Amy Dolan says that in the fast-growing companies she works with, "We know we need to evolve with the world." To Amy, that looks like changing manager training to include empathy, expanding benefits packages to include mindfulness programs and personal development stipends, and integrating sustainability metrics into bonus calculations.

Similarly, investment advisor Geeta Aiyer has come to see that she has the power and responsibility to replace investors' shoulds about how they evaluate companies. She recalls, "I asked an analyst about their company's policy on promoting women after their competitor was sued for failing to promote men and women equitably. I realized it was incumbent on me to ask these questions—not only to drive the equity I wanted to see, but in my role as a fiduciary, given the business risk of the issue. We were needlessly complicit if we were silent."

We can make these same replacements to the shoulding we project and internalize in all the elements of our lives, including our expectations of ourselves, our families and friend groups, our communities, and money management.

A Prerequisite for Change: Failure. Replacing old shoulds with new, sustainable ones isn't always a smooth process. It will inevitably generate some confusion and misunderstanding, and it will only take hold in groups that accept or even celebrate those failures. Openness to failure starts with a growth mindset: the belief that you aren't fixed in your knowledge or capacities but can learn new ideas and skills. Then add in psychological safety, the knowledge that failure resulting from strategic experimentation (rather than willful negligence or ill intent) won't result in punishment. Later, we'll consider ways to normalize failure to make this important element of change specific and approachable.

PITFALL #3: ORTHODOXY

"There are these two young fish swimming along and they happen to meet an older fish swimming the other way, who nods at them and says, 'Morning, boys. How's the water?' And the two young fish swim on for a bit, and then eventually one of them looks over at the other and goes, 'What the hell is water?'"[47] I heard this parable during David Foster Wallace's 2005 graduation speech at Kenyon College. His theme was encouraging the class of 2005 to resist "unconsciousness, the default setting, the rat race." And that's exactly our third pitfall.

I'll label this pitfall *orthodoxy*: the messages we ingest from the water in which we swim and the air we breathe. It's a trickier version of inertia because it originates in the World dimension. These are concepts such as "Families spend holidays together," "It's hard to make money," and "No pain, no gain." This prevailing systemic resistance to change is a powerful obstacle to a healthier, fairer, and more joyful way of working.

The ideas of orthodoxy cross all spheres, and we each have our own unique set of them depending on our backgrounds. As professionals in a global economy, we share enough orthodoxy to create what can be called *consensus reality*, or "the way things are." Only they're not—or won't be for much longer.

We haven't come all this way to be discouraged by this macro-level pitfall. Like all pitfalls, it's surmountable by our own action and all the ripple effects that action has. Recall anthropologist Margaret Mead's inspiration: "Never doubt that a small group of thoughtful, committed citizens can change the world; indeed, it's the only thing that ever has."[48] If you respond better to negative imagery, use an African proverb's encouragement: "If you think you are too small to make a difference, try sleeping with a mosquito."[49]

WHY WE FALL INTO ORTHODOXY

Between globalized media and communication technologies, cultural expectations have become more similar than different as we all see, consume, and talk about more and more of the same things. Further, these messages have become louder and more frequent. As humans, we want to fit into those predominant ideas, but we also want to be distinct. And to be purposeful, we need to buck a lot of the more out-dated ideas. But it's difficult to unseat this compelling set of ideas of what leadership, health, success, family, and other elements of our lives look like. Research has demonstrated some of the forces that explain the strength of orthodoxy.

Conformity. We succumb to the resistance posed by media and other cultural norms about the way we do things because of the psychological phenomenon known as *conformity bias.* Arthur Jenness first labeled the concept in 1932, so it's nothing new. Conformity bias means we tend to go along with the group. We do this for a variety of reasons, maybe because we want to be liked, look smart, or fit the image we think others have of us. It's such a powerful force that we do it even when it means betraying our true feelings or opinions, putting ourselves or others at risk (Google "Smoky Room Experiment" for a striking example), or contradicting observable facts.

There are different types of conformity. Sometimes we conform just to avoid punishment, impress someone, or strengthen our membership in a group. Other times, we internalize a cultural norm and make it part of our own value systems and identities. That type of internalized conformity is the most insidious because overcoming it means recognizing and then extracting external norms from our own brains and hearts. Asha Curran is a deeply purposeful leader, yet she, too, has an "inner voice of doubt, whether it's impostor syndrome or otherwise, that gets quieter every year as I get clearer and clearer on my purpose and how to activate it in each moment of my day and life. But the voice is still there."

Optimal Distinctiveness. Another psychological driver that comes into play here is *optimal distinctiveness*. Marilynn B. Brewer identified optimal distinctiveness as the balance we seek between similarity to and difference from the groups to which we belong.[50] We wear yoga pants or sweats to workouts and dresses or suits to weddings, but we want those items in a color and cut that shows our unique style. We're careful to speak up in meetings, but with ideas that fit solidly within our boss's known position on each issue. We want to make a great first impression with a new colleague or potential in-law, but we also want to be remembered for exactly how we do it in our own way. In other words, optimal distinctiveness is not about resisting all conformity. What *is* required is that we invest our time, energy, and attention in understanding what we actually care about changing and focus on resisting the external metrics and priorities that prevent such change.

Optimal distinctiveness explains the power of Going First. We can stand to be only so different from our context. So until someone in a group or organization—ideally someone with some form of authority—has Gone First to express their commitment to a higher purpose, no one else is likely to speak up about their own. As soon as there's some recognition that purpose drives performance—think of the corporate purpose statements that proliferated during the early 2000s—it becomes exponentially easier for people throughout an organization to lead with purpose. They can experience this level of inclusion and express their distinctiveness through whatever divergent behaviors are required to overcome the resistance to change they care about.

WHAT HAPPENS WHEN WE FALL INTO ORTHODOXY

When we let orthodoxy dominate, we don't make the changes that will move us toward a fairer, healthier, and sustainable future for people or our planet. This World-dimension pitfall is often the final obstacle between us and leading purposefully to live a life we're proud of. We've decided to take action, ignored or transformed the shoulds of our group, and now we're cowed by the dominant narrative at hand. We've been taught that hard workers don't sleep eight hours a night and that powerful leaders don't admit they made an offensive comment based on ignorance about an ethnic group.

A vivid example comes from Michael Pirron, founder and CEO of Impact Makers, a consulting firm with a unique ownership structure that ensures the company's service to employees and the community. He was pushed out by his own board after running his company for more than 10 years. (He did manage to regain control, but not without a struggle.) He blames the ordeal on "Hubris. I thought I had changed traditional businesspeople into employees and board members who would uphold our somewhat radical business model of redistributing profits. But I hadn't. We had taken action and changed our internal norms, but when push came to shove, in the face of external pressure, they reverted to the cultural norms [orthodoxy] of how a business is run."

What does this resistance to change look like on a more meta level? Economists have measured the cost of inequality in education, employment, and wages, and it's massive: nearly $22.9 trillion in the US between 1990 and 2021, according to one study whose authors include San Francisco Federal Reserve Board President Mary Daly.[51] Globally, the gender gap in earnings collectively costs us twice as much as the global GDP, or $160 trillion, according to the World Bank.[52] So the choice to join this Purpose Party and summon the courage to do things differently is not a trivial matter.

WHAT TO DO IN THE FACE OF ORTHODOXY

Imagine yourself weakening orthodoxy by spotlighting change makers to normalize them, balancing inclusion and distinctiveness, and changing the business culture. Given the collective cost in economic, human, and environmental terms, let's move right along to how we can overcome this World-dimension pitfall to purposeful leadership.

See It to Believe It. A powerful antidote to inaction in the World dimension is to shine a light on people who are leading and living purposefully. It's far too common to tell stories of violence, corruption, and chaos, particularly in a market for which those are the stories that sell ad space and sustain our commercial media industry. We have to normalize and celebrate people who are taking action, however small it might be, to make their world a better place. Stories require readers and listeners, so we have to pay attention when people talk about changemakers, those people Going First.

Kari Warberg Block is founder and CEO of EarthKind, which develops and sells plant-based pest control products. She explains, "We learn by seeing and doing, so when it comes to doing business or living our lives differently, people really need to see it to believe it. You don't know what you don't know when the dominant narrative is so pervasive."

Resisting the dominant narrative means resisting the allure of shiny, well-positioned stories about the tragedies that grab far too much of our collective attention. Global media most often uphold resistance to change by portraying the status quo. But they can also be leveraged to show more of us than ever what's possible and provide a level of transparency that enables us to hold people, companies, and governments accountable. Part of my intent with this book is to shine just that light on just these people who are leading and living purposefully in a huge variety of industries and differently sized companies, roles, and geographies. The ongoing community behind the book is an open one; your invitation goes beyond these pages to our digital and intangible group of folks who are Going First.

Balance Inclusion and Distinctiveness. Jeremy Heimans, who offered chaos as an antidote to inertia, our first pitfall, also sees a way to leverage optimal distinctiveness for change. In *New Power*, co-written with Henry Timms, Jeremy sees big potential for change in organizations that enable people to strike a balance between inclusion and distinctiveness. For example, leaders who Go First offer a clear organizational purpose that people can identify with. They model their own ways of living and leading purposefully as individuals. Those We- and Me-level examples of purpose offer the opportunity to feel included in a team working toward a common goal or as a like-minded colleague.

But to actually catalyze purpose throughout their organizations, purposeful leaders also empower each individual to identify and live out their distinctiveness. They do this by investing in their colleagues' understandings of their unique individual purposes. It's then that professionals feel included and valued for the specific ways they want to contribute within and beyond the organization.

Change the Business Culture. If cultural norms rob us of what could be healthy, fair, and joyful ways of working and living, why not build new norms? Purpose-driven entrepreneurs are eager to be part of exactly that transition.

Andrew Kassoy and his cofounders started B Lab, the not-for-profit that developed the globally recognized certification of businesses that are good for the world. Their goal, in Andrew's words, is to "Change the culture of business. We know that we need new norms, expectations, and ultimately a narrative about the private sector if it's going to be sustainable long-term."

To get there, Bryan de Lottinville, founder of field-leading corporate social responsibility software Benevity, knows that "We need mindset change. We need to help employees see the *why* behind these programs. Some elements of the flywheel are in place to make and magnify that change. Ultimately, we need people with power to make different decisions about who to hire as CEO, how to treat suppliers, and what products to design and offer." Those decisions are the substance of building new norms and Going First.

What's more, Jeremy Heimans reminds us, "It's not enough to be right. We need to spread values with creativity and passion, ensuring that they are strategically communicated to attract the broad support they deserve, given that a fairer and healthier way of working stands to benefit all of us." In other words, we can expect more of ourselves, each other, our organizations, and capitalism as a system.

As Chid Liberty stated, "I'm as pro-free-market as you can get. But the currently operating global economy is so biased that it's not free at all. We've regressed to such low expectations of humanity in the Industrial Age's quest for efficiency."

With its globalism and smart technologies, the knowledge economy enables a new set of expectations. Recall John Replogle's warning that "The end is in sight for zero-summers." It's now possible to sell more while enhancing employees' lives, paying suppliers more, and growing our market share. We need to make this the norm!

Make a New Playbook. This new norm has become the playbook of many conscientious businesses, not least of which is Unilever's Sustainable Living Brands, which delivered 75 percent of the conglomerate's growth in 2019, growing 69 percent faster than their other lines. However, this focus doesn't mean that Unilever is doing everything right or that their business doesn't cause some harm to some people or elements of our planet.

Patagonia is very clear about their extreme efforts at minimizing harm being just that: a reduction in the harm their business inherently does, not actually leaving the planet better off than if they didn't exist.

Nick Francis, founder and CEO of a help-desk software called HelpScout, is clear that help-desk optimization isn't really his highest calling. He started the company to "influence the next generation of entrepreneurs by providing a new playbook in which businesses balance profit and purpose, leaving customers, employees, shareholders, their community, and the environment better off."

Similarly, Pernell Cezar became an entrepreneur making coffee as a path to reducing the wealth gap as much as selling beans to shift his own benchmarks. Now, he defines success as "parity across ethnocommunities" and works toward that by growing his own business and paving a path for other historically under-resourced people to benefit from large corporate buyers.

Pick Your Wins. While we collaboratively write our new playbook, it can be an important change strategy to choose the chapters that we implement rather than trying to do it all at once.

Sandi Kronick, CEO and cofounder of Happy Dirt, a B Corp-certified purveyor of organic produce and packaged foods, relates to the process of resisting orthodoxy in her work and life: "More people don't do it because it's scary. It's exhausting. If you don't have gumption and determination everywhere in your body, heart, and mind, even in the tiniest, most random cells, you're going to fold at some point and give in to some element of the dominant narrative. And by the way, it can sometimes be healthy to do so!"

Thankfully, as we've discussed, the upside of resisting at least some of the cultural norms in the ways we work and live is huge. It benefits our mental and physical well-being, increases our performance on the individual and team levels, and ultimately enables equity, justice, and joy.

We have limited willpower related to our limited attention budget, so it's true that we have to "pick our battles," as they say. It's not sustainable to counter every norm we unearth every day; we'd collapse from fatigue or frustration and probably make some bad decisions. Some norms are good ideas and lead to well-being for ourselves, other people, and the planet. Again, the way forward is to get clear about the problems you care about solving so you can focus your attention on resisting the norms that represent obstacles to your chosen actions.

As longtime leader Katy Gaul-Stigge, CEO of Goodwill NY/NJ, points out, "Behavior change simply takes time. As our individual attention spans shorten and organizational time frames contract, it can be hard to allow the time required to make real changes." Effective purposeful leaders recognize this and choose their wins accordingly, finding satisfying short-term ones to sustain the energy that's necessary for the long-term ones.

Onward!

I encourage you to take a break after this chapter. Treat yourself with a moment in the sunshine, a cuddle with your dog, or a goofy meme spree on your phone. The pitfalls are critical to cover, but they're as heavy as the risks of succumbing to them.

So give yourself a pause. Know that you'll come back in part 3 to the most actionable and inspiring part of the purposeful leadership journey. We'll map your Dashboard sphere by sphere, celebrating the ways you're already having impact and finding feasible and uplifting ways to get even closer to the purposeful life you want to be living. See you there!

Reflection Questions

Our "why nots" can be the biggest barrier to achieving our "why." It's important to really get familiar with what will get in your way. Download these questions as a worksheet at www.inspiringcowgirl.com/goingfirst. For even more guidance in overcoming your unique pitfalls—check out the Going First Purpose Party Playbook.

- Which of the pitfalls do you foresee being the biggest challenge for your purpose work and why?
- What do recognize right now to be your go-to responses to each pitfall?
- What can you start doing right now to prepare yourself for facing each pitfall?

Part 3

Your Impact Dashboard

You now have all the tools to live and lead with purpose, including the science of why to do it, a framework with which to measure it, and the reasons you might not do it along with ways to overcome them. Now it's time to roll up your sleeves and use the Impact Dashboard to get a snapshot of where you are now.

For some of you, this is an exciting prospect. You can't wait to brainstorm what you're doing and what you'd like to do more of. You love a specific, action-oriented guided reflection. Fabulous! For others, you might be feeling a bit anxious. You love the theory of purposeful leadership, and you have a feeling you're doing it in some parts of your life, but the idea of really putting pen to paper and capturing how your efforts do or do not align with the impact you want to have sounds scary, overwhelming, or discouraging.

If you're in the latter camp, flip back through chapter 4 (Why You Want to Accept This Invitation) and/or the first section of chapter 8 (about the pitfalls of inaction). Or just sit with this quote for a minute:

Action is a great restorer and builder of confidence. Inaction is not only the result, but the cause of, fear. Perhaps the action you take will be successful; perhaps different action or adjustments will have to follow. But any action is better than no action at all.

~Norman Vincent Peale

If you're still a bit hesitant about proceeding, I ask you to trust me. What I'm going to share with you integrates two decades of study, reflection, and experience with thousands of leaders from a broad array of backgrounds. That work has revealed myriad obstacles, confusion, aha moments, inspiration, and stuckness, all of which have informed this version of the process. So let's do it. There will be all of those things for you, but the result is SO worth it!

The Roadmap

In the next six chapters, I'll share the ways purposeful leaders invest in each of the six spheres. To help make this work approachable for you, I use a blend of examples from my own life, the lives of our Purpose Seekers (Gabriela, David, and Lisa), and the lives of over 150 leaders I interviewed for this book.

The idea is not to present an exact blueprint, but to help you envision the ways you do and can invest in each sphere to live and lead purposefully. By learning the framework, hearing others' examples, and doing the activities, you will make the Dashboard your own.

In each sphere, I'll describe the way the pitfalls from the last chapter can manifest and provide specific tactics to overcome them. Then I'll provide some practical ways to optimize your investments of time, effort, and attention in each sphere. I'll also point out some of the many ways that the spheres interact so that you can be on the lookout for ways to optimize your complete Dashboard—or rather, the impact you have throughout your whole life. Finally, you'll find a recap of our process from chapter 7 to guide you through filling out your Dashboard sphere by sphere.

Throughout these chapters, you'll find abbreviated versions of reflection questions and activities. To get the most out of working with your Dashboard, I encourage you to use the companion *Going First* Purpose Party Playbook while reading these chapters. There you'll find more detailed and specific guidance, provocations, and practice to engage with as well as additional resources to further guide you through the process.

By the end of part 3, you'll have a robust understanding of all six spheres as an action-oriented framework for your own purposeful growth.

Chapter 9

The Self Sphere

The first and most central element of purposeful leadership is the Self Sphere. It's very intentionally the foundation of the Dashboard graphic because this sphere includes all the ways we invest in our physical, intellectual, emotional, and spiritual well-being. Without adequate investments here, our purposeful leadership is doomed to fail.

Figure 13. The Self Sphere's place in the Impact Dashboard.

Investing in the Self Sphere is about putting on your own oxygen mask before helping others on the plane, filling your cup so you have a saucerful of overflow to pour into those around you, or simply knowing that you can't give from an empty vessel. Whatever image helps you see the point here, your holistic health is a nonnegotiable requirement for being purposeful.

The specific actions required for holistic well-being are about as diverse as the number of humans on the planet. That said, we're all human beings with remarkably similar genes and resulting biological makeups, so there are a few incontrovertible elements of a solid foundation for purposeful leadership in the Self Sphere.

The ultimate underpinning of this foundational sphere is mindfulness. We haven't gotten closer to a silver bullet for well-being than this,[53] so find the flavor of mindfulness that works for you and use it. It could be meditation (neuroscience would agree, and there are many forms from which to find one that works for you), but other activities such as exercise, time in nature, cuddles with animals, and simple breathing exercises also work.

Once you start zeroing in on the mindfulness practices that work for you, you need to pursue holistic well-being by integrating other investments into the sphere as well:

- *Physical.* Physical well-being requires sleep, healthy and balanced nutrition, and physical activity.

- *Intellectual.* We're satisfied when we're operating with the right balance of competence and learning new things.

- *Emotional.* Well-being derives from a healthy sense of who you are and why that matters as well as strong, regular, interpersonal connections.

- *Spiritual.* Having a connection to some force greater than ourselves, whether through institutionalized religion, individual relationship with nature, or anything in between, provides spiritual well-being.

It's worth your time to understand the actions that keep you well in all these aspects. Here are some examples:

- Optimizing your sleep (leave your phone out of the bedroom; keep a regular schedule)
- Cultivating loving relationships (with yourself first and foremost)
- Staying active (weekend hikes, midday stretch or plank breaks, longer-than-necessary dog walks)
- Eating well ("Not too much and mostly plants," according to Michael Pollan[54])
- Meditating (or any activity that gets you in the present and mindful)
- Dancing (just a few minutes to move freely and enjoy music you love)
- Journaling (in any form for as long or short as you like; whatever enables you to get thoughts out of your head)
- Laughing (especially with a friend, child, parent, or pet)
- Reading (for pleasure or learning; no judgment about the quality! Just what brings you joy or expands your mind)
- Praying (with or without a spiritual leader, in a place or worship or under a tree)
- Setting boundaries (about anything, like when you're available for phone calls or how many meetings or social activities you can handle in a week)
- And so much more . . . .

Hopefully you're getting the idea from this list that there's a lot that might compose your "self-care cocktail" (more on that below). The important thing is to figure out what works for you and in what measure to maintain holistic well-being. Make your routines nonnegotiable and continuously improving.

How I Learned About the Self Sphere

I've always been more of a nerd than an athlete. While I succumbed to pressure from friends and my grandmother to stick with JV lacrosse through my junior year of high school, my activities of choice were reading, working, and horseback riding (which is athletic, but not in the hit-the-gym, go-for-a-run way).

After college, I lived abroad in cities where gyms weren't mainstream and very few people had a practice of working out. So when I moved to Nablus, a Palestinian city in the West Bank, I wasn't too disappointed by local partners' advice that we couldn't run, or even really walk, around town. Similarly, when an American colleague was called out (indirectly, through the proper community leaders) for doing aerobics on our patio (visible to many neighbors, thanks to the hilly landscape), I didn't mourn this limitation either.

Our work was hard. We were building a brand-new model of early childhood education that supported mental health with auxiliary programs for mothers, local university students, and international interns. We were trying to do so in the most collaborative way, working closely with local partners and following the lead of our Palestinian staff. Days were long, from the traditional start time of 8 a.m. to at least 8 p.m., when our founder was having lunch in Washington DC and would often want to catch up. Weeks were long, too, since the Palestinian workweek is Sunday through Thursday, and Friday was still very much a day to be in touch with US partners, candidates, and colleagues.

In addition, my American colleagues and I lived together on the top floor of the community center where we worked. So my desk was exactly 12 feet below my bed, or a 90-second walk, since I couldn't actually descend through the floor to get there.

All these logistics combined with the intensity of living and working in a community plagued by decades of political violence, poverty, and turmoil made for intense conditions—particularly compared to the dolce vita I had come from as a not-for-profit program director in Rome. Motivated by the learning, excitement, progress, and demands of the work, I didn't give too much thought to this intensity. But smartly, my colleague did.

A former fire jumper in her home state of Montana, my colleague knew something about coping with extreme situations. She did the research and made a well-crafted pitch to our boss and founder to buy a treadmill for our residential floor. I didn't pay much attention to her campaign. I may have been somewhat skeptical, or even resentful, of her trips to the gym supply store (which were not on every corner, as you can imagine) and time spent on materials to make her case. Somewhat to my surprise, her pitch was approved on the spot, despite our shoestring budget and focus on costs that directly and efficiently served the folks we were there to support.

A few days later, a treadmill was installed in the open room across the hall from my bedroom. Still, I hardly paid attention to all the fuss required to get the delivery men safely into our living area without scandal. I don't think I saw the machine with my own eyes for at least a few days after it arrived.

After a particularly long day, amid a heated conversation about the pros and cons of working with a new partner, my colleague excused herself for a run while I sat on the couch watching TV and eating dinner. She emerged 20 minutes later, clearly a whole new person. Sweaty and chipper, she brightly shared a new angle on this potential partnership and then trotted off to the kitchen to serve herself dinner.

I may not consider myself an athlete, but I'm not an idiot, either. The next day, I cut myself off from my to-do list at 5:30 p.m. and suited up. That walk/jog was the first two miles of at least 1,000 that I logged on that treadmill during my five years of work at Nablus. And while there are many elements and people behind the ongoing success of that organization and my contributions to it, for me the treadmill makes the top 10 list of critical success factors.

Just like purpose statements, there are nearly eight billion different versions of holistic well-being on this planet. What's more, we all know we need to do this stuff. It's not rocket science. So why don't we do it?

Let's start by exploring your specific case of activity (or lack thereof) in the Self Sphere. Don't worry; no one's watching or listening, and there's a super simple guide to the thinking I've seen work for so many people coming up. After that, I'll share myriad more examples and plenty of practical advice about the pitfalls that might be getting in the way of your Self Sphere investments, along with some proven tips to overcome them.

Making It Yours

Now it's time to do your own work! Head to the *Going First* Purpose Party Playbook for a guided process. If you don't have the workbook, go to chapter 7 and apply the process found there to your Self Sphere. If you need a reminder of the five steps, review the section in that chapter called "Zeroing in on Each Sphere."

STEP 1: BASELINE ASSESSMENT

Here's where you assess your investments in the Self Sphere. You already did most of this step back in the Baseline Assessment we did in chapter 7. Now go to the Impact Dashboard Excel Worksheet available at www.inspiringcowgirl.com/goingfirst, the *Going First* Purpose Party Playbook, or wherever you did the practice work and review the activities you identified in your Self Sphere. Edit or add to that list so that it feels complete.

When you're satisfied that you've captured the activities you do in your Self Sphere, review the total number of hours you're spending here per week. You can also determine the percentage of time each week this sphere takes (if you're using my Excel template, it's programmed into the spreadsheet for zero effort on your part).

I hate being prescriptive but, knowing that you'll want guidance on the percentage of time each sphere gets, here goes (I just ask that you trust yourself more than anything I share): If you've included sleep (an immediate 33 percent of the week, hopefully) in your Self Sphere activities, I'd recommend budgeting 40–50 percent of your time to Self Sphere investments. If that sounds shockingly self-indulgent, recognize that it's actually only one to two hours a day (other than sleep) for exercise, healthy eating, journaling, and whatever else keeps you functioning at your best.

With this reality check about the hours you have available for the activities in your Self Sphere, take one more look at your current activity list. Fill in whether you want to do each activity more, less, or the same (Column D on my spreadsheet).

Now, rate these three statements as they apply to your Self Sphere. At the risk of redundancy, I want to remind you that *perfect is the enemy of good*. Don't overthink your answers:

1. *I invest time, energy, and attention in the Self Sphere.* _____

2. *I am satisfied with the quantity and quality of my investments in the Self Sphere.* _____

3. *I see the outcomes of my investments in the Self Sphere.* _____

Next, rate the statements as you were this time last year:

1. *Last year, I was investing time, energy, and attention in the Self Sphere.*
    _____

2. *I was satisfied with the quantity and quality of my investments in the Self Sphere.* _____

3. *I saw the outcomes of my investments in the Self Sphere.* _____

Finally, rate the statements as you'd like to be this time next year:

1. *Next year, I'll invest time, energy, and attention in the Self Sphere.* _____

2. *I'll be satisfied with the quantity and quality of my investments in the Self Sphere.* _____

3. *I'll see the outcomes of my investments in the Self Sphere.* _____

STEP 2: WHAT DO YOU NEED IN THIS SPHERE?

Is there a change you can make in the Self Sphere that you really believe will increase your well-being, performance, and/or fulfillment? This might be a significant shift, like getting an extra hour of sleep, or more trivial, like meditating before breakfast rather than after. It's time to identify *one* change you're willing to make over the next month, whether it's doing something you already do more regularly, stopping something you do, or trying a new activity.

Conversely, you might decide that you're doing a pretty good job of investing in your Self Sphere and that it's really not the area you need to prioritize to live and lead more purposefully. That's fine! I encourage you to think through the questions below before you decide for sure, though.

- What Self Sphere activities are working for you now? (By "working," I mean that they feel inherently rewarding, you notice how they improve your well-being and/or performance, and you enjoy doing them—at least once you're over the initial inertia and in the act.)

- What are you doing that isn't working for you? Why not? Can you stop or swap it for something else?

- In terms of what you're doing and/or who you're doing it with or for, how varied are the investments you make in your Self Sphere?

- Would you like to diversify the kind of activities in this sphere or double down on a few things you already know work or are willing to test out?

- What blind spots might you have about the power of investments in the Self Sphere, or what types of Self Sphere activities are there that you haven't tried? Are there people, books, podcasts, or other resources that might be able to reveal these blind spots for you? (If not, check out my Reader Resources list at the end of the book.) Are you willing to spend 15 minutes this week with one of those resources to overcome those blind spots?

Now, draft a belief statement about what you want to change in your Self Sphere. Ideally, it will be simple, clear, and measurable. Here are a few examples:

- I need and want to swap my outdated commitment to running with something that provides me more rest and joy.

- I need and want to develop a sleep routine that gets me back to the 7.5 hours I need every night to have the impact I seek.

- I need and want a self-care routine that fits me better rather than the default one I use now, because I know it'll be effective and efficient.

Notice that the belief statement doesn't include exactly *how* you'll achieve the goal you're setting; just *what* you're going to do and *why* it matters.

STEP 3: YOUR ONE NEXT STEP

Now that you believe *what* the outcome will be of changing what you do in your Self Sphere, let's figure out *how* to achieve that change.

Some of you may be on to me by now and are imagining that there will be six "One Things," one per sphere. Correct! But you're still here.

For now, just focus on choosing your One Thing for the Self Sphere, and then get really specific about exactly what this activity is going to look like (at least to start; you can revise the details as you learn). Here, in the playbook, or on the Excel template, answer these specific questions in writing:

- When are you going to do it?
- For how long?
- With whom? (Alone is a fine answer.)
- In what location?
- Is there any equipment you need? (If so, do you already have it? Do you know where it is? Can you get to it today? If you don't have it, when and where are you going to buy it?)
- What's going to keep you from building your new habit? What obstacles have prevented you from getting there in the past?
- How are you going to hold yourself accountable (e.g., a habit tracker app, a friend, gold stars on the fridge or your desktop)?
- What reward will you give yourself for doing it the first three times and then weekly for keeping it up?
- If it's the right new investment in this sphere, how will you feel after doing this activity for a month?

STEP 4: SUPPORTING THAT STEP

After all of this reflection and knowing there's more to come in our next section on pitfalls, you have just one more step to take. Like your belief statement, write a simple, clear, and measurable behavioral plan to keep you on track. Here are a few examples:

- When I think I don't have enough time for my morning meditation, I'll remember that awful meeting where I blew up at my poor colleague because I was stressed about my own deadlines.

- Every time I forget to leave my phone out of the bedroom, I'll bring it back to the kitchen and do 10 pushups.

- If I revert to the "no-breakfast rush" that leaves me crashing at 10 a.m., I'll stop everything and find a piece of fruit or some nuts to get me through to the next healthy option (not devour a stale muffin).

As we go on to explore the most common pitfalls to making change play out in the Self Sphere, you may see some familiar stumbling blocks and be able to strengthen your behavioral plan. But for now, combine your belief statement, behavioral plan, and tracking choice into one succinct paragraph.

STEP 5: KEEP AN EYE OUT

By definition, this next step can't be done now, but it can be started. Remember my suggestion to track your new habits with an app like Momentum Habit Tracker or a journal (either old-school pen and paper or an app such as Day One). Hold yourself—and/or a buddy, if you decide to pair up—accountable for making the change you said you wanted to.

The point here is not to beat yourself up if you don't get exactly where you want to be. It's just to be able to see how it's going. Does the new activity actually have your desired impact? Does it fit into your life, or does it reveal something else you'd rather spend your time on?

As your outlook, work, life, and world evolve, so should your purposeful habits. But the only way to keep up with these changes and the necessary adaptations is to keep an eye on what you're doing and the consequences it's having. So pick your preferred method of tracking change and use it.

Pitfalls in the Self Sphere

I know some of you broke the rule of choosing just One Thing to do in your Self Sphere. You have a shortlist of five and another dozen you can try if those don't work. What's more, I'd guess you wanted to do at least five of those things before you ever picked up this book. The magic of Going First that I'm hoping to share with you is not only about revealing new activities that you can do to invest in the Self Sphere or any of the other spheres. The power is in identifying the *motivation* to actually do these new things, the *pitfalls* likely to prevent your progress, and the *strategies* to eliminate or overcome those pitfalls. So let's dig deeper into how the pitfalls show up in the Self Sphere.

PITFALL #1: INACTION

The Self Sphere is unique in terms of combating inaction. Our investments in other spheres usually have someone waiting on the other end: a spouse counting on date night, kids who need a bath, a colleague waiting for our edits, a client expecting a proposal, a board meeting to attend, and so on. And most of us are very reluctant to let someone else down. But in the Self Sphere, we're the only ones counting on ourselves to show up for that run, bedtime, dance break, balanced breakfast, or morning meditation.

The vast majority of leaders I've worked with choose to let themselves down rather than a colleague, friend, or family member. But this calculus is an illusion. In reality, those people *are* counting on you to show up for yourself and invest in your Self Sphere so you can show up for them.

So how do we fight the call of the couch? Let's examine inaction in the Self Sphere so we're sure to recognize the problem, which is always the first step in remedying one!

Inaction Leads to Underinvestment. Ultimately, inaction in the Self Sphere means we simply don't do the things (or at least not enough of them) to keep ourselves holistically well. Because no one is explicitly waiting on us to take that time out to meditate or choose a nourishing lunch over quick and dirty takeout, we just don't do it. But then, especially over time, we feel less and less well—and that ripples out and affects those around us.

We've all had an interaction, whether a meeting, client pitch, bedtime negotiation with a kid, or training session with a dog, in which we weren't proud of the way we behaved. Take a minute to remember your most recent one. How would it have been different if you had taken the time for self-care that morning?

Inaction Looks Like Burnout. For the psychology nerds out there who enjoy the biases underlying these tendencies, we can credit *loss aversion* with many foregone Self Sphere investments. We worry that by spending more time caring for our holistic well-being, we might lose a reputation (of being a hard worker), relationship (with a favorite fellow grinder who's always online late), or even a job (for not being available all the time). This line of reasoning is particularly common among purpose-driven people who are loath to take one second away from their work (which they see as service to others) to invest in their own well-being. But it's most critical for these people to fill up their cups to have something to give. Unfortunately, the incredible upside of being stronger, more rested, or more patient isn't as clear.

I remember a vivid example of this in a workshop I held for a fast-growing logistics company. The workshop focused on the importance of the Me–We connection, especially for first-time managers. We'll call this manager Bryan. He had been promoted to his first-ever people manager role during the COVID-19 pandemic. Having been in the same role until his promotion, he was keen to support his new direct reports, especially knowing how much more complicated and demanding it had become in the last six months.

In the first month, Bryan scheduled weekly one-on-ones with all three of his direct reports in addition to their morning stand-ups. He had a professional development chat with each of them to get aligned on their medium-term priorities and ambitions. Their different time zones meant that these often happened during his afternoon walk window, which got pushed later and eroded his time to cook dinner with his daughter. His own work piled up and got done only after his daughter's bedtime.

By the end of the month, Bryan was averaging an hour less of sleep each night, missing his daughter, and struggling to put on a happy face for team stand-ups each morning. In his own one-on-one with a longtime mentor in a different department, he realized that putting himself after his team had been the worst way to serve them.

Counter Inaction with What Feels Good. As with all forms of inaction, the best antidote is to start somewhere. This is true in the Self Sphere, too, and the advice about overcoming this pitfall in chapter 8 remains valid. But more specifically, when it comes to taking action in the Self Sphere, I encourage you to *start with what feels good.* Is there a hobby you dropped that you miss? Can you build it back in on weekends or one evening a week? Have you always wanted to try meditation or a new kind of workout? Can you rope a friend in to try it with you next week? Has your partner been looking tired too? Can you ask them to help you get to bed earlier this week, without your phones?

As a first-time people leader, Bryan's overzealous approach to serving his team illustrated exactly how the habits he had built up were critical for his own well-being. After that aha moment in conversation with a mentor, he adjusted the meeting tenor with his new team. Less frequent, longer meetings enabled a level of connectivity that worked for all of them and didn't squeeze out his afternoon walks, daddy–daughter dinner, or sleep. When we last spoke, Bryan was a few days into trying out the mini midday stretch breaks that his mentor had recommended as a great way to transition between doing his own work and managing his team.

My recommendation is to do just what Bryan did: reduce the friction of inertia and start with a new Self Sphere investment that you're excited about, either because you've done it before and found it effective or because you're curious about what it might do for you. It's already hard enough to add any activity to your busy days without jumping in at the deep end with those activities you know you should do but have always struggled with.

As you do this new activity, recognize and track its benefits using whatever tools work for you. Because you're the only direct stakeholder, it's helpful to have external data (qualitative and quantitative; remember that feelings and intuition are data too) that show the returns on these investments. Once you see that you're actually more efficient after a meditation, more creative after a workout, or a better parent with a good night's sleep, you'll have the motivation to make more difficult Self Sphere investments.

Finally, recognize the trade-offs of making the necessary Self Sphere investments you need, and make choices accordingly. If you know you just can't be who you want to be without a run and a healthy, sit-down breakfast in the morning after seven to eight hours of sleep, you might have to say no to that leadership program or sustainability committee that meets at 8:00 a.m.

PITFALL #2: SHOULDING IN THE SELF SPHERE

Even though shoulding originates in the We dimension, it's hugely influential over our Self Sphere investments. Whether from media, friends, colleagues, or that "perfect self" angel/devil on our shoulder, we have very strong ideas about what we should eat, how much to sleep, how and when to work out, and all the other possible activities we can do for our holistic well-being.

It's great that this kind of information and positive pressure is out there. Why wouldn't we take advantage of the growing research about what drives human performance? But remember that everyone's composition is a bit different, so your recipe for success will be unique too.

Shoulding Leads to Performative Self-Care. We live and work in groups, and those groups strongly influence our behavior. The culture that undervalues self-care is made up of myriad groups. Chances are good that one or many of the groups you belong to (colleagues, family, friends, etc.) don't have a culture of prioritizing self-care. In this case, your investments in the Self Sphere will be seen as changes, which can threaten your approval within the group. As social creatures, we need a certain level of uniformity and predictability to feel safe, so your changes—which might be seen as deviance from the group norms—lead to the phenomenon we shared in chapter 8 that Dr. Mario Martinez calls tribal shaming.

Have you ever asked to delay a meeting to 9:30 to fit in a morning workout or blocked out a 30-minute lunch break on your calendar? Did anyone say something like, "Good for you. I've never been able to work out in the morning and feel prepared for my day" or "Don't you get bored eating lunch on your own rather than in a meeting?" Or maybe you've heard something more actively aggressive like, "We've got so much going on—are you sure you'll be able to take care of your responsibilities starting the day so late?" These are all examples of tribal shaming. Again, though, they rarely come from meanness. (Note that to start a culture-changing momentum it takes only one person to follow your lead. Google "one guy starts a dance party" if you're a visual learner!)

Other than this tribal shaming, which is often directed at discouraging any self-care at all, listening to shoulds can have another dangerous outcome. Shoulding can lead to every kind of outcome other than the unique mix of activity in your Self Sphere that you need to be well. The point is, to protect your investments in your Self Sphere, you need to make them work for you.

Shoulding Looks Like Following the Lemmings Off a Cliff. I had always seen working out as primarily a tool to control my weight. Having lived in Western European cities where lifestyles are inherently active (walking) and food is de facto healthier than the US (smaller portions, fewer preservatives), I followed the norm of not bothering with intentional exercise. Since I wasn't gaining weight, I felt I didn't need to worry about working out.

What I learned from my colleague, though, is how limiting that belief was. The mental health benefits of working out, particularly in this new, stressful job, were critical to my holistic well-being regardless of what the scale reported. I was eating healthier than ever in Nablus; there wasn't any alcohol being served, and our food was local and organic by default. So I wasn't worried about weight gain or other physical symptoms. But seeing what exercise did *for my leadership* is at the root of what I now see as a nonnegotiable commitment to fitting in some kind of workout on most days of my life.

Similarly, Lisa, the Purpose Seeker we met in chapter 7, is reflecting a lot on her Self Sphere investments as she nears the post-retirement phase of her career. After some burnout and illness in the early part of her career, she learned what it took to stay well (eating balanced meals and avoiding red meat, walking to meetings to mix up her posture during the day, and taking weekend runs). But now she realizes that these Self Sphere investments have been based more on *shoulds* than what really makes her feel good.

Lisa hates running and is having increasing knee pain. She likes yoga but, because it conflicts with a standing team meeting, only gets to the class that really makes her feel refreshed once a month. And she has always preferred noshing frequently throughout the day rather than saving up for a big sit-down dinner with her daughter and/or parents.

After reviewing her Dashboard, Lisa has resolved to swap out her runs for a long weekend walk-and-talk with her daughter. Now that she's an empty nester, she can give up the evening meal she held onto as a relic of family life. And she's decided to experiment with a new seven-and-a-half-hour sleep schedule that she spurned earlier in her career but seems to line up with research she's read about wellness in middle age.

Counter Shoulding with Experimentation. To counter shoulding, start with the overall recommendation to overcome it in the Self Sphere: adopt a growth mindset and get comfortable with failure.

It can feel absurd that we don't know what it takes for us to really feel good, but that's the natural result of all this shoulding! Accept that none of us is one-size-fits-all and that our Self Sphere investments need to change over time. Then you're free to play—and I do mean play—with all of the variations of Self Sphere investments and how they affect your well-being and performance.

Here's an example of what I mean: In coping with burnout, Bryan experimented with his afternoon walks, adding music one day, a podcast the next, and finally returning to silence, which he found most effective in providing the break he needed. He was a bit skeptical of the stretch breaks his mentor suggested, but he acquiesced to her and himself that he would try it for two weeks, varying the duration and types of stretches to zero in on a version that worked for him.

Be sure you're using the same process of customization to resist shoulding in the Self Sphere. Next time you read an article about the importance of meditation, ask yourself, *Do I need more of that outcome in my life? Has my experience shown that to be true for me?*

Carissa Reiniger, a lifelong purpose-driven entrepreneur and founder and CEO of Small Business Silver Lining and Silver Lining Finance, found sitting still to meditate absolutely torturous. But she was keenly aware of the neuroscience of mindfulness and that the demands of her fast-paced, high-stakes job required her best mental and emotional presence. So she found a workout studio with pool workouts that was a 30-minute walk from her home (and office). She made sure to book at least one class a week, sometimes a double-header. The combination of the walk—often coupled with a phone chat with her nieces—the underwater movement, and the walk back provided the grounding reset she needed to be present, empathetic, and creative for the rest of her week.

Of course, the human body and brain have certain ways of working that are relatively uniform, as reflected in research. But we also have our own fingerprints and styles for what we find rejuvenating versus ineffective or anxiety-producing. The Self Sphere is the ripest for experimentation because *you* are the only direct stakeholder. Your roommates might be confused by your fluctuating bedtimes, but your experiments won't disturb anyone as much as if you were switching up a meeting agenda or presentation format to find what works. (Not that there aren't ways to do those experiments too; they're just a little more delicate.)

PITFALL #3: ORTHODOXY IN THE SELF SPHERE

The Industrial Era instilled the notion that time spent not working—particularly on the indulgent notion of investing in self—is useless and costly. So much of our world, including how we work, shop, and interact, is still based on rules from that era.

Even more anachronistically, our brains are suited to our former lives as cavepeople, especially the limbic system. That pesky "lizard brain" adapted to help us quickly avoid tigers, but it remains the first to the party, even though tigers are rarely on the top 10 list of threats we face at any given moment.

We are not cogs or cavepeople. What we have come to know through research and firsthand experience is that our bodies and minds require rest, among other elements of self-care, to function at their best—especially if that performance includes higher-order skills like creativity, collaboration, and resilience. We're on the cusp of change, but for now, much of the modern world still treats workers as machines to be optimized for productivity and output.

The rules of life and work in the 21st century have changed, and success requires that we adapt accordingly. That's exactly where this pitfall of orthodoxy is so problematic, particularly when it comes to the Self Sphere. What got us here (outsmarting tigers) will not get us there (optimizing for the global well-being of all people and our one shared planet).

> *Orthodoxy Leads to Zero Impact.* If there's one point I hope you take from this book, it's that not doing what you need to do to stay well will sooner or later prevent you from having any positive impact at all. Succumbing to cultural ideas about the nature or amount of Self Sphere investments that you need or deserve is anathema to purposeful leadership. Picture one of those days when you hadn't had enough sleep, fought with your partner over coffee, or skipped lunch. Were you able to be creative in your work? Or even accurate? Were you a supportive manager, helping your direct reports do their best work? How loving were you to friends or family you came across?

For those of us with any leadership role, whether formal or informal, at work or at home, making the necessary investments in our Self Sphere has an immediate ripple effect. It models to those around us that they, too, can and must make similar investments. As the Dalai Lama advised, "If you feel burnout setting in, if you feel demoralized and exhausted, it is best, for the sake of everyone, to withdraw and restore yourself."[55] And if you're particularly committed to the equity-building element of purposeful leadership, heed Audre Lorde's words: "Caring for myself is not self-indulgence, it is self-preservation, and that is an act of political warfare."[56]

Following orthodoxy in the Self Sphere leads to an inability to have the impact we aspire to have.

Orthodoxy Looks Like Disease. Since orthodoxy sits in the World dimension, the relevant manifestations are all the global trends toward unwellness and unsustainability. Medical research found that during the first year of the COVID-19 pandemic, diagnoses of anxiety increased by 25.6 percent and depression by 27.6 percent.[57] Unfortunately, this trend did not begin with the pandemic. Between 1990 and 2019, incidences of anxiety disorders increased by 47 percent.[58] Apart from the individual suffering, this skyrocketing rate of anxiety has a global cost estimated around $45 billion.[59]

In other words, the ramifications of underinvesting in ourselves are no joke. There's no inferring to be done in terms of the collective cost. It's not that we just *suspect* that meditation enhances collaboration; we *know* it. In his eponymous book *Dying for a Paycheck*, Stanford professor Jeffrey Pfeffer asserts, "Work is killing us."[60] And it's not just work; it's the way we sleep, rest, eat, move, and play (or don't, as the case may far too often be).

While there are clinical treatments for anxiety, the most commonly recommended antidotes are the self-administered activities we're talking about in the Self Sphere. And when we don't do them, anxiety proliferates.

Counter Orthodoxy by Compiling Evidence. Instead of bowing under the weight of global norms about how to take care of ourselves, we can surround ourselves with sources and people who model and support thoughtful investments in self-care.

The general advice about ways to overcome orthodoxy apply to the Self Sphere. For starters, look for examples of the ways that Self Sphere investments pay off. You can look at other people you know for this evidence, but beware of those insights becoming shoulds. Because we each have a relatively unique fingerprint of ideal Self Sphere investments, the best place to look is in your own life.

What Self Sphere investments were you making on a day or phase of your life when you were feeling particularly good? If you're not sure, start using a tracking tool and figure it out. Then be really intentional about connecting the results to your Self Sphere activities. When you calendar your workout sessions, for example, label them "Sweat for endorphins" or "Stretch for creativity" to remind yourself why you're taking the time. *Develop your own tracking practices.* Eventually, you'll build a more effortless awareness of all the dimensions of your well-being and the efforts that can get it back on track.

Next, *expect more of yourself and the people around you* in the Self Sphere, and set up processes and systems to back up those expectations with others as well as yourself. For example, our team includes a well-being rating (1–10) alongside customers in the pipeline and deals lost in our weekly wrap-up meetings. Making the rating and having a historical record allows us to check ourselves and each other to ensure there aren't too many weeks in a row under 7 or a downward trend over time.

Finally, *blend inclusion and distinctiveness* in pursuit of optimal distinctiveness. The research on mindfulness is compelling, so that's likely going to be part of your self-investment routine. But maybe you're just not at a moment in your life when you enjoy stillness for more than a few minutes. Find your own path to mindfulness, whether it's chopping carrots, running, or massaging your cat.

Do the same thing for people around you when modeling Self Sphere activities. Point out *why* you make the various investments you make rather than harping on *what* you do. This will allow others to see the outcomes they can aspire to when they determine their healthiest form of sleep, diet, etc.

Crafting Your Self Sphere Cocktail

Most great parties do include a cocktail, regardless of its alcohol content, so let's look at mixing your Self Sphere investments to make them the most delicious. For the most part, we know what is good for us to do—or at least what advertisers think we "should" be doing—and the counter-narratives of the increasingly commercial self-care industry. But the exact nature and mix of actions in your Self Sphere is truly unique to you. It will evolve over time as you go through different stages of life, work, and identity.

As with all of the spheres, achieving well-being for yourself isn't a "set it and forget it" task. To stay in touch with how you're feeling in the various dimensions, you have to mix in some review and reflection and then course correct as necessary to make your actions fit your evolving needs. How you craft your evolving wellness cocktail can also be a fun project. I'll share some of my own current Self Sphere cocktail: the Cowgirl Chiller, as I like to call it. I use a daily habit tracker and journaling app, and I keep a purposeful growth tracker of my own creation. You can download the Weekly Purposeful Habit Tracker at www.inspiringcowgirl.com/goingfirst as a starting point for making your own. Each Friday, I take my daily stats (which I've gathered in an app) and enter them into my spreadsheet.

Figure 14. Screenshot of my Momentum Habit Tracker.
Yikes! With editing pressures this week, I'm neglecting friends and a ski trip with my husband! This is a good example of how great activities can squeeze out other worthy investments sometimes.

My quantitative metrics include how many days I meditated, worked out, ate vegetarian, avoided alcohol, talked to friends and my mom, and did something loving for my husband (acts of service is his number one love language). I also record the balances of my bank and investment accounts and any significant expenditures I made that week, whether debt repayment, purchases to support well-being, or investments. Next, I rate the week 1–10 in the Me, We, and World dimensions and add a note describing the week in each area. Another tab in the spreadsheet captures quarterly, yearly, five-year, and moonshot goals, which I calendar to review periodically.

Using some sort of standing tool like this is essential for ensuring you're mixing your cocktail based on what works for *you*. It might be less structured than a spreadsheet, maybe journal entries or a regularly updated vision board. Or maybe it's more structured and/or social, such as using a coach or accountability group to stay on track. What you track and how you track it should be resonant for you. The important thing is that you keep an eye on what you're doing to stay well and whether it's working.

There are choices to be made in the Self Sphere. I often tell clients, "You can't have it all, but you can have *your* all." In other words, choose what you want consciously and identify the things that set you up for success in that area. Perhaps flexibility to work out in the middle of the day is hugely important to you. Great! Be sure that you choose jobs and personal relationships that can accommodate that need. Similarly, if having peer support for your mindfulness practice is important to you, choose to spend proportionate amounts of your time with friends, colleagues, or strangers who provide that.

There will be choices in one sphere that influence your actions in the others. Adopting a baby or launching a company is not an excuse to abandon all things well-being, but either choice presents some trade-offs in how you use the limited number of hours in a day. The purposeful approach is to make these choices conscientiously and pair them with continued commitment to the Self Sphere so you can realize the best outcomes of your choices. And because enjoyment can be motivating, give your Self Sphere blend a fun cocktail name!

Overlapping Spheres

Well-being in the Self Sphere has to come from, well, ourselves. But pretending that our actions in this area aren't influenced by our context and investments in the other spheres is fruitless. The Self Sphere habits of the people around us—friends, family, colleagues, characters we admire on TV and social media—influence ours. Which is a(nother) good reason to choose those people carefully!

Different stages of our lives also influence our Self Sphere needs and investments. For example, when starting a new job, launching a new product, having a baby, or caring for a sick loved one, we may not manage to fit in our ideal self-care routines. These situations don't call for abandoning our Self Sphere investments completely; remember the oxygen mask metaphor? But they are reasons to examine ways to compress your exercise routine, meditation practice, or healthy homemade lunches. Maybe you add ankle weights to make dog walks more rigorous, meditate for 5 minutes instead of 20, or find a meal delivery service you like. On the other hand, in some particularly difficult moments such as a divorce, moving houses or jobs, or learning a new role or set of responsibilities, I've found it critical to double down on my self-sustaining habits. During these times, I think of the saying, "If you don't have time to meditate for an hour every day, you should meditate for two hours."

During the shift (and eventual end) of my working relationship with the dear colleague I shared as an example of balancing care and challenge in chapter 6, I was particularly careful to prepare for our one-on-ones. I would make time for lunch (or at least an energizing snack) beforehand, put a 15-minute buffer on my calendar so I wouldn't be rushing into our call, and protect 5 minutes at the start of our call for a non-work check-in about her wedding planning or my puppy's latest goofiness.

The best way I can advise you to manage these interactions similarly is to build as sensitive a connection as possible to your real well-being. Ask yourself at least once a day, "How am I?" and then really listen to your body, mind, and heart. The tools I recommended in the previous section help me track my well-being in the moment and over time, so I can course correct as needed before it's too late and I've bitten someone's head off.

Every choice about how we invest our time and energy requires trade-offs with activities in other spheres, so spend a little time thinking about the interactions between your Self Sphere and the others spheres so you can anticipate those trade-offs most effectively.

Whew! That was a lot. But hopefully you're convinced that a strong Self Sphere is the foundation to success in every other part of your life and have some insights about what additional activities might move the needle for you to be more well.

Remember not to become overwhelmed. There are a million changes you could make, but it's counterproductive to leap in and burn out. You have five more spheres to explore first; *then* you'll have the insight to choose what's most important to start with and establish priorities for future work as well.

Reflection Questions

Like all the chapters, these questions are available as a free worksheet at www.inspiringcowgirl.com/goingfirst. But if you're tempted to play with each Sphere, you'll love the Going First Purpose Party Playbook!

- What's the One Thing you want to do in the Self Sphere that would feel good?

- Where do you see yourself succumbing to inaction in the Self Sphere? Do you recognize the root cause?

- Do you recognize the concept of tribal shaming? What has a colleague, friend, or family member said to you that might fit into that category of unintentionally calling attention to a change you made? When have you commented to a friend, colleague, or family member about a change that they made? Which of those comments were supportive? Do any of them look like tribal shaming now that you're familiar with the concept?

- Are you making any investments in your Self Sphere that are driven more by shoulding than the actual effects they have on your well-being? What are they, and how will you change that?

- What investments in your Self Sphere do you remember making during a great phase or day of your life? How did they make you feel? How can you remind yourself of that impact as an incentive to continue or restart those activities?

- Consider your Self Sphere holistically. What are you doing? What are you not doing? Is the blend authentic to you and aligned with your desired impact?

- What connections do your current and desired investments in the Self Sphere have to the other spheres? How do you want to revise the investments you're making in your Self Sphere to optimize those connections between spheres?

Chapter 10

The Family and Friends Sphere

Surrounding the Self Sphere is the Family and Friends Sphere. The people in this sphere are those we choose to love, support, care for, learn from, and grow with. Perhaps we work to raise empathetic children, support friends in their own purpose journeys, or provide dignified care to our elders. Our efforts in this sphere directly impact those humans and increase collective well-being. Importantly, these efforts also set an example for others around us, strengthening the web of essential personal support networks for everyone. And our investments in the Family and Friends Sphere pay us back as well. Having loving, trusting, and reliable relationships increases our likelihood of survival by 50 percent at all ages![61]

Despite the huge potential influence we can have in this area, it's often overlooked and undervalued in our culture, and therefore by ourselves and each other. This work is often invisible or taken as mere obligation (or pleasure). It's assumed to take second fiddle to professional obligations or even Community or Money Sphere activities. Either way, it isn't recognized for its potential potency. Culturally, our efforts in building our family or community are explicitly ignored. Increasing attention has been paid to the value of the so-called "invisible labor" of raising children and caring for elders or family members with disabilities. In 2021, the global economic value of that work was quantified at over $10 trillion.[62] (Curious what you're "earning" at home? Check out the Invisible Labor Calculator, which Amy Westervelt created to help bring awareness to the value of this work.[63])

Alongside their economic value, our efforts in the Family and Friends Sphere have a massive impact and contribute very powerfully to purposeful living. By creating secure attachments, imbuing a growth mindset, fostering a sense of curiosity and empathy, and facilitating a wide variety of experiences for our kids or other family and friends, we shape (and are shaped by) humans who are more able to lead and live purposefully.

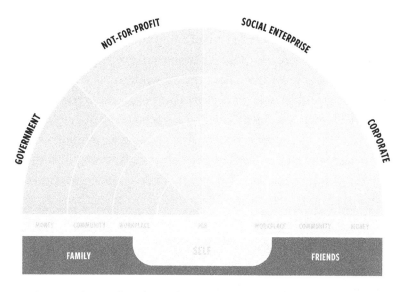

Figure 15. The Family and Friends Sphere's place in the Impact Dashboard.

To appreciate the depth of this influence, reflect for a minute on what you learned from your parents and/or the other adults who were present in your childhood. What did they teach you about food and mealtimes? About work? Money? Relationships? Trust? Responsibility? These might've been implicit or explicit lessons and more or less positive or desirable from your vantage today. But there's no denying that our intimate relationships have huge sway on the people we become—who go on to impact other generations. What do those moments of influence on someone else do for you?

Family Care

Raising children makes arguably the deepest impact any of us can have. Whether as a biological parent or not, the behavior we model, teach, and reward is arguably the most direct influence we have on the next generation. By providing physical and emotional safety, the secure attachments required to foster curiosity, and the exposure to diverse experiences that foster empathy, we empower the next generation of humans.

Parents don't have full control over their children's outcomes, but there are certainly ways to shape their course, and that matters far beyond the context of your own family. Many parents' Dashboards reflect the fulfillment that can result, particularly after they think about their parenting activities in this way.

Michelle Penczak says, "I'm clear that, first and foremost, my family is taken care of. But how I do that matters too. I want to show my boys how hard work can help people. Not only does it get you toys, [but] it can make your heart happy in so many ways." Modeling purpose like this for our families is a hugely powerful form of influence in the Family and Friends Sphere.

Kate Williams is the CEO of 1% For the Planet, a network of brands and companies such as Honest Tea and Patagonia that donate 1 percent of their gross sales to environmental causes. She explained her family-and-friends choices in this way: "My husband and I have made professional choices to have meaningful work *and* be present at home. I know that's part of why my kids are who they are." These choices required some trade-offs, such as not being able to travel as much or stay as long at the office. But Kate was committed to maintaining that presence at home, had the privilege to make it work, and has had influence on shaping her kids' values, behavior, and life choices accordingly.

Providing dignified aging for parents and other elders is another powerful contribution we rarely recognize. Whether because of the unpaid nature of this work or our reluctance to talk about dying and death, many generous caretakers don't acknowledge the impact they're having on themselves or receiving from others. The invisibility of caretaking efforts is problematic because they often compete directly with other forms of investment that are externally recognized and valued. We put people in the no-win position of choosing to forgo caregiving responsibilities, leaving elders in danger or other siblings or family members overburdened; forgo responsibilities in other spheres, risking loss of relationships, employment, compensation, or well-being; or do it all for as long as possible—which is inevitably not forever—and burn out.

Our current model is a lose-lose-lose situation that ripples far beyond caregivers themselves. We need to change our policies and attitudes toward caregiving, particularly as life expectancies grow (with bias for income level and race, unfortunately). Employers must provide accommodation logistically and culturally for employees who are also caregivers. Entrepreneurs (such as the Danielsens below) must continue to create new models that provide affordable quality care to support caregivers' efforts. Investors need to support those models with a thoughtful understanding of the real needs of caregivers and their charges. And not-for-profits can step in to support those who can't afford these improved forms of support.

Some people are starting to take these steps, often based on their own experience supporting people with invisible or visible disabilities. Melissa Danielsen and her twin sister were largely responsible for managing their brother's developmental disability and epilepsy. These duties and his death at 29 years old had many implications for their life and job choices as young adults. Now they've started a company, Joshin, which provides adequate care for employees who have family members with disabilities. Melissa explains that her personal experience makes her "willing to say the tough things about disability as a form of diversity" to achieve her mission of getting employers to offer care solutions that really work for families.

Friendly Influence

As birthrates fall and geographic tendencies pull us farther from our nuclear families, relationships with friends—our "chosen family"—become more important. These connections provide the same range of ways to support each other in overcoming challenges and reaching our full potentials.

A perfect example is the concept of "pods" that became such a popular (and problematic, in many ways) coping mechanism for families whose children's schools were closed during the height of the COVID-19 pandemic. By sharing or outsourcing the responsibility for supervising their kids' remote schooling, friends enabled others to keep their jobs. COVID pods are a specific case of mutual support that has long been a factor in child rearing, like carpooling and playdates. Without grandparents in the home, parents—most often mothers—have had to find other forms of childcare.

Of course, the actions in your Family and Friends Sphere become sustainable only if you maintain a solid foundation in your Self Sphere, ensuring that your cup is full enough to spill the abundance over to serve others.

How I Learned about the Family and Friends Sphere

As I mentioned in my Dashboard example, I spent the first decade of my career living internationally, thousands of miles and at least six time zones away from my family and longtime friends. Of course, relationships can traverse distance, but for me, living abroad meant that I was not in close or regular touch with most people from my past.

It's not that I cared or valued our relationships any less than friends I saw regularly. And when I did return for holidays or weddings or they came to see me, we picked up right where we left off, enjoying deep closeness. But as my mom pointed out a few years ago, sporadic visits can't substitute for the intimacy of daily (or at least more frequent than Christmas and birthdays) contact. I also realized in my early 30s that I didn't want to have children of my own, one of the biggest investments one can make in the Family Sphere. In multiple ways, I wasn't particularly tuned in to my impact, or lack thereof, in this sphere.

I don't mean to say that I had no influence on my family members and friends (or they on me). Indeed, my very presence abroad was consequential to the people closest to me, encouraging multiple trips abroad, if nothing else, and inspiring some of them to explore their own international stints. But for much of my life, I didn't contemplate my family and friends as part of my impact portfolio.

It's easy to think of family as static—the hand you've been dealt—and proceed according to orthodoxy nuanced by your own family unit's shoulds. And friendships can be reduced to a "nice-to-have"—a fun way to unwind on the weekends or cheaper alternative to a therapist's ear. On the other hand, these relationships can also feel like conflicts to our paid or familial commitments and thus become a source of stress. These perspectives undervalue the powerful impact that friendships can have on us and our friends. They can be thought-provoking, heart-healing, and even career-boosting relationships, with major impact in both directions. Our physical and mental well-being depends on such personal connections: they aren't just a "nice-to-have"; they're an important source of prevention and resilience.[64] Further, connections to family and friends provide support for our identities and contributions in other dimensions. These people can be our greatest supporters, helping encourage us in spirit or with specific resources to achieve our desired impact. And we can do the same for them.

Having had the chance to build strong relationships with my three stepchildren changed my outlook on the importance of including family and friends as part of my impact portfolio, particularly when we had the chance to live together while we quarantined during COVID-19. It was then that I learned the power of day-in day-out interactions. While I'm proud to have always been someone who family and friends seek out for advice, that's a different form of influence than shaping household dynamics. During our pandemic-provoked householding (the kids were in their late 20s and working full time), I saw the results of my choices of what to buy and cook, how to organize my days, and what to talk about. And vice versa, they (and my husband/their father) had influence on me.

I'm grateful to have had this opportunity to understand the potential ramifications of the Family and Friends Sphere more deeply. The inherently personal nature of these relationships makes the learning that happens within them more intimate and so often more profound and/or lasting than what we experience in our external or professional lives.

Of course, investments in the Family and Friends Sphere are not immune from the same pitfalls as the other spheres. Let's examine what they look like more closely.

Making It Yours

It's time to do your own work! Head to the *Going First* Purpose Party Playbook for a guided process. If you don't have the playbook, go to chapter 7 and apply the process found there to your Family and

Friends Sphere. If you need a reminder of the five steps, review the section in that chapter called "Zeroing in on Each Sphere."

Avoiding the Pitfalls in the Family and Friends Sphere

PITFALL #1: INACTION IN THE FAMILY AND FRIENDS SPHERE

It's not that we tend not to do anything about, with, or for our family and friends. But too often we miss the opportunity to do so with an intention about the positive influence we do, could, and want to have on them.

Inaction Leads to Missed Opportunities and Incongruence. Failure to act purposefully in our closest personal relationships leaves a lot of untapped impact on the table. Even though many of us spend more waking hours at work than at home, the depth of impact we can have on our family (biological or chosen) far outweighs the leverage we have in most, if not all, professional relationships. The personal depth of family and friend relationships means we're better positioned to influence the well-being, beliefs, and performance of our family and friends than we are our colleagues. Yet we often overlook the potential effect we have. Particularly those of us who choose not to be parents (biologically or elsewise) miss opportunities to influence the people we do have familial relationships with, whether those are nieces, nephews, siblings, parents, or non-biological kin such as godchildren.

Inaction also risks missing opportunities for impact on our friends because, at least in some cultures, friendships are seen as separate from the domains of politics, money, religion, and/ or spirituality. But much of our influence inhabits those realms, so how are we to invest in the Family and Friends Sphere if these topics are off-limits?

I'm not suggesting you attempt to convert all of your cousins or friends to your perspective on self-care or environmentalism, or, on the other hand, invest only in family and friends who already align with your opinions, purpose, and desired outcomes. But it's worth considering what investments you can make with care *and* challenge in the Family and Friends Sphere to live and lead more purposefully.

The next most common result of inaction I see in the Family and Friends Sphere is *incongruence*. When we aren't intentional about spending time, energy, and attention with family and friends in ways that connect to our desired influence, we don't feel fully ourselves in those relationships. That lack of authenticity ultimately prevents intimacy, making what should be our closest ties feel lonely and unsatisfying.

Incongruence can also happen in our Job and Workplace Spheres, but I've seen it to be particularly painful in the personal realm because that's where we expect to be most at ease and authentic.

Inaction Looks Like Compartmentalization. It's easy to see our family-and-friends activities as things we simply have to or want to do and then get them done accordingly. But a purposeful approach leverages these relationships as arenas for our desired impact.

If we simply make meals, get our kids to the doctor, send our friends birthday cards each year, or invite family for dinner periodically, we're delivering on the expectations of being "good" parents and friends. But we're doing so in a compartmentalized way. Our family and friends may be safe, healthy, and feel taken care of or loved, but we're delivering those benefits as generic commodities rather than with the full impact of our unique approaches.

Let's consider some examples to bring this all to life. Purpose Seeker Lisa took great care of her daughter and parents. She was thoughtful about what she bought for their households and cooked for meals because of her own commitment to responsible consumption and local, fresh, plant-focused meals. But since she didn't share these choices or the desires that led her to make them, over time she realized that her daughter hadn't picked up Lisa's values.

By delivering on her familial commitments without communicating her own values and the desired impact that informed how she did so, Lisa missed an opportunity. Further, she hadn't gotten as close to her daughter or parents as she could have if she had invited the conversation about how they think about their purpose or true selves.

In my own case, I've realized that I've left the values and impact I seek at work out of most of my personal relationships. It's in my work—in my efforts to enable fairer, healthier, and more joyful work for everyone—that I feel most purpose-aligned. As I've gotten more comfortable sharing those efforts with family and friends, I've felt those relationships deepen. As a result of sharing more about my purpose and the influence I seek, my mom has approached me about helping her carve out more time to invest in her own self-care amid her busy life of caregiving, building her portfolio career, and being involved with the community in her neighborhood. Similarly, now that they're more in the loop with how much I care about advancing fair and healthy work, my stepkids approach me more regularly with their questions about career transitions and longer-term plans.

Whatever your desired outcomes are, leaving them out of your personal relationships because those are only for fun, caregiving, or easy unconditional love creates unnecessary barriers to the depth of those relationships.

Counter Inaction with Conversation. When we break down this compartmentalization and integrate our true selves—our purpose—into these interactions, we can have real impact. In the Family and Friends Sphere, the recommended antidote to inaction—*start somewhere*—can be simply asking a question!

Open the conversation with a friend or family member about their feelings on whatever flavor of impact you're thinking about, such as why you made the dinner you made that night or why you buy the laundry detergent you buy. Invite them to shape the conversation by asking if they'd be curious to hear what you've been working on at work, in your retirement account, or on that new board you joined. Or let them lead. Ask what the best moment of their day or week was, or the hardest. In asking these questions, we get at our best, authentic, purposeful selves, going beyond our role in a family or friend group. Showing your interest in this way and offering your own honest answers will deepen your personal relationships.

Adding this depth in your Family and Friends Sphere pays off in two ways. First, it expands your potential contributions by airing and applying your purpose to the people you interact with in personal ways. Those people, who love and trust you at least somewhat implicitly, are likely to take your choices into advisement as they think about their own. Second, this sharing of what you want most deepens your relationships. When we know more about what makes each other tick, we develop more appreciation for each other. By sharing your truest self and inviting your family and friends to do the same, you create that mutual understanding.

PITFALL #2: SHOULDING IN THE FAMILY AND FRIENDS SPHERE

Our own family-and-friend groups can strongly should us: how often we "should" be together, what we "should" do in that time, and even what we "should" or "shouldn't" do or talk about when we're together. But like every aspect of 21st-century life, family and friendships are changing rapidly. We're moving farther and more often than we used to, separating from family members and childhood friends. We also have far more access to advanced and relatively cheap communication technologies to stay in touch.

Myriad factors influence our modern relationships, but the takeaway is that they're vastly different since the shoulds we're exposed to were developed. What does that mean for a purposeful approach to family and friends?

Shoulding Leads to Loneliness. Whatever the flavor of shoulds you're subject to, they lead to a one-size-fits-all approach to relationships. And for the nearly eight billion of us on this planet who aren't the ones the approach was built to fit, the approach is suboptimal. If we try to fit into it, we won't give or get all that we could out of that relationship.

One of my favorite explanations of this concept is in Glennon Doyle's reaction to potential new friend Elizabeth Gilbert's interest in becoming friends. In *Untamed*, Doyle wrote, "I am not a good friend. I have never been capable of or willing to commit to the maintenance that the rules of friendship dictate" (like remembering birthdays, meeting for coffee, and texting back). Doyle's reaction to these failures was, "I decided I would stop trying. I don't want to live in constant debt."[65]

But opting out of friendship is a worse health decision than smoking 15 cigarettes a day.[66] As I mentioned before, people who feel lonely are 50 percent more likely to die prematurely. Loneliness is the longest-lasting and potentially most fatal pandemic of the 21st century. In addition, marriage rates are declining; if current trends continue, married people will soon be the minority.[67] Of course, marriage is not a guaranteed antidote to loneliness, but this is a stark trend in our decision to commit formally to intimate relationships. More generally, research has shown that 36 percent of all Americans feel "serious loneliness," including 61 percent of young adults and 50 percent of mothers with young children.[68]

To thrive, we need social relationships with family, biological or chosen (a.k.a. our dearest friends). But to be sustainable and provide us with the benefits of social interaction, the connections must be purposeful (aligned with our own styles, needs, and preferences). This isn't selfish; it just requires us to be reflective and honest so that we can find the other people whose styles, needs, and preferences match our own enough to be mutually beneficial.

Shoulding Looks Like Meeting Obligations. Let's revisit our Purpose Seeker Lisa to see how shoulding influenced the way she supports her parents and daughter. In an effort to maintain the cultural obligation to family meals that her Korean parents held, she went to eat with them on as many weeknights as possible, even after a late night on a client project. This meant they all ate later than they'd have liked, and Lisa was tired and often cranky at the visits.

In my case, for the first few years I was with my husband, I scheduled a manic few days from December 23 to 26 to fit in visits with my mom and stepfather, in-laws, and stepkids, as well as go to our friends' annual Christmas party. It was exhausting, and every visit was a bit too short to be satisfying. Now I've realized that the date doesn't much influence the intimacy or joy we can get from a visit, so I spread all these wonderful gatherings out over a few weeks at the end of the year, making room for a getaway with my husband and stepkids to rest after the busy year-end.

Counter Shoulding with New Expectations. Swapping out your shoulds by changing the people and expectations you're exposed to can be a great way forward in terms of friends. That said, it can be harder with family, because if you want to keep the family you were born with (and you don't have to!), they are who they are.

In the case of these forever relationships, the path forward is about changing your relationship to the shoulding. Can you let go of the idea that your mom thinks you should be married at 32 and can't enjoy time with you if you're not? It might be a lot louder in your head than it is in hers. As soon as you overcome inaction in the Family and Friends Sphere by asking questions to get to know them more deeply, the shoulding might fade on its own.

Especially in families, we often have very strong identities as Mom, Dad, or the middle, youngest, or older sibling, and so on. Those roles can shape who we are, but they're likely not our whole story, especially 20 or 50 years after all those family dinners. So here, too, get clear about your expectations for the family relationships in which you'd like to feel more impactful, and then try sharing those expectations. You might be surprised at the willingness you find to scrapping a should.

Lisa realized she could suggest a longer, more relaxed weekend visit to have a leisurely lunch, revisit old pictures, and play cards with her parents. That would provide the quality time that she craved with them without exhausting her during the week. When she broached the idea, they were equally enthusiastic and relieved at the idea of eating their dinner earlier without having to wait for her to finish work.

As for me, I'm still working on creating new expectations for my own friendships. Having lived abroad for 10 years without the time, money, or desire to travel back for every bachelorette party, wedding, baby shower, or birthday in my 20s, traditional friendship rules suggest that most of my childhood and college friends "should" have given up on me. But I still treasure very close relationships with many of them. We challenged the traditional expectations and won.

That said, I share Doyle's lack of friendship skills. I just don't like the phone, I fall into deep holes around my work, and I'm a profound introvert. So I may not call back for months, am probably not up for dinner on Tuesday, and have likely forgotten your kids' names and certainly their ages. Yet I promise I have deeply intimate, satisfying, and impactful (in both ways) friendships with a formidable group of people for whom those limitations work just fine.

Rewriting new shoulds is also a great path to purposeful relationships. When Doyle declined Gilbert's suggestion that they become friends because of her inability to follow friendship "rules," Gilbert's response was to create new terms. Doyle explains that Gilbert "offered a new friendship memo: that for us there would be no arbitrary rules, obligations, or expectations. We would not owe each other anything other than admiration, respect, love—and that was all done already. We became friends."[69]

The same can be true for parents and children, stepparents and stepchildren, siblings, second cousins, college roommates, spouses, life partners, and unlabeled people who love each other and are committed to each other's well-being. What's important, as in every sphere, is that you're clear on what you need and have to offer and that you're open and receptive to hearing those things from the other person. If you can share that and still decide there's some result you both value in developing or maintaining a relationship, you're in good shape for a purposeful connection.

PITFALL #3: ORTHODOXY IN THE FAMILY AND FRIENDS SPHERE

The water in which we swim has a particularly strong, if invisible, current in our Family and Friends Sphere. Of course, family relations and friendships are highly culturally determined, even within different groups and regions of the US. So the nature of the shoulds you're most exposed to depends on your nationality, geographic origin, religion, racial and gender identity, and more.

But what's universally true is that, much like all the other spheres, those group norms have not kept up with the pace of change. Further, since our culture doesn't consider this a "productive" part of our lives, most of us spend less time and energy optimizing our personal relationships than we do our career personas and interactions.

But, as I've pointed out in this chapter, investments in the Family and Friends Sphere have huge opportunities for impact. In some ways, they're the most delicate opportunities because of their personal and intimate nature. Without the theorizing, studying, and practice that we're more likely to do when it comes to our work lives, community involvement, or money, our commonly held ideas—the water in which we swim—have a lot of influence over our choices in the Family and Friends Sphere. Let's consider the results of that influence.

Orthodoxy Leads to Invisibility. Recall the $10 trillion of invisible labor that's performed globally each year? That effort is almost entirely made up of investments in the Family and Friends Sphere. This huge number illustrates the extent to which orthodoxy obscures the investments we make as caregivers, whether for our kids, parents, neighbors, or friends.

Vast efforts in our Family and Friends Sphere are not only made invisible by the water in which we swim, but are overlooked by any person, relationship, or activity that doesn't fit the most common script for our family or friendships. That leads to a downward spiral: we don't value our own efforts to invest in our family and friends purposefully, so we do less of it, and the idea that these activities are inconsequential is reinforced. Further, nontraditional family relationships or friendships aren't valued or even recognized, and our "traditional" models for these relationships are strengthened.

Orthodoxy Looks Like Constraints. When we allow our family and friendships to be governed by orthodoxy, we miss out on fulfilling relationships. My own family makeup has always been more of an elaborate cocktail than the fluoride-enriched tap water of the American nuclear family. My parents separated when I was a toddler and divorced shortly thereafter; my mom remarried when I was six. From then on, I celebrated at least three Christmases: at home, often with three parents; at my maternal grandparents', sometimes including their ex-son-in-law (my dad); and at my paternal grandparents', often without their son but with their ex-daughter-in-law (my mom) and her new husband (my stepfather). If we had followed the "rule" that divorce ends relationships, we all would've missed out on many memories.

When my mother was caring for my father through his struggle with brain cancer more than 20 years after their divorce, we faced a new mountain to climb. Because she was no longer a relation by law, we needed to establish her as the primary point of contact at each doctor's office and care center. This added effort was unwelcome during an already exhausting phase of caregiving, as well as slowing critical care to my dad on more than one occasion.

Of course, in the modern era, this experience is not uncommon. Blended families are the new norm, yet I've heard dozens of similar stories about the challenges facing nontraditional families in medical, legal, and educational settings. We haven't officially expanded the menu beyond the same old orthodoxy in terms of what we expect family to look like for ourselves and others.

Counter Orthodoxy with Intentionality. In the words of Riane Eisler, a systems scientist, "In our time of rapidly changing technological and social conditions, we have to go much deeper, to matters that conventional economic analyses and theories have ignored. There's a common denominator underlying our mounting personal, social, and environmental problems: lack of caring. We need an economic system that takes us beyond communism, capitalism, and other old isms. We need economic models, rules, and policies that support caring for ourselves, others, and our Mother Earth."[70]

Investments in our Family and Friends Sphere are often about quality over quantity. Generally, it's hard to avoid seeing these people. We live with some of them. The purposeful approach is to resist orthodoxy and get more intentional about the ways you're spending that time together, like Lisa's shift to longer, more relaxed weekend visits with her parents.

Factors That Influence Our Impact in the Family and Friends Sphere

Now that we've explored several ways to influence our personal relationships as well as the pitfalls that prevent us from doing so, let's consider some factors that influence the impact we can have in our Family and Friends Sphere.

DEMOGRAPHICS AND LIFE SPAN

Investments in the Family and Friends Sphere tend to fluctuate and evolve over the course of our lives not only naturally but also as a result of inaction, shoulding, and orthodoxy. The traditional flow is for young adults to spend a lot of time with friends, shift toward building families as they get married, partner, and/or have kids, and then revert to friends and peers as their kids move on to launch their own families. Some of these tendencies are biological, logical, and/or convenient. But others are either invalid from the start or outdated for the 21st century.

Make no mistake, we don't just impose this traditional order of operations for family-and-friends activities on each other; we do it to ourselves, choosing our investments in the Family and Friends Sphere based on our age and life stage. Dr. Mario Martinez, the clinical neuropsychologist who brought us the concept of tribal shaming, also has a strong view on this point. Here's his take from a podcast interview with Tami Simon:

> So, for example, you are . . . a little older than middle age. You can't have a sports car anymore because 'what's this old guy or this old woman doing with that car?' [Your idea of age] is already setting you up for failure. The first time your back hurts [after a drive in your sports car] you think, 'Ah, I'm too old for this.' You give up the joy. You buy a bigger car, and you enter the tunnel of helplessness of, '[Now] I need anti-inflammatories.' *That's* how you age.[71]

Demographics are changing fast, including longer life spans (particularly for wealthy White folks, given the health costs of being poor and non-White), reduced marriage rates, and delayed and reduced childbearing. These factors, as well as the changing preferences for relationships in 21st-century economy, make our traditional views incredibly ineffective at quenching the thirst for supportive and loving relationships with blood relatives and chosen family.

MODELING AND LENDING PRIVILEGE

Another thing to consider about the investments in your Family and Friends Sphere is how you use your privilege in these relationships. Accumulating and then lending privilege to your family and friends generates a powerful ripple effect.

Dia Bryant, now executive director at the Education Trust, was the first in her family to go to college. Once she graduated, she "came to New York with $1,000 and my suitcase. I lived on couches, ate hot dogs, and worked my way to and through a master's degree. Once I was established and had a couch for [him] to crash on, my brother came. And then our other brother joined us."

Setting an example in this way is a form of impact not to be underestimated. Dia felt the "tension of betraying one side to be with the other" in her choice to move to New York and attend graduate school. But she's equally clear that this choice is responsible for her massive "opportunities to be one of the few people who can move between worlds, learning what works and what doesn't," and then paying that insight—a form of privilege—forward to family and friends.

You, too, can lend the privilege you have as a result of your gender, race, educational background, financial means, or otherwise to your chosen family or friends. While family members often share the same privileges, like Dia, some siblings may be more able or inclined to accumulate more access to resources and power over the course of their lives. Providing a personal reference for a friend who didn't go to school with many professionals in their field of work, or helping them navigate a corporate culture they're not familiar with, are both ways you can use your own privilege to help someone else realize their potential.

Crafting Your Family and Friends Sphere Cocktail

Now that you've learned about the Family and Friends Sphere, the pitfalls to avoid, the impact you can have there, and the factors that influence that impact, it's time to apply the five-step model to this sphere. If you're using the playbook, turn to chapter 10 for a more detailed process.

STEP 1: BASELINE ASSESSMENT

Assess your investments in the Family and Friends Sphere by reviewing the activities you identified on your Impact Dashboard Excel Worksheet, the Purpose Party Playbook, or wherever you've been doing the work. Edit or add to that list so that it feels complete. When you're satisfied that you've captured the activities you do in your Family and Friends Sphere, review the total number of hours you're spending there per week. You can also determine the percentage of time each week this sphere takes. Fill in whether you want to do each activity more, less, or the same, and then rate these three statements as they apply to your Family and Friends Sphere now, last year, and a year from now:

> *I invest time, energy, and attention in the Family and Friends Sphere.*
>
> *I am satisfied with the quantity and quality of my investments in the Family and Friends Sphere.*
>
> *I see the outcomes of my investments in the Family and Friends Sphere.*

STEP 2: WHAT DO YOU NEED IN THIS SPHERE?

Determine whether there's a change you can make in your Family and Friends Sphere that will increase your well-being and/or the well-being of your family and friends. Identify a change in this sphere that you're willing to make over the next month, whether it's doing something you already do more regularly, stopping something you do now, or trying a new activity. You might instead realize that it's really not the area you need to prioritize. Before you decide for sure, think through the questions from pages 162–163 of this book as they apply to your Family and Friends Sphere. When you're done, draft a simple, clear, and measurable belief statement about what you want to change in your Family and Friends Sphere. Remember that your belief statement doesn't include exactly *how* you'll achieve the goal you're setting; you're just identifying *what* you're going to do and *why* it matters.

STEP 3: YOUR ONE NEXT STEP

Once you believe *what* the outcome will be of changing something in your Family and Friends Sphere and *why* it matters, figure out *how* to achieve that change. Focus on choosing your One Thing for this sphere, then get really specific about exactly what this activity is going to look like (at least to start; you can revise the details as you learn). Here, in the playbook, or on the Excel worksheet, answer the questions from page 164 of this book as they apply to your Family and Friends Sphere.

STEP 4: SUPPORTING THAT STEP

Having a motivating belief statement helps keep you focused on why you're doing all this purpose work. Think about or write down your answers to the following questions that will help guide you in creating one.

- What's going to keep you from building this new habit, whether from the pitfalls we discussed in this chapter or otherwise?

- How can you overcome those obstacles?

Now write a simple, clear, and measurable behavioral plan to keep you on track. Be sure that this plan connects to the results you want to see from your Family and Friends activities.

STEP 5: KEEP AN EYE OUT

The only way to keep up with changes in your outlook, work, life, and the world and make the necessary adaptations is to keep an eye on what you're doing and the consequences it's having. Pick your preferred method of tracking change and use it. Remember, the point here is not to beat yourself up if you don't get exactly where you want to be. It's just to be able to see how it's going. Does the new activity actually have your desired impact? Does it fit into your life, or does it reveal something else you'd rather spend your time on?

Overlapping Spheres

Our family and friend activities certainly affect the other areas of our lives, and vice versa. Of course, I'll start with the way that our self-investments, or lack thereof, influence our ability to be present for family and friends—and model self-care for others. The caregivers must be tended to first if they are to sustain that support.

The life-stage expectations for family and friendships that we explored often influence our expectations of our own or others' job and workplace activities. We expect young employees to work late and pick up weekend work or travel since they "don't have anyone waiting at home." We hesitate to hire newly married women because they're likely to call on our maternity leave policy. We shift big accounts and projects away from later-career folks who are "on their way out to the golf course" anyhow.

Family and friends can blend seamlessly into community activities as well. We meet friends in our community activities, and we may choose to get involved in the community investments that our family members or friends make. This overlap strengthens our communities and our families, providing precious social capital that's such a clear driver of well-being. Further, our family relationships are one of the most potent drivers of our attitudes about money. Thus, the way that we model, teach, and reward attitudes to and use of money in our families has significant sway over the ways our family members deal with money.

When people think about the influence they want to have, the next four spheres (Job, Workplace, Community, and Money) usually come to mind more readily than the first two. Certainly these four spheres are important, powerful levers for impact. However, I've yet to meet a human who has successfully reached fulfillment by exerting effort only in the more professional spheres. So even as we proceed from home out into the world through the Dashboard, find ways to maintain your attention and effort on the more personal spheres.

Reflection Questions

Like all the chapters, these questions are available as a free worksheet at www.inspiringcowgirl.com/goingfirst. But if you're tempted to play with each Sphere, you'll love the Going First Purpose Party Playbook! And if you're already there, you'll find these questions in Chapter 10.

- Consider your Family and Friends Sphere holistically. What are you doing? What are you not doing? Is the blend authentic to you and aligned with your desired impact?

- With whom will you try out some conversation starters first? What's the worst thing that can happen if you try them? What do you hope will happen?

- What examples of shoulding occur in your Family and Friends Sphere? Which of those shoulds fit with your desired impact just fine? Which don't? What will it take to reject some of the shoulding that isn't aligned with your purpose in this sphere?

- What other pitfalls have you experienced in this sphere?

- How can you recognize and track the value of your investments in your personal relationships and help others do the same?

- Where are you achieving quantity in your family and friends investments, but not quality? What shift will increase the quality of those activities?

- Are you following "rules" in your friendships or family that are outdated and unhelpful? Which ones? Who can you speak with about the potential upside of breaking those rules?

- Are there ways you can lend your privileges to your family members or friends? Have they ever extended their privilege to you? Did it influence your well-being or career at all?

Chapter 11

The Job Sphere

The Job Sphere is made up of the professional activities you're some-how compensated for. Note that these job activities may not fit the mold of a full-time employee role with specific responsibilities and deliverables, particularly in the 21st-century version of work. Your job investments might be part of an official, contracted, full- or part-time job, or a contractor role for one or several clients. Or maybe your Job Sphere is pro bono, and your compensation is experience in a new field or fulfillment after retirement from full-time work. For now, use the LinkedIn test: where on your LinkedIn profile would you put a particular job investment in your Impact Dashboard: your experience section (likely fits in the Job Sphere), your projects section (per-haps Self, Job, or Workplace Sphere), or your volunteer experience section (Community Sphere)? Most importantly, remember that the Dashboard is a tool with no right or wrong answers, so go with whatever classification helps you measure and shape your investment mix toward living and leading with purpose.

Whatever specific form your job takes in terms of the role you're in and the form of compensation you earn, you have opportunities for influence in two primary ways: *what you do* and *how you do it*. Before we look more closely at Job Sphere investments and the pitfalls that block them, I want to make these two elements of job impact clear.

The content marketer we met briefly on Purpose Seeker Gabriela's team writes company blog posts about their customers, retail partners, and suppliers. Their last post highlighted a small, independent business owned by a Black woman who recently became a retail partner to the brand. The article got a lot of traffic and doubled the shop's online orders that week. Simply by doing their job of telling the story of various stakeholders, Gabriela's colleague had the effect of directing financial resources to a historically under-resourced person.

On the other hand, when Gabriela facilitates her team's weekly meeting, she has control of the agenda and tone of the meeting. Given her desire to pay forward her own approach to her Self Sphere investments, she could build in a brief mindfulness practice to mitigate stress and overwhelm. This is a way for Gabriela to shape her influence by how she does her job.

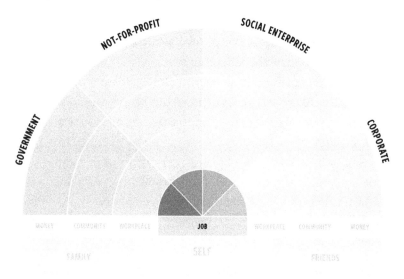

Figure 16. The Job Sphere's place in the Impact Dashboard.

These examples illustrate that both what you do and how you do it in the Job Sphere can have rippling positive effects that mirror your values regardless of where you work (that's where the Workplace

Sphere comes in). But if it were that easy to leverage our jobs for impact, we'd all be doing it, wouldn't we? Let's look more closely at investments in the Job Sphere and the pitfalls we fall into on our way to making them

How I Learned About the Job Sphere

I learned a lot about the Job Sphere during my time in the not-for-profit sector (though I didn't call it that at the time). Let's start with *what* we were doing. By the IRS's definition, as employees of 501c3 organizations, what we were doing was "good" for the people we served, as described in our mission statement. In reality, I saw a lot of useless efforts: some of what we did didn't meet those people's needs and, worse, some caused harm due to *how* we did it.

I was hired to do a needs assessment of local youth centers in Palestine that a major global funder was considering as grant recipients. The funding came with a requirement to meet a 50/50 gender mix for participants in the centers' programs within one year. There were a few brave families in this conservative community who started sending their daughters to one of the centers after having gotten over concerns of physical safety, philosophical differences, and conflicts with the students' school obligations. Still, there were usually conditions for joining, such as having to be in a girls-only program with a female facilitator or staying in the same classroom or activity as their brother. Building trust with families was a long, slow path. Clearly, the center wouldn't get to that 50/50 mix within a year unless they reduced the size of the programs to the handful of girls whose families permitted them to come with a matching number of boys. But this approach would underutilize both the centers' capacity to serve youth and the funding provided.

I relayed all this to the funder. Hoping to leverage my privilege as a White American with deep commitment to equity, I explained the center leader's commitment to equity and the need to pursue it in a more realistic time frame and format that would work in his community. A few days later, the global funder made the grant to this center and four others—which included a requirement of equal participation by gender within 12 months at risk of rescinding funding in the second year. By demanding equal gender participation to serve their own vision rather than honoring the cultural context, this major international funder caused great harm to staff of these youth centers as well as hundreds of youths and their families, to say nothing of reinforcing the image of international development as paternalistic and inept at solving real problems.

So even in the not-for-profit sector, where the IRS is in charge of mandating that organizations do work that's intended to be good for the world, the specific choices people make about what to do and how to do it can cause harm.

Indeed, I was the example of a bad leader in some situations! I remember with great discomfort several phone calls, workshops, and staff meetings in which I barked at a youth leader, community member, or colleague. Whether they were late with a deliverable, misunderstanding my point, or refusing to try my brilliant idea, I applied some combination of withholding approval, shame, and unconstructive criticism.

Over time, I was able to recognize these errors within a matter of days or hours and apologize. Sometimes I was able to repair the relationship during that conversation and revisit the issue at hand to reach a solution that worked for everyone involved—most importantly, the people we were trying to serve. But in other cases, my errors led to a trust deficit for days or weeks that (rightly) took me days or weeks to repair. And in that time, none of us was able to do the work we were there to do as effectively as we could have. This might've been different had I been making the Self Sphere investments necessary to stay empathetic, non-judgmental, and present in listening to the challenge presented.

I certainly don't intend to suggest that the not-for-profit sector does no good in the world; on the contrary. But I want these examples to illuminate the fact that having impact in the Job Sphere is more complex than having a job that saves lives or shapes young minds. There are plenty of ways to have great outcomes and align with your purpose in every single job on the planet. Let's dig in and see how!

Making It Yours

It's time to do your own work! Head to the *Going First* Purpose Party Playbook for a guided process. If you don't have the playbook, go to chapter 7 and apply the process found there to your Job Sphere. If you need a reminder of the five steps, review the section in that chapter called "Zeroing in on Each Sphere."

Avoiding the Pitfalls in the Job Sphere

If you've come this far, you're at least open to the idea that you can have positive leverage in your job, whatever your industry, sector, or function. Before we get into all that magic, let's address the reasons you aren't already having it (or at least not as much as you'd like).

PITFALL #1: INACTION IN THE JOB SPHERE

In the Job Sphere as much as any other, we tend to not make changes. We keep doing the things we do the way we've been doing them. Especially during over-busy days, it's hard to make the extra effort required to identify what we'd like to change, much less actually make those changes. This risk of inaction applies to what we do as well as how we do it.

Inaction Leads to Learned Helplessness. Inaction in our Job Sphere is part of a nasty downward spiral to *learned helplessness*, which *Psychology Today* defines as "when an individual continuously faces a negative, uncontrollable situation and stops trying to change their circumstances, even when they have the ability to do so."[72] We can agree that the 2020s have provided more than enough aversive stimuli (bad news) that we can't control. When most of us see a news story about a natural disaster, read a report about racial violence, or see the latest statistics about the gender wealth gap, we aren't catalyzed to action because these are just the latest in a long string of big, complicated problems. We don't see them as directly connected to what we do in our job on any given day.

This learned helplessness results from paying attention and feeling compelled to solve *all* problems, or at least solve all of one really big problem. Investing our attention in all the bad news we're exposed to leads to inaction because we're simply too overwhelmed to do anything. The less we do, the more overwhelming these problems seem and the more helpless we feel, and so on down the spiral. But remember how we assigned you only one eight-billionth of the world problems to work on? I haven't figured out exactly what that looks like yet, but I can assure you that it isn't single-handedly ending racism in your city or your team! Nor do you have to single-handedly take on eliminating ocean plastic or littering in your town.

Inaction Looks Like Inflexibility. If we don't approach our job activities purposefully, identifying the small elements of a single problem that we *can* have a positive influence on, we lose out on the win-win-win of doing work that's fulfilling for us, motivating for our teams, and good for the world. Particularly as the world changes faster than ever around us, if we don't find ways to connect our jobs to impact, we won't keep ourselves or our team members engaged in the work we need done, much less solve our increasingly urgent challenges.

In my experience with the youth centers in Palestine, the donor succumbed to inaction by sticking with their demand for either a perfect gender mix or no engagement at all. They weren't willing to act collaboratively with the leaders whom they were purportedly aiming to support. It would've been far more impactful for the donor to evolve their expectations toward a more realistic path that led to gender equity, ideally in collaboration with the local partner, to arrive at a mutually acceptable midpoint.

You might recall Andrew Glazier, CEO of Defy Ventures (helping formerly incarcerated people find dignified careers) and his journey to leading purposefully in a way that was motivating to him and his team. He explained that it took a while: "It's a lot of work! In our jam-packed workdays, it can feel like there's no time, especially with the urgency of our other tasks. So we make the false choice: 'either I do my work or think about purpose.'"

Over time, failing to creatively revise our Job Sphere activities to align with our desired contributions leads to lower productivity, less creativity, and eventual burnout. Andrew saw this firsthand in himself and at Defy: "If you don't make time for [finding impact at work], bad things happen! At worst, it affects your ability to do the work. In the best case, you proceed, but toxicity builds up and you do work that isn't aligned with your purpose, which will eventually lose effectiveness. Like a termite infestation, your house may not fall down right away, but the misalignment is costly long-term."

This inflexibility also shows up as what Chid Liberty has witnessed as a version of the NIMBY effect:

> It's easy to think you're on the right side of history globally speaking but not follow through when it comes to your own

personal case. One senior leader whose company we invested in supported the plan to bring diverse candidates into their executive team all throughout the due diligence process. But apparently it never occurred to him that it could be his role taken by someone of a different gender or race. And so even though he recognized that this transition was essential for the business's survival, he resisted the new hire we made with the full support of the board, other investors, and executive team members. It's really a case of NIMBY applied to people and power that leads us not to take the action our purpose would lead us to take.

Not evolving to find some results you feel good about from your day-to-day work is not a sustainable path forward; you cannot maintain the effort, creativity, and resilience that lead to success in today's economy. So let go of the overwhelming and paralyzing inflexibility that either you fix this problem or you walk away from it and continue business as usual. Evolve your unique way to have positive influence.

Counter Inaction with Specificity. To get over inaction in your Job Sphere, get specific about the outcomes you want. Then be honest about what it will take to have that impact. This step will call on the willingness to change your ideas that we recommended you pack in your Purpose Party bag, and it leads to the psychological remedy for learned helplessness: self-efficacy.

Self-efficacy is a person's belief in their ability to do what it takes to achieve certain outcomes. It's facilitated by having a growth mindset; recognizing that even massive, complex issues can get better; and believing that you can learn to contribute to them from where you sit right now.

Remember, don't conceive your impact at work as needing to fix all things. Work on getting clear and specific about the contributions you can make toward solving the problem you care about. Believing that you can do so and then seeing yourself have even tiny incremental effects increases your self-efficacy. In turn, this stops the downward spiral of learned helplessness, transforming it into a positively reinforcing cycle of action and satisfaction that improves your well-being and performance.[73] As Stuart Landesberg recognizes, reducing plastic from consumer goods is "not the only problem, but the one I feel most personally drawn to."

If you don't see some way that your efforts have a positive impact on the planet or people around you, you'll lose the motivation that's essential for success in the demanding, fast-moving, competitive 21st century.

PITFALL #2: SHOULDING IN THE JOB SPHERE

Shoulding shows up in the Job Sphere in terms of *how* you do your job. Let's take a closer look.

Shoulding Leads to 20th-Century Leadership. Current shoulding in the Job Sphere is a product of the Industrial Era and the extractive form of capitalism that still informs mainstream work in the early 21st century. It's taught explicitly in MBA programs, the official training ground of private sectors. Fred Keller, founder of B Corp Cascade Engineering, is in good company with his fear that our embrace of purposeful leadership "is not going to change significantly until we change the MBA curriculum."

Of course, we're all socialized to what leadership "should" look like, whether we've ever sat in a business school classroom or not. Asha Curran laments that "As a leader, we're still taught to distrust others. And these days, we don't want what we say to be taken in the wrong way lest it be broadcast on social media, which is so black/white, right/wrong."

Mike Vien, cofounder and CEO of Wallit, a startup offering wellness spending programs for employees, admits that "There is no playbook. We are all like deer in headlights" in 21st-century leadership. In far too many cases, we revert to the playbook that most of us do have access to, which is for hierarchical, command-and-control, short-term, financial-only management.

Shoulding Looks Like Fear. Even when we might want to say or do something in our Job Sphere differently from the ways we "should" be more in line with the impact we want to have, it's scary to break that existing script.

I recognize that the colleagues at the donor organization for the youth centers in Palestine were scared. They felt great responsibility to ensure that their funds never reached anyone the US government would have a problem with. And their 20th-century approach to upholding that responsibility was to follow the rigid rules their superiors had set, including a perfect 50/50 gender mix (which made perfect sense in their American context). My suggestion to apply this rule in a way that reflected the local context was threatening to their sense of control and safety. They stuck with the externally generated 50/50 rule and ultimately missed the chance to have any positive impact at all with the ample funds they were able to provide.

This fear can also show up as discomfort. "Everyone wants to do the right thing and gets in their own head. We don't know how to talk to just humans anymore in today's fast-moving and changing world," said Britney Pierini, a people professional at global and fast-growing startups.

Mark Atkinson thinks a lot about purposeful leadership, both in his own role as cofounder and CEO and for his clients. In reference to our so-called best practices (shoulding) not applying anymore, he said, "I see a lot of insecurity among well-intentioned leaders.

Then they become protective of info, defensive of ideas, and read malintent into their colleague's most benign actions, often colored by their own insecurities."

Fear can also play a role in deeply purposeful organizations. Becca Van Nederynen, a people professional in purpose-driven tech and biotech companies, often sees this among her new hires: "They're ecstatic about the values-alignment throughout the hiring process, and then there's a honeymoon when they start and see purposeful leadership in action. But then, because none of us is perfect, I often see impostor syndrome set in after about a month. They get scared of the high bar for integrity and whether they'll be able to keep living up to it."

Counter Shoulding with the Grandmother Rule. Our work today is certainly more complex, resulting in more potential for harm on all the people it touches across an entire supply chain. What's more, thanks to our interconnected world and technology-driven transparency, we know a lot more about that potential harm done by the companies we work for, buy from, partner with, and invest in.

It remains true that the vast majority of humans aspire to leave the world a bit better than they found it when they wake up each morning. But until we have a completely updated playbook for the way we work that's more purpose-driven and impactful, I offer the *Grandmother* (/Grandchild/Dog) *Rule* to inform your decisions at work (use whichever version resonates most strongly with you of these three corollaries): Do your job the way you want to tell your grandmother/grandchildren/dog that you do it.

Emily Barron, chief people person for fast-growing tech companies, lives by this rule. She explained, "A lot of it just comes down to doing the right thing. If something happens in an employee's family, don't put the leave of absence paperwork in front of them right away. Couldn't they just take a few days off to deal with the immediate issues and then handle our paperwork after that?"

When it comes to the insecurities he sees as so damaging to purposeful leadership, Mark Atkinson advised, "Experience is the best way to get over it. You have to decide that you want to do things differently and what you're ready to learn."

And that decision can only go one way if you're a people leader in any form, according to Annie Lin, chief people officer of Swiftly and other fast-growing tech companies before that: "Regardless of your role and level, if you take a people role, you are signing up to be a leader."

Purposeful leadership calls on us to step up courageously to counter shoulding in the Job Sphere. Cecilia Saez, chief people officer of B Corp-certified and public benefit corporation bank Aspiration, sees that fear allows people to "get sucked into the vortex of how others do their work. It takes courage to say, 'No, I do not want to do it that way. Who wants to follow me this other way?' In some cases, you won't gather a following, but instead of shifting back to the status quo, you can move on."

Christie Smith of Accenture points out that 21st-century leadership "requires us to authentically own topics that we had previously abdicated to human resources; corporate social responsibility teams; or a diversity, equity, and inclusion colleague. Managing leadership training, community outreach programs, or bias training is not natural for most CEOs and other business leaders, for whom the measurement of value has traditionally been shareholder value and how many widgets they got out the door on a quarterly basis."

Christie's point is a critical one and brings us to the next pitfall in the Job Sphere: how orthodoxy manifests as the standards we're measured against.

PITFALL #3: ORTHODOXY IN THE JOB SPHERE

Orthodoxy is no less problematic in the Job Sphere than the others. Here, it affects what we do in our day-to-day work, showing up specifically as the notion that work that is good for the world cannot earn money—at least not as much as traditional work in the private sector—and that there must be some discount for impactful work.

Before we dive into this pitfall, we need to examine this notion of what's good for the world more closely. Recall the Spectrum of Impact: what's good for the world isn't limited to the most dramatic, frontline, lifesaving forms of work that are usually done by not-for-profit organizations. While cancer research, elephant repopulation, and ocean plastic capture are worthy endeavors, so are equitable contract writing, healthy sustainable food production, and dignified affordable housing design. And those latter activities are generally done by for-profits, whether Businesses for Good or traditional corporations.

The false belief that only the most explicit forms of influence (and thus not-for-profit roles) can be aligned to purpose holds us back from finding the win-win-win ways to do any element of our jobs in any sector of the economy. If we don't believe that we can or should be paid for doing work that is good for the world, our journey to leading purposefully is doomed before we begin.

Orthodoxy Leads to Unintended Harm. By focusing on dramatic, lifesaving issues such as deforestation in the Amazon or stubbornly high rates of malaria in Nigeria as what you want to solve through your work, you limit your potential to achieve impact in your Job Sphere. Taking this approach can cause unintended harm to yourself—in the form of frustration and misalignment—as well as to the people or ecosystem you're trying to help.

Dramatic problems are certainly important and deserve solving; indeed, our collective well-being relies on them being solved! But they're also complex and technical, requiring specific expertise and ways of working.

So if you're that content marketer on Gabriela's team who we met at the beginning of the chapter, these problems are not for you to solve. Fixating on their solutions as your desired outcomes in your Job Sphere will leave you unfulfilled, rob your team of your best efforts, and do nothing to help the Amazon or malaria rates. It would also have kept that local business you profiled for your employer's blog from getting the bump in sales that resulted from your post about them and led to an increase in wealth for its owner, a Black woman.

Orthodoxy Looks Like Declining Performance. Not feeling good about the impact you're having through your day-to-day work is also not a sustainable path forward. If you don't see some positive effect on people or the planet as a result of your Job Sphere investments, you can lose the motivation and resilience that underpin success in the demanding, fast-moving 21st century.

Cognitive dissonance is the psychological concept that because holding two conflicting ideas in our heads at once takes effort (and is thus undesirable), we align our behavior with our ideas to maintain the notion that we are good people, which is essential to our well-being. In other words, if we work hard at something, we want to believe that it's worth doing and ultimately has some value. If we don't believe that our work has a positive impact on someone or some ecosystem, we won't be able to justify the level of effort it requires.

Vincent Stanley is Patagonia's director of philosophy and a wise and vocal proponent of responsible business through his writing, teaching at Yale, and many other Job Sphere activities. He warns, "Ultimately, your work has to align somehow with your purpose.

It just won't last if it doesn't. You'll get burnt out or demotivated and you won't be able to perform."

If this risk to your own effectiveness doesn't spur you to action in finding impact in your Job Sphere, know that you'll soon be evaluated on these metrics (if you're not already). As increasingly more investors demand that companies address social and environmental sustainability, the pressure is rising on CEOs and leadership teams to improve the social and environmental metrics for each of their domains. That impact is achieved by people throughout the organization, so the demand for improvement will eventually trickle down to you, no matter your position in the company. Christie Smith sees this happening fast among Accenture clients:

> Now leaders are being measured on how they invest in making employees 'net better off.' They're held accountable for the effects of their engagement with employees, customers, and really all stakeholders. Until now, the ends have justified the means, and as long as your widgets were on time, on budget, and up to quality specs, you passed. Now we have moved into an era of leadership where the skills that haven't been measured or valued are the real differentiators, including empathy, collaboration, and ultimately the impact we have on people and our planet.

Counter Orthodoxy with Learning. To keep up with these expectations—and more importantly, to reach your full potential—it's time to get serious about finding and crafting ways to increase your impact in the Job Sphere.

Follow the Grandmother Rule to increase that influence today. But do not tarry in starting or accelerating the lifelong learning and continuous improvement required to reduce the harm your work causes and increase its positive outcome. For better or worse, recognize that Arthur Woods, cofounder and CEO of Mathison—who could be considered an expert on diversity and inclusion himself—said during our interview, "There aren't any experts in this work."

Plenty of people have been thinking deeply about purposeful leadership for a long time, and I strongly encourage you to learn from and work with them. For his part, Vincent Stanley understands that not everyone works at a company that integrates impact as wholly as Patagonia does. So he encourages professionals to take a broad view of impact, recognizing where a given company is in the evolution toward business being good for the world. It's not about letting employers off the hook; it's about being curious and creative in looking for ways that your job can have positive leverage, even if it feels micro or hyperlocal.

Once you've gotten specific about the problems you care about solving and implemented the Grandmother Rule to improve your day-to-day choices, it's time to take the next step.

Almost any global problem will have antecedents that are within your sphere of influence and can be addressed by some of your capabilities and responsibilities. While purposeful leaders take the time to understand the problems they care about deeply enough to reveal the approachable elements of their root causes, they stay within their sphere of influence while expanding their impact.

Luann Abrams, founder and CEO of Project CEOX, has demonstrated how deep understanding enables alignment of job activities with purpose. Luann wanted her two sons to have significant and prosperous careers as well as the possibility to be present to their own families. But she knew that even if she instilled these values in her boys, she couldn't influence every company they might work for to enable her wish for them. When she read some research indicating that female CEOs have happier employees,[74] she saw a path to advance her wish for her sons. She started Project CEOX to place more female CEOs at growing companies, thereby increasing her sons' likelihood of engaging in balanced and impactful careers.

Again, Luann is under no illusion that she's changed the entire workforce or eliminated her sons' risk of having inadequate parental leave. But she has found an issue she cares about with a root cause that her skills and interests can address.

David, our Purpose Seeker, has always been grateful for an internship he got through a local not-for-profit during college. He is cognizant of the way it shaped his career early on. As he contemplates ways to integrate his background more intentionally into his Job Sphere, he's curious about offering a senior at his alma mater an internship similar to the one he had. However, it's been over a decade, and the school, students, industry, and hiring pipeline have all changed. If David doesn't learn more about all these elements of the problem he sees—that he doesn't meet many people from his hometown in finance—he could miss an opportunity to have the influence he seeks or even create additional unintended harm. The answer is to gather insights from all the stakeholders involved with the problem so David can identify the best possible way he can contribute.

Factors That Influence Our Impact in the Job Sphere

Now that you know the Job Sphere pitfalls to look out for and some tips to avoid them, let's zoom back out and consider the factors that influence the purposeful choices you make in your Job Sphere.

DO YOU

At the risk of boring you, I'll say once more that today's biggest problems are complex and ever-changing. This is why we work on the ABCs: simple awareness that your job can be part of solving problems; belief in your ability to do so; and then the clarity, confidence, and courage to do your specific part. So as you identify investments in your Job Sphere that have the impact you seek, be where you are. Do what you are qualified and uniquely positioned to do.

If these immediate steps don't provide the sense of purpose you had hoped for, you might need to change your role or learn a new skill or industry so you can make a change. But unless you already know that's your next step, start by increasing your influence from right where you are.

FOLLOW YOUR INTUITION

When considering your Job Sphere investments, your internal compass is an important source of data. The number and severity of crises we face today makes it hard to identify the appropriate level of urgency. The best guide any of us have as to when we need to take action toward a given problem is our intuition.

After years of seeing bias, discrimination, and violence against his Vietnamese American parents as well as other Asian Americans, Jeff Le shared those experiences more publicly than he ever had: "It just finally felt like I had to. I had never had the belief that my voice mattered, but finally, it seemed like the options were all so bleak, why wouldn't I go big? [This choice] was not without risks, like starting to receive hate mail, and the massive additional time commitment on top of full-time work, an infant daughter, and ample community activities to evaluate 60 writing requests and then write 23 articles."

But Jeff is grateful that he trusted his instinct to take action when he did. He's received plenty of feedback that his perspectives affected others' viewpoints on Asian American hate and inspired many to come forward with their own stories. Finally, he finds fulfillment in what he's doing as a writer and activist, even as it makes for longer days.

TALK IT UP

The other factor to consider as you shape investments in your Job Sphere is an easy multiplier for whatever you choose to do: talk about it candidly and often. Sharing the impact we're having and aspire to have is a powerful antidote to all of our pitfalls. First, it becomes a self-fulfilling prophecy, countering inertia and saving you—and others around you—from inaction. Second, it offers a new model in contrast to the legacy shouldering that opposes purposeful leadership by normalizing intentional and impactful investments in our Job Spheres. Third, in sharing your current and desired impacts, you provide real-life learning about the potential leverage of the jobs of everyone around you.

Clay Adams reflected on the consequences of his Job Sphere investments: "You have to talk about it a lot. One of our values is mutual respect and trust, so in the past few years, I spoke up about how this value influenced my approach to the murder of George Floyd as well as our COVID-19 vaccine policy." Of course, the way you talk about your job may overflow into your other spheres, so at the end of this chapter, we'll look at how they overlap.

Crafting Your Job Sphere Cocktail

Now that you've learned about the Job Sphere, the pitfalls to avoid, the impact you can have there, and what influences that impact, it's time to apply the five-step model to this sphere. If you're using the playbook, turn to chapter 11 for a more detailed process.

STEP 1: BASELINE ASSESSMENT

Assess your investments in the Job Sphere by reviewing the activities you identified on your Impact Dashboard Excel Worksheet, the Purpose Party Playbook, or wherever you've been doing the work. Edit or add to that list so that it feels complete. When you're satisfied that you've captured the activities you do in your Job Sphere, review the total number of hours you're spending there per week. You can also determine the percentage of time each week this sphere takes. Fill in whether you want to do each activity more, less, or the same, then rate these three statements as they apply to your Job Sphere now, last year, and a year from now:

> *I invest time, energy, and attention in the Job Sphere.*
>
> *I am satisfied with the quantity and quality of my investments in the Job Sphere.*
>
> *I see the outcomes of my investments in the Job Sphere.*

STEP 2: WHAT DO YOU NEED IN THIS SPHERE?

Determine whether there's a change you can make in your Job Sphere that you really believe will increase your well-being and/or the well-being of your colleagues. Identify a change in this sphere that you're willing to make over the next month, whether it's doing something you already do more regularly, stopping something you do, or trying a new activity. You might instead realize that it's really not the area you need to prioritize. Before you decide for sure, think through the questions from pages 162–163 of this book as they apply to your Job Sphere. When you're done, draft a simple, clear, and measurable belief statement about what you want to change in this sphere. Remember that your belief statement doesn't include exactly *how* you'll achieve the goal you're setting; you're just identifying *what* you're going to do and *why* it matters.

STEP 3: YOUR ONE NEXT STEP

Once you believe *what* the outcome will be of changing something in your Job Sphere and *why* it matters, figure out *how* to achieve that change. Focus on choosing your One Thing for this sphere, then get really specific about exactly what this activity is going to look like (at least to start; you can revise the details as you learn). Here, in the playbook, or on the Excel worksheet, answer the questions from page 164 of this book as they apply to your Job Sphere.

STEP 4: SUPPORTING THAT STEP

Having a motivating belief statement helps keep you focused on why you're doing all this purpose work. Think about or write down your answers to the following questions that will help guide you in creating one.

- What's going to keep you from building this new habit, whether from the pitfalls we discussed in this chapter or otherwise?

- How can you overcome those obstacles?

Now write a simple, clear, and measurable behavioral plan to keep you on track. Be sure that this plan connects to the results you want to see from your job activities.

STEP 5: KEEP AN EYE OUT

The only way to keep up with changes in your outlook, work, life, and the world and make the necessary adaptations is to keep an eye on what you're doing and the consequences it's having. Pick your preferred method of tracking change and use it. Remember, the point here is not to beat yourself up if you don't get exactly where you want to be. It's just to be able to see how it's going. Does the new activity actually have your desired impact? Does it fit into your life, or does it reveal something else you'd rather spend your time on?

Overlapping Spheres

Since we all have only 24 hours in a day, our investments in the Job Sphere have a very real impact on the activities in our Self Sphere and our Family and Friends Sphere. As our job activities become more and more consequential, it's rewarding to see and feel these results, but it can have a shadow side: all that success can lead to overwork, which affects your personal life.

Amy Peterson, founder of social enterprise Rebel Nell, is deeply motivated and fulfilled by her work of providing dignified livelihoods for hard-to-employ women who were incarcerated or addicted. Her passion for this work cut into her ability to make the investments she wanted in both her Self Sphere and her Family and Friends Sphere. Now she's gotten better at "knowing when to turn it off. I stay mindful of how the challenges and weight of my work can carry over so I can stay present for the times I need to be a mom or spouse." Ironically, if you're not careful to set boundaries and keep an eye on your desired blend of investments in all spheres, this challenge often increases as you become more purposeful about your work.

There are also times that job and community investments might overlap, particularly if you're doing pro bono work for a nonfinancial form of compensation, whether that's experience, credibility, or fulfillment. The only guideline for differentiating Job Sphere and

Community Sphere activities is how you see these activities fitting in. If they feel like a primary focus and are in line with your career path, they probably fit best in the Job Sphere. If, on the other hand, you see them as more of a side hustle or extracurricular, they're probably a Community Sphere investment.

Community Sphere investments can be brilliant ways of addressing any gaps you identified in the learning required to overcome orthodoxy. You might learn something about the problems you care about solving and see gaps in the ways you're currently equipped to contribute. Those gaps are opportunities for investment in your Community Sphere or Self Sphere so you can increase your Job Sphere impact later on. If some of the problems you care deeply about are too dramatic and distant to address from your Job Sphere, you may be able to contribute to their solutions through other spheres. For example, you could support people who are qualified to solve those problems by spreading the word or volunteering your time in the Community Sphere. Or you could leverage your Money Sphere—what you buy and invest in and to whom you donate—to address the problems you aren't equipped to in your job.

Speaking of money, it's important to think about your desire for accumulating financial wealth when you choose your job. Some jobs have earning potential that's directly tied to the time you spend doing them, whereas others are more scalable with opportunities to increase your earnings regardless of the hours you put in. If you want to earn enough to fund a safe and secure lifestyle, the former model should be adequate (assuming lots of things about the labor force that I shouldn't about fair wages, healthcare, and so on, but that's work for another volume).

On the other hand, if you aspire to accumulate great wealth as a path to expanding your influence, you should look for ways you can exponentially increase your earnings. That can usually be accomplished through the ownership of property, whether in the form of real estate, public or private equities, or ideas. I have no judgment about your aspirations to wealth, but getting clear about where you want to be will facilitate your journey to living and leading with purpose.

Of course, the activities in your Job Sphere are closely linked to choices about your workplace investments, which we'll explore in the next chapter. But first, consider the following:

Reflection Questions

Again, you can grab these questions as a free worksheet at www.inspiring-cowgirl.com/goingfirst. But if you've already downloaded three others, take the plunge and get yourself a Going First Purpose Party Playbook! And if you're already there, you'll find these questions in Chapter 11.

- Identify the skills, talents, experiences, knowledge, and relationships you can bring to your Job Sphere. What ways do you make positive change from things you already do in your job? How does it feel to recognize those impacts?

- What insights do you have about the investments you're making in your Job Sphere? What are you *not* doing in this sphere? Does this impact feel authentic to you? Are there ways you can do your job that are more "you"?

- How can you adjust your media intake to reduce any overwhelm you might feel by absorbing bad news?

- Which problems can you see have some link to your day-to-day work? Are any of these the ones you care most about? Given this, what's your next step in identifying a specific job activity you can pick up that will lead to the outcomes you seek? If you know the problem you'd like to address but aren't sure how your job connects, who might you ask, or where could you look into it?

- What form of shoulding have you encountered recently in your job? Did you follow along or break with tradition? How did either path feel? Would you do anything differently next time?

- What connections do your current and desired investments in the Job Sphere have to the other spheres? How do you want to revise the investments in your Job Sphere or other spheres to optimize the connections between them?

Chapter 12

The Workplace Sphere

The Job Sphere was concerned with what you do and how you perform the duties of your position, whether that's a traditional full-time or part-time role or something less formal like pro bono consulting. The Workplace Sphere represents ways you have impact by virtue of the entity for which you choose to do that work and the ways that entity influences the world.

On our Dashboard, we define a workplace simply as the entity for which we do the work that we identify as our main professional activity. We can change the dynamics of our workplaces by influencing what the organization does and how it does it.

The choice of where to work is the primary avenue of impact in the Workplace Sphere. Ideally you direct your skills to an organization with values and a mission that match your own and that has an influence on the world to which you are proud to contribute. Power dynamics are shifting in the 21st century such that even the lowest-paid employees have more power than ever before. If nothing else, workers can, and are increasingly seen to, vote with their feet and work somewhere else in a tight labor market.

The second avenue of impact in the Workplace Sphere is our ability to shape *how* our workplaces operate. Culture is built from the bottom up, by each employee's choices and behavior. Of course, there are policies, procedures, and power that shape these contributions, but especially in the hybrid or remote (and increasingly freelance) 21st-century workplace, our *how* trickles down and back up through the organization.

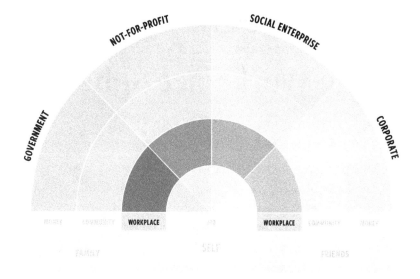

Figure 17. The Workplace Sphere's place in the Impact Dashboard.

The Spectrum of Impact: The What of the Workplace Sphere

The Spectrum of Impact is particularly important to keep in mind as you consider your Workplace Sphere investments. What an organization does is strongly influenced by where it sits on the Spectrum. Government agencies and not-for-profits are bound by external constraints to do work in service of the public or a specific group of beneficiaries. Social enterprises—a varied group of entities that I'll define as for-profit, for-purpose companies—seek to create results while generating profit. And many traditional for-profits are still wrapped up in the idea that a business's sole social purpose is to maximize profits for shareholders, though this perspective is rapidly losing currency.

An organization's place on the Spectrum of Impact is not a perfect or complete predictor of its outcomes or approach, but it is a helpful starting point to understanding how an organization operates in the world. And as we discussed in chapter 5, organizations at any point on the Spectrum can absolutely have positive impact; they just go about creating it differently.

Specifically, government agencies offer important basic services for entire populations. Their efforts are not usually directed at change as much as ongoing maintenance (think roads, water, and schools). Of course, all these services, along with others provided by the government and the policies underlying them, have huge ramifications on our well-being as well as our natural environment. Not-for-profits, on the other hand, tend to have deeper influence on smaller groups of people and often have more of an orientation toward changing circumstances for people or the environment. And for-profits—whether for-purpose social enterprises or more traditional corporations—can also have massive significance. For-profit companies must earn their own financial sustainability rather than relying on taxpayer funding, grants, donations, or service contracts like public and not-for-profit sector organizations do. This need for profitability, or at least to break even, means that their ways of creating impact are different and often less dramatic, but their financial sustainability often enables greater scale.

We'll say more about this in the upcoming pitfalls section, but a major obstacle to optimizing our influence in the Workplace Sphere is the notion that for-profit companies don't need to, can't, or shouldn't have a positive impact. This 20th-century perspective is dead, even if not everyone knows it yet.

I'll leave you with the Spectrum of Impact to make your choices about which type of organization to work for. I wish I'd been familiar with it when choosing where to spend the first part of my career; it would've helped me realize that not-for-profits were not the only option!

Culture: The How of the Workplace

Alongside what an organization does, *how* it does those things also matters. The latter can be broadly seen as the culture of an organization. And employees *are* culture, so we each have significant opportunity for impact by influencing how things are done at our workplaces. Let's look at a few quick examples to illustrate how we can use this leverage in our Workplace Sphere.

As CPrO/CTO of Real Self, Ward Vuillemot is focused on creating psychological safety for his teams and the entire organization: "The irony is, you have to mean it. I didn't talk about psychological safety for a year after starting work here. What matters is if you tell me I'm making a psychologically safe environment." Later in this chapter we'll hear more about *how* Ward creates psychological safety at RealSelf.

Our Purpose Seeker Lisa has aligned her Workplace Sphere by virtue of having chosen to work for a consulting firm that better aligned with her values than the top global firm where she started. While the projects look similar to what she did at her previous firm, this firm does them differently. When pitching for work, the partners include a statement of social and/or environmental consequences that would or could result from the project. In an effort to reduce burnout, their staffers include wellness ratings when assigning consultants at all levels to projects. They encourage month-long sabbaticals every four years to facilitate personal growth as well as rest from the demanding client service they do.

How I Learned about the Workplace Sphere

I experienced the influence of the *how* of a workplace vividly early in my career. I landed a dream job at an international not-for-profit organization headquartered in Rome. There I had the opportunity to facilitate a global community of youth activists by building their capacity as changemakers and deepening the connections and collaborations among them. It was a fabulously challenging, engaging, and rewarding role.

The founder of the organization was a creative, wise, and empathetic leader. He was a mentor to me, opened doors that advanced our work, and kept our team motivated even during our annual stressful and busy conference season. When he got sick and decided to spend what was now more obviously limited time with his family, he stepped back from the organization in all but name and promoted the organization's COO to executive director. This man had been excellent at his operational duties, but he was not creative, wise, or empathetic. Within months, morale at the organization plummeted.

As we approached our next annual conference, my colleagues and I were tired, frustrated, and cranky. Our moods permeated the event, and my youth activists generated significantly fewer new ideas and collaborations than they had in previous years. The closing party didn't have the same joy or satisfaction it usually did. I—and many colleagues—left the organization within weeks of wrapping the event. This experience was a formative one for me in realizing how much impact an organization's culture has. Choose your workplace carefully, not only for what it does but for how it does it.

Making It Yours

It's time to do your own work! Head to the *Going First* Purpose Party Playbook for a guided process. If you don't have the playbook, go to chapter 7 and apply the process found there to your Workplace Sphere. If you need a reminder of the five steps, review the section in that chapter called "Zeroing in on Each Sphere."

Avoiding the Pitfalls in the Workplace Sphere

PITFALL #1: INACTION

Inaction in the Workplace Sphere explains why not every organization has recognized and adapted to the fact that a zero-sum, either/or approach to profit and purpose is dead.

Inaction Leads to Extinction. Employees, customers, and investors are more regularly and loudly demanding that companies speak to the social and environmental ramifications of what they do. In this environment, it's less about who has the smallest microchips or lowest cost of capital and more about who humans want to work for, buy from, and invest in.

If all workplaces have positive impact, it means that all employees can have positive impact, and that's the precondition for a dignified, inspired, and equitable workforce. This is a huge opportunity, but only for companies that dare to consider and revise their effect on people and the planet.

Companies that don't begin to optimize what they do and how they do it for its outcomes on people and the planet will fail to engage and retain the 21st-century consumers who demand value alignment. And access to talent is a must-have for success. Jimmy Etheredge is very aware that Accenture's growth "is paced by the talent we can attract."

Inaction Looks Like the Same Old. Inaction in the workplace shows up as a lack of innovation, which is paramount to a death knell for 21st-century organizations. Both what we do and how we do it need to be rethought to survive. There are myriad ways to make what we do better for people and the planet, enough to fill plenty of other volumes. (Several are included in the Workplace Sphere section of my Reader Resources at the end of the book.)

As Joey Bergstein, repeat CEO of cutting-edge purpose-driven companies including Seventh Generation, explained, "Our goal is to move the industry [toward sustainability] without becoming irrelevant. So we have to stay innovative, on the cutting edge." That approach is undoubtedly what led Sabra to hire him to grow their business in a sustainable way.

Yet, as Stuart Landesberg explains, Grove Collective is working toward "Two things that seem incompatible: business targets, including focus, quality engineering, and financials, along with being a perfect B Corp, scoring as high as possible on how 'good for the world' we are. These often pull on opposite sides of the same thread, so leaders revert to the side they're more comfortable with."

This reversion to the comfort zone is exactly the problem. Not enough decision-makers are Going First to recognize the mandate for innovation and behave accordingly. A major and perhaps primary root cause of this failure is the lack of diversity in organizations. We need to attract, engage, and retain workforces that reflect the diversity of identity, thought, and style of our population (and customers, by the way), using the truly "holistic definition of diversity" that Arthur Woods calls for as cofounder and CEO of Mathison.

Such a view of diversity includes gender, sexuality, race, and ethnicity, but also religion, spirituality, cognitive styles and abilities, geographic origins, physical ability and identity, and personality. Having people who represent a full range of identities and then building the inclusive culture that enables them to contribute at their highest levels is the prerequisite for effective innovation. As Mark Atkinson says, "If we're not being inclusive, we're making dumb decisions. It's not easy to build a company that serves our customers, much less employees or investors, in the future of work if we are operating in old norms of White guys deciding the future of our business over beers."

Counter Inaction with Yes-And. Because of their understanding about the importance of diverse talent, Jimmy Etheredge and Accenture's other leaders are innovating like crazy. They have a "yes-and" philosophy: developing new approaches to all elements of their business and fundamentally rethinking how they do what they've always done. And when it comes to talent strategy, Accenture has developed an apprenticeship program that will bring in 20 percent of their entry-level full-time hires in just five years after the program's pilot. Their "Care to Do Better" strategy informs this program, as well as their overall approach to promoting holistic well-being for all employees at all stages of their experience.

In relation, Paul Polman, who established Unilever's Sustainable Living Brands as chair, said, "More and more businesses are seeing the potential of a more sustainable business model, driven both by the firm belief that business can be a force for good and by the realization that the cost of inaction often exceeds the cost of action—notably when it comes to the growing threat of climate change and water scarcity."

Raj Thakkar, whose social enterprises serve other social enterprises and not-for-profits, has no choice but to do business in a way that aligns with their customers' desired impact. His approach to innovation is "Listening to the team. The quieter I've gotten, the more expressive and effective they've become. Every leader's job is to get out of the way."

Similarly, Mark Atkinson's focus at Mursion is to "Make people feel heard, bought in, ownership. That's the path to having the best idea win."

Jana Rich, a career-long recruiter and now founder and president of Rich Talent Group, prioritizes flexibility and open-mindedness to achieve this yes-and approach. In her case, she's working to shift the "perception of what qualified means" to achieve all of her stakeholders' goals, including their employer clients and the professionals they hire Rich Talent Group to recruit for them.

But what are the traits of a yes-and organization? Lara Galinsky, a longtime thinker, practitioner, and coach for purposeful leadership, has seen that several conditions enable the pursuit of profit and purpose: "Ideas must be allowed to funnel from anywhere in the company through formal and informal channels. There must also be a framework for unintended consequences conversations to catch the ways that best intentions can create harm."

The organizations that achieve those workplace conditions have made failure a shame-free part of progress. Their people feel psychologically safe, as we mentioned Ward Vuillemot works to realize at RealSelf. He built that psychological safety through a number of actions, including evolving Amazon's Correction of Errors framework into the "Celebration of Errors" he practices regularly with his teams. During these functions, team members share all the mistakes that were made on a weekly basis and complete a thorough review, which includes the consequences of the error on all stakeholders, short- and long-term resolutions, and an assessment of the error's root cause. Ward explains, "Our goal isn't to be perfect. The question is, do you keep on rethinking the problem or eventually realize it can't be done and find another answer altogether? But if you're scared to fail, you risk becoming frozen or apathetic to the situation."

Comfort with failure is essential if we are to write a new playbook that guides organizations toward creating a balance of environmental and financial sustainability that meets the needs of all of their stakeholders.

Ultimately what's most important is that we recognize *all* entities have the potential to positively affect people and the planet, not just not-for-profits, public agencies, or social enterprises. It's not about profit or purpose; the winning strategy for the

21st century is "*Yes*, we sustain ourselves financially, *and* we make the world a better place in the process!" But that isn't the status quo approach, so getting there requires action.

PITFALL #2: SHOULDING IN THE WORKPLACE SPHERE

Shoulding is how the 20th-century's profit-versus-purpose status quo is maintained. Through formal incentives, informal norms, and cultural pressure, we keep people behaving the way our workplaces always have. We shun financial considerations at not-for-profits and dismiss social and environmental impact as nice-to-haves—at least once we've achieved some level of profitability (which often increases each time we hit our target).

Shoulding Leads to Misaligned Incentives. Like our black-and-white notion that jobs should either have positive significance (nurses, teachers, cancer researchers) or be highly profitable (bankers, famous actors, and high-ticket salespeople), our vision of work-places is similarly limited.

Some organizations can and should be good for the world. Generally, this list includes not-for-profits, maybe government agencies (depending on the era and your political views), and, if you're plugged into the "Business as a Force for Good" move-ment, companies like Patagonia, Unilever, and Aspiration Bank. But, as we often amend, traditional for-profits should keep their heads down and make money to pay employees just enough and shareholders as much as they can manage.

Though the COVID-19 pandemic and racial reckoning provoked by George Floyd's murder provided a highly credible counter to this approach, companies' response times have been varied and slow. Most organizations still use financial-first or -only metrics to reward their people. Similarly, investment decisions are driven primarily by short-term economic metrics. These narrow incentives are a major obstacle to a truly equitable, just, and thriving global economy. That vision requires every organization on this planet to become a proactive steward of its impact. And that requires all employees to be incentivized to optimize their workplaces for profit *and* purpose.

Shoulding Looks Like Mixed Messages. As Stuart Landesberg explains, "One of the greatest problems in today's economy is that the smartest people are being motivated by financial ends that aren't correlated with the societal change we need. Economic rewards and societal rewards are uncorrelated."

Some traditional corporate CEOs have begun speaking loudly about the social and environmental effect their companies can and will have in the 21st century. But very few have changed their performance management systems to reflect this dual approach to pursuing profit and purpose. This misalignment means that in many organizations, employees have to work against their own financial best interest to work for their desired impact. There are examples of employees making just such choices, but it won't become the norm until workplace incentives are properly aligned.

Even at deeply purpose-driven companies like Guayaki, people must relearn this approach to pursuing purpose alongside profit. Guayaki's cofounder and chair, Chris Mann, bumped into this challenge when rolling out a hiring program designed to employ formerly incarcerated people. His team was very enthusiastic about it, but "didn't do a great job of getting the specific mission and vision to everyone. There's an intuitive component that got them excited, but our practices didn't line up. We have to learn how to embed our desired impact into practices and policies as we grow."

It's important to anticipate the new challenges of initiatives so that teams are prepared for the ripple effects, like the fact that new hires need extra training on workplace basics such as email and meeting etiquette.

Counter Shoulding with New Shoulds. Regardless of whether your workplace is a global financial powerhouse or a community-based organization helping kids find their way to higher education, there is opportunity for social and environmental influence. But as Chris found at Guayaki, those impact opportunities must be recognized and incentivized throughout the organization to be realized and sustained.

A real visionary approach is offered by Didier Elzinga, entrepreneur, purposeful culture diehard, and founder and CEO of Culture AMP. Didier suggests that we "change the burden of proof. Why don't we have to prove that a non-diverse company performs better?" This should-flipping around what companies look like is a powerful thought experiment! But to get there, we can leverage formal incentive structures.

Indeed, the transformation to valuing nonfinancial outcomes is already underway. Joey Bergstein changed incentive structures to elicit the priorities he knows he needs his teams to have: "We align people's work and objectives to our sustainability goal. Twenty percent of everyone's bonus is based on their team's sustainability and advocacy goals. And no one's bonus is paid out unless they have done 20 hours of volunteering."

Another new model comes from MassMutual, which built diversity into its Annual Incentive Plan. It measures leaders on the demographics of their team for now, with a plan to integrate inclusion when they have more reliable measurement tools. Lorie Valle-Yañez, MassMutual's head of diversity and inclusion, explained that the shift in how the company was training for and tracking inclusion started strong thanks to "CEO support from the start even when he didn't know what we were going to do. And the board was also very supportive, pushing us to do more, go faster."

This alignment of incentives is happening even at the organizational level. BPN Paribas is a leading international bank, and Danone is a company that's committed to making food and beverages that are good for us and the environment. BNP Paribas tied the interest rate on its loan to Danone to the company's performance on the environmental standards for which it already reports. The more Danone reduces its environmental impact, the lower its cost of capital: a critical financial metric for executives.

Vanessa Barboni Hallik is conscientious of the power of incentives for her people and the organization as she builds Another Tomorrow: "How do we create alignment so that the vision can be translated into action and ultimately into incentive structures? That's why we became a B Corp."

Many other organizations, B Corp-certified or not, are making similar moves to ensure that financial incentives account for not just economic performance but also social and environmental metrics. These metrics are often team-based, which creates a secondary benefit of rewarding collaboration, a critical 21st-century business skill.

Formal performance management systems are notoriously resistant to change and are certainly not the only driver of our behaviors at work. At MassMutual, Lorie has found that even the first pilot of a White Ally program and limited performance management incentives added enough "transparency and clarity to drive our leaders to want to get better. They're seeking education, exposure, and experience to be more inclusive leaders. Everyone started joining Business Resource Groups as allies."

Geeta Aiyer has been a mission-driven investor for her entire career. She founded Boston Common Asset Management to invest customers' assets in a fully impact-seeking way. She knows she "can't ask companies to do this and not do it ourselves. So we started a 'Walk the Talk' committee to think about our impact on all levels. They've organized movies as part of our Friday continuing education programs that lead to incredibly emotional conversations and the deepened trust that results. They helped us figure out compost for the office, volunteer activities, and protests to attend together." With executive level buy-in, this committee provides a new set of shoulds for employees regardless of their job role.

Both old and new shoulds can be even less explicit, however. Kari Warberg Block created a graphic of the EarthKind ecosystem "using the metaphor of stakeholders as the soil, given the company's focus on controlling pests without harming the environment. It hangs in all offices and lives on most employees' desktops, providing clarity and focus on what is expected of them."

PITFALL #3: ORTHODOXY IN THE WORKPLACE SPHERE

As in the Job Sphere, orthodoxy rejects the blend of purpose and profit at the workplace level as well. Our extractive form of capitalism combined with a puritanical approach to money has led to a widely accepted belief that organizations that make money cannot possibly be good for anyone. Similarly, we promote the constraint that entities that improve people's lives or the environment cannot make money and still be doing good.

The Friedman Doctrine of 1970 stated that the only social responsibility of business is to "use its resources and engage in activities designed to increase its profits."[75] This notion, despite coming from a relatively obscure economist at the time, combined with Industrial-Era mentality led to an overly narrow focus on financial performance. Leadership habits follow that orthodoxy.

Orthodoxy Leads to Missed Opportunities. The dualistic orthodoxy that for-profits create profit and not-for-profits create impact is out of date. On the organizational level, an either/or approach to profit and purpose closes off many of the most exciting business opportunities in today's economy. Unilever's Sustainable Living Brands, for example, drove 75 percent of the multinational's growth in recent years, because while most of us buy as much soap and ketchup as we need, we're motivated to shift and expand our buying to brands that align with our values.

Similarly, orthodoxy for individuals leads us to stay at workplaces that aren't aligned with our desired impact because we don't believe it's possible to make money and do good for people and the planet. Regardless of the satisfaction you may take from your job role, a disconnect with the entity for which you're doing it will lead to distress.

While it wasn't uncommon for our parents or grandparents to tolerate a morally neutral or dubious employer, this approach is far more damaging now. Most of us carry a good deal of our work product and communication in our pockets or purses. We do much or all of our work in the same space where we raise our kids, sleep, and exercise. This integration of our work into our lives makes any disconnect between our values and the values of our workplaces particularly uncomfortable. We no longer have the distance of "leaving work at work."

Another 20th-century approach was to wait until retirement to give back and do the things that have the outcomes we seek. I've already suggested that if we don't take too much, we don't have to "give back." But there's also no reason to wait to create positive change! With shifts in demographics and the financial realities of retirement funds, our definition of "working age" has extended by decades.

As the boundaries between work and life melt away, the cognitive dissonance of working in a place that doesn't match our desired impact is particularly uncomfortable. For all the reasons mentioned, staying at a workplace after we recognize that it's not aligned with our values is a sure path to frustration and demotivation. Ultimately, we experience a decline in career performance and influence in both the Workplace and Job Spheres.

Orthodoxy Looks Like Firewalls. I started my career in the not-for-profit sector because of my belief that all "good" work happened on that side of the imaginary firewall between for-profit and for-purpose organizations. I don't regret that decade, but I do wonder what impact I would've been able to create earlier on if I had approached that work with more openness to which organizations it would be worthwhile to join as an employee.

Vanessa of Another Tomorrow has also moved between sectors, recognizing that her career is following "a vision that guides me, and then I do whatever I have to get there, regardless [of] what type of organization that might mean I'm contributing to."

Likewise, our Purpose Seeker Lisa has been able to work across the full Spectrum of Impact as a consultant. She's gotten such a variety of client work because she was the one who developed the tools and performance indicators that respected the hybrid goal of her not-for-profit and public sector clients to generate both profit and purpose. Many of the firm's original frameworks didn't work for these clients. Because of her desire to work across the Spectrum, Lisa worked to evolve her approach and won over a lot of purpose-driven businesses. Interestingly, more traditional for-profit clients have started asking for Lisa's input to help find ways to integrate purpose alongside their profitability plans.

Counter Orthodoxy with Integration. Indeed, the integration of purpose into business models (or the reverse, integrating business models for sustainability of purpose-driven not-for-profits) is the key to successfully resisting orthodoxy and thriving in the 21st century. The fundamental belief for purposeful leadership in the Workplace Sphere is the integration of all outcomes, including financial, human, and environmental, with a long-term perspective.

With an integrated approach, we can see the opportunities for our workplaces to affect the world. As a marketer, our Purpose Seeker Gabriela isn't directly responsible for her company's product stories, ingredients, or packaging. But she can find ways in her Workplace Sphere to build relationships and exert informal influence on the ramifications of those elements of the products. By expanding her firm's frameworks, Lisa has contributed to shaping the offerings and talent strategies (and consequently their impact) of those who aren't her clients and aren't directly in her Job Sphere. Even these forms of indirect involvement in our companies' influences can be powerful if we connect to them intentionally and help our teams to do the same.

Joey Bergstein recognizes the value of an integrated approach in his workplace: "Everyone has a role in what we're doing. It's just a matter of helping them see where they fit. This is an ongoing communications challenge, so we do regular meetings with different teams. For example, we're talking to the sales team again this week on how they are the key in changing the industry by selling our new single-dose detergent caps that reduce product usage and thus plastic."

As entrepreneurs start companies that seek profit and purpose from their very inception, increasingly more opportunities for integration are emerging. Nina Tandon, CEO and founder of EpiBone, which could be thought of as a "traditional" biotech firm, is very clear on the way the company does good as they also do well in business: "We're enabling patients' healing by engaging the power of their own cells. It's so subversive! I'm incredibly proud to be re-centering healing in the patients' own bodies as a female CEO."

Nina founded EpiBone as a for-profit startup, not a not-for-profit advocacy organization with the mission of helping patients take charge of their own healing. That organization surely exists and is a worthy pursuit. But the potential of integrating profit and purpose, as Nina, Chris, John, and so many more in this book and beyond are doing, is leveraging the entire Spectrum of Impact to achieve the systems change we need—and giving every employee an opportunity to affect their Workplace Sphere.

Factors That Influence Our Impact in the Workplace Sphere

The primary factor that influences the impact we can make in the Workplace Sphere is choosing the organization where we'll do our jobs. The first way you can determine this is by considering the Spectrum of Impact and asking yourself whether you're committed to a workplace in one particular sector or part of the Spectrum. There's no right answer here. Like Lisa, you may want to help find win-win-wins for clients that increase their performance, bring in customers, and positively impact people and the planet. In my case, I've learned that I'm more motivated by integrating purposeful leadership into private sector companies that are less comfortable with the forms of impact they can have.

Next, try to understand as much as you can about how a company interacts with all their stakeholders, including employees, suppliers, customers, investors, community members, and the planet. These insights will help you make intentional choices about the workplace you choose.

In choosing the most aligned workplace for you at a given moment in your life, it's also valuable to consider your *change profile*. Are you most motivated and fulfilled by making incremental change at a broad scale, or do you feel better about contributing to deep change that's smaller in scope and perhaps sets an example for others to follow? Maybe you fall somewhere in the middle or don't know yet, so this is a question to explore in your next job search.

We need people who are making change from inside of big, complex organizations. But that kind of change takes time and skillful relationship management. While that's rewarding and incredibly impactful for the right person, it will be unsustainably frustrating for someone who wants to move quickly and see immediate progress.

Generally speaking, traditional corporations have a slower, more incremental approach to change, and so do government agencies, but that's not always the case. There may be turnaround moments or regime changes that enable broad-reaching, fast change in those sectors. Of course, it's impossible to understand everything about an organization from the outside. Luckily, no matter where you land, you'll have opportunities to design, participate in, model, or strengthen the culture. How you show up each day influences other people's experiences, whether you're leading meetings and designing strategies or are "just" an individual contributor.

Along the journey of increasing your influence in the Workplace Sphere, it's valuable to keep perspective and recognize that trade-offs do happen. Even the most purpose-driven businesses bump into these trade-offs, as do not-for-profits. Every organization ultimately has limited resources, whether of time, money, or technology, and has to make choices about their impact. As Chris Mann explained, Guayakí had made a plan "to shift our distribution to electric vehicles to minimize our carbon footprint. The EVs we could get were small! And so they made our drivers' lives harder and days longer. We went back to gas vehicles until we [could] get larger EVs. It was a matter of balancing exhaust with our drivers' well-being."

One last avenue of influence on our investments in the Workplace Sphere lies in working with a company's explicit policies and practices. This is one reason HR or people operations roles can be so deeply purposeful. By shaping the way *any* organization treats its people, we have direct and significant influence on at least one stakeholder group.

Ultimately, the best blend of investments in your Workplace Sphere relies on the self-awareness I advised you to bring to the Purpose Party. You must identify how you're most gratified and best equipped to contribute before you can find a workplace that's a match.

Crafting Your Workplace Sphere Cocktail

Now that you've learned about the Workplace Sphere, the pitfalls to avoid, the impact you can have there, and what influences that impact, it's time to apply the five-step model to this sphere. If you're using the playbook, turn to chapter 12 for a more detailed process.

STEP 1: BASELINE ASSESSMENT

Assess your investments in the Workplace Sphere by reviewing the activities you identified on your Impact Dashboard Excel Worksheet, the Purpose Party Playbook, or wherever you've been doing the work. Edit or add to that list so that it feels complete. When you're satisfied that you've captured the activities you do in this sphere, review the total number of hours you're spending there per week. You can also determine the percentage of time each week this sphere takes. Fill in whether you want to do each activity more, less, or the same; then rate these three statements as they apply to your Workplace Sphere now, last year, and a year from now:

I invest time, energy, and attention in the Workplace Sphere.

I am satisfied with the quantity and quality of my investments in the Workplace Sphere.

I see the outcomes of my investments in the Workplace Sphere.

STEP 2: WHAT DO YOU NEED IN THIS SPHERE?

Determine whether there's a change you can make in the Workplace Sphere that you really believe will increase your well-being and/or the well-being of your workplace and those within it. Identify a change in this sphere that you're willing to make over the next month, whether it's doing something you already do more regularly, stopping something you do, or trying a new activity. You might instead realize that it's really not the area you need to prioritize. Before you decide for sure, think through the questions from pages 162–163 of this book as they apply to your Workplace Sphere. When you're done, draft a simple, clear, and measurable belief statement about what you want to change in this sphere. Remember that your belief statement doesn't include exactly *how* you'll achieve the goal you're setting; you're just identifying *what* you're going to do and *why* it matters.

STEP 3: YOUR ONE NEXT STEP

Once you believe *what* the outcome will be of changing something in your Workplace Sphere and *why* it matters, figure out *how* to achieve that change. Focus on choosing your One Thing for this sphere, and then get really specific about exactly what this activity is going to look like (at least to start; you can revise the details as you learn). Here, in the playbook, or on the Excel worksheet, answer the questions from page 164 of this book as they apply to your Workplace Sphere.

STEP 4: SUPPORTING THAT STEP

Having a motivating belief statement helps keep you focused on why you're doing all this purpose work. Think about or write down your answers to the following questions that will help guide you in creating one.

- What's going to keep you from building this new habit, whether from the pitfalls we discussed in this chapter or otherwise?
- How can you overcome those obstacles?

Now write a simple, clear, and measurable behavioral plan to keep you on track. Be sure that this plan connects to the results you want to see from your workplace activities.

STEP 5: KEEP AN EYE OUT

The only way to keep up with changes in your outlook, work, life, and the world and make the necessary adaptations is to keep an eye on what you're doing and the consequences it's having. Pick your preferred method of tracking change and use it. Remember, the point here is not to beat yourself up if you don't get exactly where you want to be. It's just to be able to see how it's going. Does the new activity actually have your desired impact? Does it fit into your life, or does it reveal something else you'd rather spend your time on?

Overlapping Spheres

Economic needs and the current dominance of extractive capitalism mean that many of us will work for an organization at some point in our careers that doesn't perfectly align with our values or priorities. The Dashboard is helpful in those moments.

In the Workplace Sphere, there are three main things to consider when it comes to where you can have the best results: becoming a change agent at your current organization, finding impact in other spheres until you can change your employer situation, or changing jobs to work for a more aligned organization. The job you want has some influence on where you do it, but not as much as some people would think. Particularly today, as industries are changing so quickly, it's becoming more common to apply our training, experience, and ways of thinking and working to a totally different industry. The same can be said about crossing sector lines from the not-for-profit sector to the private (as I did) or, perhaps more commonly, in the opposite direction.

So maybe it's time to apply your skillsets to an organization at a different point on your Spectrum of Impact. Most organizations need all the basic functional skills, and there's increasing openness to professionals who come from other backgrounds. Indeed, research by Toni LaBelle shows that the leaders who were ranked as most effective by their peers were the ones who had experience in multiple sectors, whether public, private, or not-for-profit, rather than a consistent career in one or the other.[76]

By nature of the benefits and culture that are offered, the workplaces we choose influence our ability and likelihood to invest in all of our other spheres. For example, does your workplace offer wellness spending accounts or other benefits like fitness or meditation tools to enhance your investments in your Self Sphere? Is there a culture of actually using those benefits, even when work is busy? Does your workplace offer reasonable paid leave for parents (of any gender and circumstance of birth, whether natural, surrogate, or adoption) and caregivers (for elders, family members with disabilities or illness, and other cases beyond parenting)? What about flexible work in terms of time and place? In the Money Sphere, do you get matching funds for your retirement or for your charitable donations? Do you use those benefits, or do you want to move to a company that offers them if you don't have access where you are?

Your workplace can also support your Community Sphere with volunteer opportunities, small business support through supplier programs or other partnerships, or not-for-profit board membership programs. Are these accessible to you? Are they well-run and values-aligned? And with that, we'll look next at the Community Sphere in greater detail. But first, consider the questions below.

Reflection Questions

Speaking of your workplace, use that office printer to print these questions as a free worksheet, downloadable at www.inspiringcowgirl.com/goingfirst. I'll hold back this time from telling you to check out the Going First Purpose Party Playbook. But for the lucky and wise who are already have the Playbook, you'll find these questions in Chapter 12.

- Consider your Workplace Sphere activities holistically. When you zoom out, what do see you're doing? What are you *not* doing? Does this mix feel authentic to you?

- How do you feel about the work you do when you talk about it at your dinner table or during your kids' homework time? Are there times it's been uncomfortable because of a values misalignment or times when you've been particularly proud to bring up your workplace in a personal setting?

- What forms of inaction, shoulding, and orthodoxy do you recognize in your organization and how do they threaten the organization's thriving or even survival going forward?

- Where might you find a way to update your workplace's *what* or *how* to seize the opportunities of being a yes-and organization, supporting impact as well as business success? What's one first step you can take toward investigating or activating such opportunities for integration of profit and purpose?

- How do you think you "should" be contributing to your Workplace Sphere, and what do you expect, formally and informally, of your employees, bosses, and/or colleagues?

- What ways can you think of that you "should" the people around you at work, such as your direct reports, colleagues, mentees, customers, or suppliers? Which of these shoulds align with your desired impact? Which don't? What's one new should that you'd like to bring into your workplace? How will you start?

- What's the change profile of your current workplace? Are you pursuing marginal but wide-reaching change or more extreme change with more limited scope?

- What's your ideal change profile? Have you most enjoyed past experiences that led to small change on a broad scale or dramatic change with a smaller audience?

- What connections do your current and desired investments in the Workplace Sphere have to the other spheres?

- How do you want to revise your investments in your Workplace Sphere or other spheres to optimize the connections between them?

Chapter 13

The Community Sphere

Outside of work, we have formal and informal opportunities to engage in not-for-profits, government entities and committees, neighborhood associations, and other groups in our areas of interest that operate in our local communities (or remotely). Volunteering, board memberships, elected positions, and informal advisories or promotions are all examples of activities in the Community Sphere.

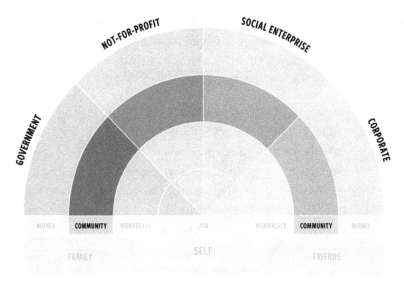

Figure 18. The Community Sphere's place in the Impact Dashboard.

Community activities can be a healthy and productive complement to our work—particularly if our current job doesn't provide the type or extent of impact we seek or is in a time of transition. These "extra-curricular activities" are also a great chance to expand our networks, build new skills, learn new industries, and have more of the positive influence that creates a meaningful life.

How I Learned about the Community Sphere

Between my upbringing in Hartford and then West Hartford; 10 years as an expat on three different continents; a career spanning public, not-for-profit, and private sectors; and a global MBA program with 71 classmates from over 40 nations, I've been part of a very wide range of communities. When I moved from New York City to a suburban town in Connecticut, I shifted to remote work and quarantined for the COVID-19 pandemic and narrowed the focus of my work to pur-poseful leadership advisory and coaching (and writing about it for this book). This conjunction of factors dramatically limited the type and makeup of the communities to which I had regular access. I realized how unusual the breadth of my community affiliations was compared to most people's experience.

When I launched a "Purpose in a Pandemic" webinar series with a few colleagues, the response was enormous. One of the most com-mon sentiments was how much participants appreciated the chance to connect with other people across a wide range of demographics, industries, and career stages. That sense of community was a particu-larly important comfort during a time of such uncertainty, as many sources of community had paused during the early days of quaran-tine. Since then, I've realized that one of the main benefits I bring to the startups I advise, the not-for-profits I support by committee or board, and the horseback riding associations of which I'm a member is expanding the group's perspective based on the diversity of my community connections.

Making It Yours

It's time to do your own work! Head to the *Going First* Purpose Party Playbook for a guided process. If you don't have the playbook, go to chapter 7 and apply the process found there to your Community Sphere. If you need a reminder of the five steps, review the section in that chapter called "Zeroing in on Each Sphere."

Avoiding the Pitfalls in the Community Sphere

PITFALL #1: INACTION

In today's atomized, workaholic society, it's all too easy to make the primary error in the Community Sphere: not engaging at all. Community is the often most sparsely populated sphere, even among purposeful leaders. We're hugely dedicated to our careers, invest a lot of time in job and workplace activities, can't avoid making money decisions, and would never completely neglect our family and friends.

When reflecting on your activities in this sphere, whether as a volunteer, board member, or otherwise, you might've had this common reaction: "Life is busy. My family needs me. My boss needs me. I don't have time or energy for anything else!" While those commitments are all valid, overwork and overwhelm are also very real drivers of inaction in the Community Sphere. Even though technology and automation have reduced the human burden of production and the knowledge economy has taken over, we're working more hours than our factory-working ancestors.

Similarly, with the expectations to support our children's extra-curricular activities, social lives, and schoolwork, parenting has become an even fuller-time job. These expanded expectations in our Family and Friends, Job, and Workplace Spheres mean we have fewer hours available for community investments. And when you're particularly stretched in those spheres, whether in raising young children, starting a new job, caring for elders, or whatever else, community may well not be your primary area of investment. After all, particularly during the career-growing and family-raising part of our lives, community activities can fall by the wayside without major harm to our well-being and performance.

Or can they? Let's consider inaction in the Community Sphere more closely.

Inaction Leads to Fragility. Community involvement is more problematic to opt out of than it may seem. For our own wellbeing, the success of our organizations, and the health and prosperity of our communities, volunteering is incredibly powerful and can't be replaced by personal relationships or work.

One of the academic concepts that has stuck with me most clearly over the years is *social capital*: the notion that our relationships and human connections have actual, tangible value. I first learned of social capital from Robert Putnam's research on the erosion of community ties in the US that he published in *Bowling Alone*. The title comes from Putnam's finding that bowling leagues fell victim to busier work and family lives as people shifted from community recreation to solo endeavors or family activities. He saw this loss of human interaction outside of family members and colleagues as emblematic of the reduced connectivity between neighbors.[77] He, along with many other researchers, found this shift to be incredibly costly. When social capital is lower, everyone suffers, including businesses (transaction costs are higher in low-trust environments), communities (higher crime rates), and society (higher levels of political opposition that stymie problem-solving).

What's more, medical and psychological experts have demonstrated how a lack of community engagement leads to fragility in the individual dimension. Other-oriented community activities (such as visiting children in the hospital, pets in a shelter, or preparing meals for a soup kitchen) have been shown to counter depression and increase life satisfaction even more than self-oriented community activities (such as bowling, political action, and arts and cultural activities).[78] With depression higher than ever—up 28 percent, according to a 2021 paper[79]—there's a nasty downward spiral of people being less inclined to seek out the very engagement that could reduce their depressive symptoms.

Even without a diagnosis of clinical depression, loneliness is a serious threat to physical and mental well-being. People who are lonely are more likely to die prematurely, even more so than if they smoked a pack a day or were obese.[80] One risk, then, of underinvesting in your Community Sphere is dying before your time.

Inaction Looks Like Isolation. The less time, energy, and attention we have for community involvement, the more intimidating and overwhelming it becomes to find ways to build it back into our lives. Community activities are a challenging gray area where we're not counted on as explicitly as we usually are in blood relationships, friendships, or professional roles.

Furthermore, we're usually not paid for our community investments. We make these efforts because we want to, whether for the social connection, the sense of influence, or the building of skills or relationships. But there isn't usually a formal agreement about community engagements like there is for a job (written contract) or with family and friends (unspoken expectations). So it can be scary to offer, much less ask for, help in these informal relationships. You may wonder, *What if they don't want my help and take offense at my offer? What if they want more than I have to give and I let them down? What if I don't like engaging with them after all?*

In completing her Dashboard, our Purpose Seeker Lisa realized that the lack of community investments throughout most of her career meant she lacked opportunities for engagement as she approached the end of her formal career. She had concentrated her energy in her Job and Workplace Spheres, which provided great satisfaction and impact, but those transactional relationships would end with her retirement. Though Lisa had a sense that her skillset could be hugely helpful for some of the organizations in her community, she felt insecure about offering her services in that less formal context as a volunteer. This uncertainty about how she'd contribute and whether it would be valued made Lisa's view of retirement a lonely one, leading her to hang on even more tightly to her work for as long as she could.

Counter Inaction with Engagement. As we were all vividly reminded during the COVID-19 pandemic, each of us is interconnected with many humans other than our family members and colleagues. Our well-being depends on other humans in our communities, whether that be a neighborhood, nation, or region. Enlightened self-interest calls for us to make strategic investments in our communities in a way that matches what we're uniquely positioned to offer.

During our coaching, Purpose Seeker Lisa identified three organizations she was keen to contribute to: two not-for-profits and a startup that a former client of hers had recently launched. We worked on her approach to these organizations, including a get-to-know-you period and a process for getting really clear about what she had to give (how much time, when, to do what activities) and asking what the organization needed and wanted from her. After our initial conversations, Lisa started zeroing in on the right forms of engagement with two of those three organizations.

For my part, after years of building my business through very specific and targeted outreach to the people and organizations

I saw as potential clients, I took a different approach to writing this book. I knew that I wanted to integrate the wisdom of the global community of purpose-driven leaders, so I reached out to strangers, old friends, and prior colleagues or partners and asked them for 30 minutes for an interview on the topic.

Six months later, I had completed over 150 interviews, the fruit of which you're (hopefully!) enjoying at this very moment. As well as enhancing the insights in this book, this process reenergized me for my field of work after a period of burnout; added 1,000 professional connections to my LinkedIn network; made dozens of introductions between various interviewees that led to jobs, press, and friendships for other people; and ended up with two new advisor roles for organizations that I'm passionate about (one for-profit and one not-for-profit).

By engaging beyond my formal work-related relationships and friendships, I learned a lot, acquired some business leads, and met some awesome thought partners and potential collaborators. It's also worth noting that I was asking these people for a favor: to share their time and wisdom. Making people feel expert and valued in this way can be as potent a form of engagement as doing something that you see more explicitly as service.

So counter inaction by engaging with at least one of your various "communities," whether it's your neighborhood, other participants at your workout studio, fellow craftspeople selling on Etsy, or your high school classmates. Your investment might be as simple as getting to know their personal stories or as involved as organizing a committee to plan a reunion. Then go further by either finding a form of service that leverages some unique skill or knowledge you have to improve someone else's day or life or making others feel helpful by asking about their unique skills or knowledge.

But before you choose what you want to contribute, read on. The best contribution might not be the first thing you think of.

PITFALL #2: SHOULDING

Shoulding in the Community Sphere is the temptation to engage only as our professional selves. If you're an accountant, for example, you offer to keep the books for a local not-for-profit. As a web designer, you offer to redo the local choir's website. But why limit yourself to only your professional role? Why not join the choir instead? (Okay, maybe not if you're tone deaf. But most local choirs don't require perfect pitch, and if you offered to do your job for them for free, you'd probably have some inclination for singing.) Or if you're a singer by day, why not volunteer to keep the books for your choir? You've been wanting to learn QuickBooks to better stay on top of your many different freelance gigs anyway. Be sure you've got the support to learn properly so you don't cause any harm, of course, but volunteer engagements can be low-hanging fruit to stretch your thinking, build skills, and explore new ways of working.

So why do we keep shoulding ourselves in the Community Sphere in ways that impose limits on who we are, what we do, and how we do it? And how can we counter that shoulding?

Shoulding Looks Like Your Comfort Zone. Our Purpose Seeker Gabriela has been deeply involved in her church's Sunday school program since enrolling her kids almost seven years ago. Her marketing skills helped grow the program among church members as well as with other families in the community. She has loved the chance to build relationships with parents beyond her girls' school district and deepen her own spiritual practice with the kid-friendly activities she helped create as a volunteer.

Gabriela grew up attending Sunday school while her mom volunteered. She knew she'd do the same when she was a new mom; it's a comfortable form of community engagement. But now that her kids are busier with schoolwork and extracurriculars, they attend Sunday school only occasionally. And recently, the hours she spends supporting the church's program are starting to feel more obligatory than fulfilling, and they often conflict with time she wants to spend with her daughters rather than adding to it.

My research for this book revealed where my own comfort zone has limited my Community Sphere investments. During my time running Inspiring Capital, I was intentional about building community. It was our mission to support purpose-driven professionals in their career journeys, so I knew it mattered for me to have a network of mentors, employers, and partners. But the breadth of interviewees I interviewed for this book revealed how narrow my view had been. By interacting primarily with not-for-profit and Business for Good leaders I knew from my former life (my comfort zone), I excluded the wisdom of and opportunities to engage with leaders of publicly traded companies, other coaches and advisors, and the tech sector.

Counter Shoulding with Something New. To get away from the shoulds in your Community Sphere, you'll have to break out of your shell. Make a community investment that helps you explore a skill, group of people, activity, or interest you've been curious about that you'd never be able to or dare try in your job or at work.

Gabriela, for instance, picked up on her daughters' interest in public policy, and they've been developing a new Sunday routine of researching local and national candidates who are leading legislation to support immigrants. Their next step will be to find ways to support those candidates by volunteering for their campaigns, leveraging Gabriela's messaging expertise, or looping into their Money Sphere and donating.

As for me, my expansion beyond the not-for-profit and social enterprise communities that I had been focusing on while building Inspiring Capital resulted in an advisory relationship with a tech startup. It also led me toward coaching and facilitation engagement with a Fortune 500 company that would otherwise never have been on our invite list.

PITFALL #3: ORTHODOXY

Combined with a global pandemic and commercially powered social media, American individualism has left us more isolated in the 21st century than ever before. As early as the 19th century, Alexis de Tocqueville observed the risk of atomization: that "every citizen . . . is lost in the crowd."[81]

Indeed, in *Bowling Alone*, Robert Putnam gathers a vast array of statistics of how that atomization manifested over the 20th century as decreasing marriage rates, religious involvement, and urban residence (in favor of more distant urban sprawl and suburbs). Our isolation was made explicit through the quarantine and social distancing required during the COVID-19 pandemic of the 2020s. Despite some heartwarming examples of mutual support among communities during that crisis, such as community pantries and evening applause for healthcare workers, as the quarantine dragged on our norm became more isolated.

Further, today's orthodoxy about community is increasingly segregated by racial, socioeconomic, and religious factors. Research by UC Berkeley showed that 81 percent of urban areas became more racially segregated in 2019 than in 1990.[82]

On top of all this, we're living in a crisis of trust, which is particularly problematic for community investments because there's usually no contractual agreement for those investments. If we help out a neighbor, there's no legal document requiring them to repay the favor. Volunteer work is not a guarantee of a prestigious board seat or even appreciation.

When we aren't able to trust each other, we're very unlikely to invest in any of the communities to which our common fates are tied. Edelman's 22nd annual Trust Barometer showed that nearly 6 out of 10 people start with distrust, and nearly two-thirds say they can't have constructive conversations with other community members.[83] What do these barriers to mere conversation mean when it comes to community activity?

Orthodoxy Leads to Homogeneity. Increased segregation means that the most accessible community activities lead us to interact and connect with people who look and think like us. We may think of ourselves as community-minded and engage in multiple community activities, but do the communities in which we invest cross any lines of difference, whether race, gender, religion, geography, or otherwise?

Far too often, the answer to that question is no, and we've walled ourselves off thanks to political and school districts, media content, and the human tendency to seek sameness. Even when we realize that we operate in very homogenous communities, we may resist change because it's scary, a slightly longer drive, or there's a risk that we might offend someone. Those concerns may have some merit, but the growth and reward that results from building bridges across differences far outweigh the risks. It's also the only path to the equity and justice that Purpose Party people seek.

Community is critical to our pursuit of equity and justice. Particularly as faith in government wanes and political conflict intensifies, community becomes the domain in which we can learn about each other and collaborate across familial, organizational, or political divides. It's the connective tissue that holds us and our companies accountable to shared wellbeing. Failure to invest in the Community Sphere and grow our collective social capital results in disconnected family and organizational units that cannot possibly serve each other's needs—because they have no way to understand what those needs are.

Orthodoxy Looks Just Like You. Our Purpose Seeker David experienced the ultimately unsatisfying impact of a community investment that was limited in scope. He signed up for his firm's Junior Board program, which matched young professionals with not-for-profits that were eager to engage volunteers early in their careers as potential future donors and board members. But because this program was managed within the financial sector where he was already spending most of his time and energy, it wasn't providing a fulfilling connection to the community where he had grown up. David has his own connections to that community, but it's just no longer his day-to-day context. In the next phase of his career, he's eager to identify ways to find organizations or individuals to support that are less closely tied and similar to his Job and Workplace Spheres.

Your workplace can be a source of deeply satisfying community activities, like volunteering or board placements. But keep David's experience in mind and be sure you're able to extend beyond your (usually quite homogeneous) circles to have the impact and satisfaction that comes from connections with people who don't look and think just like you, your family members, and your colleagues.

Counter Orthodoxy with Bridges. The granddaddy of social capital, Robert Putnam, differentiated between *bonding* and *bridging* relationships. Bonding social capital reinforces strong group identities among homogeneous groups, which Putnam compared to superglue. He likened bridging social capital to WD40: a facilitator of smooth interactions and collaboration. He cautioned against defaulting to the comfort and ease of bonding social capital, as it's actually bridging social capital that provides the benefit of social capital to communities, organizations, and society.[84]

Here's an example. Susan McPherson, social capital billionaire, founder and CEO of CSR advisory firm McPherson Strategies, and bestselling author of *The Lost Art of Connecting*, realized that she was investing a ton in formal and informal community activities, but all the people she interacted with looked just like her and had very similar careers. These investments had been effective in career building—that is, they built bonding social capital—but she realized they weren't providing the outcomes she sought.

To bridge this gap, Susan got involved with the Lower East Side Girls' Club, where she mentored young women from a community adjacent to her own neighborhood but miles away in terms of racial and socioeconomic status. Those relationships were immediately fulfilling to Susan, enabling her to pay forward her privilege and connections to help the young women find jobs, internships, and career advice. As they've grown up, they've become part of her professional community and expanded Susan's perspective on the community programs she advises her clients about. Building bridging social capital was ultimately more meaningful and valuable to Susan and the people she served.

We'll talk more about the powerful interactions between community activities and the other spheres soon, but you can see how quickly these activities have ripples that improve our own performance as well as that of our organizations. To say nothing of the way we're protecting ourselves from loneliness, depression, and premature death!

Similar to Susan, when Purpose Seeker Gabriela and her daughters decided they wanted to get more active in the public sector, Gabriela realized she had zero relationships in government service. She kickstarted her Community Sphere investments with a cold call to a local representative, who was thrilled to spend an hour with the three of them while giving an overview of the landscape and ways they might start getting involved.

So when you consider your community involvement, think about building bridges. Engage across differences. The first step is to ensure you're hearing from people who are different from you. Attend town council meetings and listen to all arguments, especially those from other neighborhoods and other parties. Watch a different news show than your usual. Diversify your podcast or daily newsletter feed with creators of a different generation, religion, or racial, gender, or ethnic identity than yours. Once you begin hearing a wider variety of perspectives, building relationships across those gaps will feel less intimidating.

Some other ways to build these bridges are by participating in an ERG at work as an ally or reaching out to someone of a different age, race, or religion as a mentor or mentee at work. Welcome a neighbor of different demographics than you with an invitation to tea or just stopping to talk on the stoop or in the hallway. These simple human connections build the currency of social capital for you and the community around you.

Factors That Influence Our Impact in the Community Sphere

The Community Sphere offers powerful opportunities to expand your impact by broadening your network, expanding your skillset, and influencing issues beyond the scope of your (current) career. Because these efforts are not what we're looking to get paid for, we can try out new things.

FINDING A GOOD MATCH

Given the opportunity for learning and the importance of trust in these less formal relationships, choose community organizations with values that align with yours. Similarly, get clear about your community investments from an individual perspective. What do you want to contribute? Your time? Money? Your social connections and ability to introduce new donors, customers, investors, or partners? All of these can be valid resources, but only if you're clear on what you've got to offer and find an organization that will value it!

Additionally, how much do you want to contribute? This applies to the number of dollars, hours, or introductions you can give as well as to how much work you're willing to do on your own versus what support you need from the organization to engage and apply your contributions. Also, how long do you want to commit to your contributions? It can be more harmful than helpful if a volunteer steps in eagerly with big ideas and plans that require time, effort, and energy from a not-for-profit's staff and then disappears, having cost the team and not delivered any benefit. I always recommend setting specific project scopes for your support as a volunteer and timelines for your donations. Will you give a set amount monthly for the next year, annually for the next five, or is this a one-off donation as you move on to support other causes?

THOUGHTFUL PROBLEM-SOLVING

The Community Sphere also offers great opportunities to contribute to those urgent human and/or environmental problems that you care about but aren't equipped to address in your Job or Workplace Spheres. The modern economy requires more marketers, accountants, and service providers than we do cancer researchers or teachers, so you may not have a chance to get at those frontline impact opportunities in your work. But you *can* support the people doing that work with your community investments. Because these bigger issues are probably beyond your everyday life and work, it's important to zero in on the ones you care most about. Then be patient and open-minded in learning about the problems and best-known solutions *from the people they affect.*

We've learned so much in the not-for-profit sector about supporting people in a way that's sustainable, dignified, and aligned with what they want rather than our ideas about what they should want or need. There's a vast arena of work on identifying equitable and effective ways to solving humanity's most pressing problems. You don't have to become an expert, but get familiar with the problems you care about and the solutions you support so your Community Sphere investments don't do unintentional harm.

For example, TOMS was one of the first highly visible buy-one-give-one social enterprises, donating a pair of shoes for each pair purchased to improve comfort, mobility, and decrease risk of disease. A more holistic view revealed that importing free shoes was actually harming local economies as it eroded local retailers' and producers' revenues. TOMS responded by creating a plan to manufacture their donated shoes locally, and recently they got rid of their buy-one-give-one model altogether in favor of donating one-third of profits to a variety of causes.

There are myriad other examples of "charity gone wrong" in which well-intended efforts have less impact than they were intended to or have unintended negative consequences. Don't let this paralyze you; just do your homework, ideally by getting to know the people you're hoping to serve as well as you can.

MAKING IT A WIN-WIN-WIN

Get clear about what you're looking to get in exchange for your Community Sphere investments so you can find a good match. Community activities are usually unpaid, but that doesn't mean they're uncompensated. Remember the enlightened self-interest approach that teaches us it's best for everyone if there's some compensation for effort. The rewards for your efforts, then, might take the form of recognition and social interaction. Or perhaps you derive great fulfillment from supporting an organization's theory of change that you've seen work. You might also be seeking intellectual satisfaction or skill development for your career. These are all fair outcomes to hope for, as long as you're clear about them and choose an organization that's well-suited to provide them.

You also need to be clear about why you're making whatever investment you're making in the Community Sphere. Again, because these relationships are usually not legislated by formal contract, it's important to communicate transparently about what each side has to give and the expectations that come with it.

As Oren Heiman, former managing partner of New York-based law firm Shiboleth, came to understand, Community Sphere investments can also lead to rewards in the professional spheres by revealing a new job or workplace. His myriad community involvements were unintentionally but significantly tied to his business development successes. In light of his passion for human development, Oren served on many not-for-profit boards that advanced that cause. In those board meetings, relationships were built, initiatives were sparked, and deals were ultimately done. "It wasn't my intention," he said, "to drum up business with other board members, but because we got to know each other as humans, aware of what drove us in our work and lives, it was natural for me to see a need that my firm could serve and for them to trust me to do that work. More than half and probably closer to 80 percent of our firm's business ultimately came from my community relationships."

It's completely acceptable if you're looking to build your skills in a new industry and offer your marketing skills to a local business in that field. But be clear about this at the outset so you can address any potential conflicts of interest when you apply for a full-time job with this organization or a competitor, for example. If public recognition is valuable and motivating to you, talk about that with the leader of the organization to explore how that can be done in a mutually beneficial way.

Everything is possible as long as you're clear about what you're looking for first with yourself and then with your counterparts. You can't have it all, but if you do the work to figure out what *your* all is, you can have your all.

LOOKING BEYOND NOT-FOR-PROFITS

Consider options along the full Spectrum of Impact other than the not-for-profits that we might think of most often in this sphere. You could volunteer or run for a part-time town leadership role in the government sphere or serve on the board of a not-for-profit, social enterprise, or traditional for-profit company. Volunteers are usually most common in the government and not-for-profit sectors, but as a social enterprise founder, I can tell you that we welcome volunteers as pro bono advisors, brand ambassadors, and general champions with open arms.

Depending on the problem you're looking to solve, identify the right place on the Spectrum of Impact to get involved. For example, if reducing malaria is your goal and you learn that selling bed nets at a highly affordable rate for rural families is more effective than giving them away, you might want to choose a social enterprise or not-for-profit that uses this model. On the other hand, you might believe research that it's more effective for governments to mandate bed-net provisions at schools, so you would want to choose to support candidates or an organization in government that promotes that policy.

Keep in mind that when you use or recommend products made by traditional for-profit companies, that is also a form of community investment whether you intended to make it or not! We'll talk more about your choices of what to buy in the next chapter, but first, take a moment to reflect on the factors that inform how you craft your Community Sphere.

Crafting Your Community Sphere Cocktail

Now that you've learned about the Community Sphere, the pitfalls to avoid, the impact you can have there, and what influences that impact, it's time to apply the five-step model to this sphere. If you're using the playbook, turn to chapter 13 for a more detailed process.

STEP 1: BASELINE ASSESSMENT

Assess your investments in the Community Sphere by reviewing the activities you identified on your Impact Dashboard Excel Worksheet, the Purpose Party Playbook, or wherever you've been doing the work. Edit or add to that list so that it feels complete. When you're satisfied that you've captured the activities you do in this Sphere, review the total number of hours you're spending there per week. You can also determine the percentage of time each week this sphere takes. Fill in whether you want to do each activity more, less, or the same, and then rate these three statements as they apply to your Community Sphere now, last year, and a year from now:

> I invest time, energy, and attention in the Community Sphere.
>
> I am satisfied with the quantity and quality of my investments in the Community Sphere.
>
> I see the outcomes of my investments in the Community Sphere.

STEP 2: WHAT DO YOU NEED IN THIS SPHERE?

Determine whether there's a change you can make in the Community Sphere that you really believe will increase your well-being and/or the well-being of your community. Identify a change in this sphere that you're willing to make over the next month, whether it's doing something you already do more regularly, stopping something you do, or trying a new activity. You might instead realize that it's really not the area you need to prioritize. Before you decide for sure, think through the questions from pages 162–163 of this book as they apply to your Community Sphere. When you're done, draft a simple, clear, and measurable belief statement about what you want to change in this Sphere. Remember that your belief statement doesn't include exactly *how* you'll achieve the goal you're setting; you're just identifying *what* you're going to do and *why* it matters.

STEP 3: YOUR ONE NEXT STEP

Once you believe *what* the outcome will be of changing something in your Community Sphere and *why* it matters, figure out *how* to achieve that change. Focus on choosing your One Thing for this sphere, and then get really specific about exactly what this activity is going to look like (at least to start; you can revise the details as you learn). Here, in the playbook, or on the Excel worksheet, answer the questions from page 164 of this book as they apply to your Community Sphere.

STEP 4: SUPPORTING THAT STEP

Having a motivating belief statement helps keep you focused on why you're doing all this purpose work. Think about or write down your answers to the following questions that will help guide you in creating one.

- What's going to keep you from building this new habit, whether from the pitfalls we discussed in this chapter or otherwise?
- How can you overcome those obstacles?

Now write a simple, clear, and measurable behavioral plan to keep you on track. Be sure that this plan connects to the results you want to see from your community activities.

STEP 5: KEEP AN EYE OUT

The only way to keep up with changes in your outlook, work, life, and the world and make the necessary adaptations is to keep an eye on what you're doing and the consequences it's having. Pick your preferred method of tracking change and use it. Remember, the point here is not to beat yourself up if you don't get exactly where you want to be. It's just to be able to see how it's going. Does the new activity actually have your desired impact? Does it fit into your life, or does it reveal something else you'd rather spend your time on?

Overlapping Spheres

The investments we make in our Community Sphere are influenced by those on our Family and Friends, Workplace, and/or Money Spheres. We get involved with an organization through a family member, neighbor, or workout buddy, and we often do community activities that build on our job by offering our knowledge or skills pro bono. We might join a board through our workplace, such as a board membership program that matches employees with not-for-profit boards, or choose a not-for-profit that aligns with the industry, geography, or corporate responsibility program of our workplace. And our investments in not-for-profits are often paired to include our community activity as a volunteer or board member alongside monetary donations.

The influence flows in the other direction too. Our workplaces are determined by our communities more frequently than you might think. Over 83 percent of jobs are found through "weak ties," which are those in your Community Sphere.[85] Because we tend to have access to the same information as our family members and colleagues, it's far more likely that we'll come across a new opportunity through someone we know less intimately and have fewer overlaps with. Thus, our community activities enrich our other spheres, introducing us to significant others and investment opportunities as well as new jobs or clients.

Next up, we'll explore the Money, Money, Money Sphere. Often the most interaction within your Sphere of Impact occurs between your Community and Money Spheres. It makes sense to bolster the ways you're using your money—your financial capital—with the human capital you have to invest in your Community, Job, or Workplace Spheres. So keep in mind the investments you thought about here in the Community Sphere as we move forward to think about all the ways we can use money purposefully.

Reflection Questions

Yup, also these questions are available as a free worksheet from the book's page: www.inspiringcowgirl.com/goingfirst. There's so much more rich-ness in the Playbook—you're near the end of the book, and maybe ready for that next step!

- Consider your Community Sphere activities holistically. When you zoom out, what do see you're doing? What are you *not* doing? Does this mix feel authentic to you?

- Where are you currently in terms of isolation versus engagement with your community (whether that's local or global or simply being united by common interests)? What impact on yourself or your community might result if you engaged more (or less, if you're feeling overcommitted)?

- How broad a range of people (in terms of gender, age, religion, background and level of study, profession, personality style, etc.) do you interact with regularly? Are your current community activities broadening that range at all? Where would you like to diversify your community?

- What do you want to contribute in this sphere? Your time? Money? Your social connections and ability to introduce new donors, customers, investors, or partners? How much of this contribution do you want to make, and for how long are you willing to commit?

- Do you understand the problem you're aiming to solve and the people it affects well enough to make a thoughtful contribution to it? If you're not sure, who can you ask or what references can you consult?

- What are you hoping to gain from your community investments? Are you clear on those expectations and ready to have an honest conversation with your potential community partners about them?

- Have you explored ways beyond not-for-profits to have the impact you seek? If not, where might you learn about these alternate paths to change?

- Is there someone—or a general profile of a person—you've been eager to connect with but haven't known how? What knowledge or skills do they have that you could flatter them by asking about?

- What connections do your current and desired investments in the Community Sphere have to the other spheres? How do you want to revise the investments in your Community Sphere or other spheres to optimize the connections between them?

Chapter 14

The Money, Money, Money Sphere

The word money is repeated three times in the chapter of this title not because it's the most important sphere but because there are three specific ways to use money as a driver of impact toward our purpose: 1) what we buy, 2) where and how we bank and invest, and 3) to whom we donate.

First, the lowest-hanging fruit for working purposefully with money is found in our choices about what to buy (or not!) and from whom. The first step in the interest of our planet's well-being is to buy fewer things and buy used items. When we do need or want to buy something new, we can make thoughtful choices about what those things are and who we buy them from. Specifically, by purchasing from local and responsible businesses owned by the people to whom we want to direct wealth, we allocate our capital in a more purposeful way.

Second, as the investment industry gets more democratized, more of us have access to and choice about where our money is held, whether in retirement funds, stocks, or banks. B Corp-certified banks and locally owned credit unions provide values-driven options for basic banking. Accredited investors have access to myriad other forms of investments in every asset class, check size, and problem area to have influence with their investments. But even for those of us who don't qualify as accredited investors, crowdfunding laws and platforms have made private investments available in increments as small as $50. Investment funds composed to avoid negative industries, such as weapons or fossil fuel, deliver returns equal to or higher than market indices. An increasing number of funds actively support companies that seek positive impact, whether through gender equity, creative environmental practices, or community engagement, all of which also correlate with better financial performance and investor return.

Third, we can use our money to donate to not-for-profit organizations that effectively and efficiently improve well-being and equity for people and our planet. Small donations can still be powerful, particularly if they're direct, local, and recurring, and provide a reliable source of support for grassroots organizations.

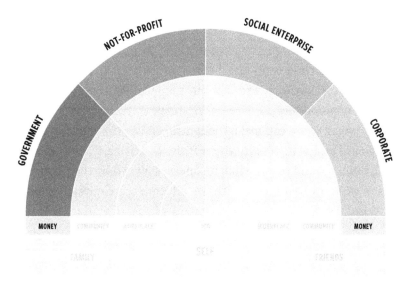

Figure 19. The Money Sphere's place in the Impact Dashboard.

How I Learned about the Money Sphere

It was during business school that I learned about (and later labeled) the Spectrum of Capital™ to go along with the Spectrum of Impact described in this book. I saw that there are simply different forms of capital, like different organizational types, to achieve different goals. From taxes and other payments that fund government agencies to philanthropic donations and investments in and purchases from private sector organizations, there are as many forms of capital as there are uses of it. As with all of our investments of time, energy, and attention, the important thing is to align our expectations of returns.

Figure 20. The Spectrum of Capital™.

These distinctions between different uses of financial capital made sense to me after a decade working in the not-for-profit sector funded by philanthropic capital. I had gotten frustrated at the low ceiling funders put on our growth, even though they knew their "investment" (donation) would be spent with only social returns, not financial. It seemed that it would be more powerful to use these generous philanthropic funds to make strategic investments in potentially life-changing programs, even if they hadn't been tried and proven. Or better yet, invest in (donate to) programs that had some kind of revenue model to generate funds that could be recycled back to expand the organization's sustainability and/or reach whenever possible.

In that vein, I proposed what I know now to be a social enterprise approach to expand our youth leadership program at Nablus with a boutique hotel that the local university's tourism students could run. It didn't get off the ground for a number of reasons, one of which was board members' and funders' inability to see the place as a commercial venture in our not-for-profit structure.

During my MBA program, my eyes were opened to the wide-ranging ways money can drive social and environmental change. These insights didn't come from the classroom, but from opportunities I had to learn from, volunteer for, and advise a variety of social enterprises. For example, I worked with a longtime purpose-driven entrepreneur to support a new fashion company that was designing clothes for children with developmental, physical, or emotional disabilities that made certain clothing difficult or impossible to put on. That prevented them from dressing themselves and feeling independent even in this basic daily function. The problem wasn't that their families couldn't afford clothes or even a caretaker to dress them, and the solution wasn't a not-for-profit organization to provide those resources. The company needed different products that met the kids' needs and enabled independence.

I also helped with the business planning and leadership development for a shea butter co-op in northern Uganda. Shea butter is a highly sought-after ingredient in high-end skin care products. The particular variety that this group grew in their region was the most desirable in the global market. These women were not lacking a source of significant income; indeed, buyers were actually chasing them for more and more of their product. They just didn't have the know-how and technology to optimize their farming and storage systems, particularly amid climate change that affected their rainfall and temperatures. So again, the answer wasn't not-for-profit donations; it was investment offered at reasonable terms that matched their revenue scale and timing, paired with capacity building.

Further, I learned about activist investors who raised environmental, social, and governance issues in the public equity markets. An excellent example is the pressure exerted by Natasha Lamb of Arjuna Capital, among others, that resulted in Citi's publishing a uniquely candid report about the global gender differences in their salaries. Much change is still needed at Citi and their competitors, but the Citi report catalyzed by Natasha and other activist investors remains an important landmark for the transparency that change requires.

Entire volumes have been written on each of these examples and others like them. The important lesson I want to pass on here is that money is merely a way of facilitating exchange. It enables certain activities to continue or not, and it needs to be the servant of our desired outcomes, not the master. In this chapter, we'll explore how to do just that: make purposeful choices about how you allocate your money to have the impact you seek.

Making It Yours

It's time to do your own work! Head to the *Going First* Purpose Party Playbook for a guided process. If you don't have the playbook, go to chapter 7 and apply the process found there to your Money Sphere. If you need a reminder of the five steps, review the section in that chapter called "Zeroing in on Each Sphere."

Avoiding the Pitfalls in the Money Sphere

PITFALL #1: INACTION

Like all the spheres, the first pitfall is simply not being intentional, in this case when it comes to how we spend, invest, and donate our money. The biggest driver of this paralysis is the orders of magnitude between the money that we individually have access to and the volume of transactions we see at work, in the media, and as the cost of fixing the problems we care about. As a result, our spending power feels insignificant and undeserving of our time, energy, or attention.

Inaction Leads to Market Failure. The result of inaction in the Money Sphere is ultimately market failure, or rather, successful markets that aren't aligned with actual demand. If we aren't intentional about using our money in a way that reflects what we want to see in the world, spending instead on what's readily available, most well-known, or recommended by celebrities or authorities we trust, we aren't funding the companies that reflect our desired future.

In the great big world of consumption, it's easy to think that our choice of milk (of which there are ever more choices, fewer and fewer of which come from cows), toilet paper, or jeans is utterly irrelevant. What difference does it really make whether we buy so-called sustainable paper towels?! But billionaires don't buy much more milk, toilet paper, or jeans than you do. Individual consumer decisions can and already do influence corporate behavior, and their influence is expanding rapidly. Particularly those of us born before 2000 are shaking off the notion of corporations as all-powerful black boxes. In the world of social media, transparency is at an all-time high, and that increases consumer—and employee—power.

Similarly, in the great big world of finance, it's easy to think that our measly IRA couldn't possibly move the needle. And as we pass hospitals and libraries named for billionaires and their companies, it's easy to think our $10, $100, or even $1,000 donation is worthless. This is simply not true. The vast majority of investment funds and not-for-profit organizations rely, at least in part, on "retail" customers. They wouldn't survive if their only support came from huge accounts or endowments.

The power of a free and well-regulated market is that it meets the demands of customers. But that can also be the danger. If we don't take the time to allocate our $10, $100, or $1,000 donations and investment savings to entities that match our values and do business in a way we respect, we'll never build the market we want to see.

Inaction Looks Like Surrendered Power. Making and using money is a core activity for the vast majority of us. Doing it in the most common or visible ways represents a huge lost opportunity. Since we're already buying, investing, and donating, the Money Sphere is arguably the sphere with the greatest potential for immediately expanding our impact. Yet because of powerful cultural taboos against talking about money and media pressure to buy certain quantities and types of things, we surrender our power as consumers, investors, and donors every day.

In my bohemian life as an international not-for-profit worker, I was thrilled to cover my student loan payments and set aside every additional yen, euro, and metical to fund my travel. I didn't think twice about buying disposable and irresponsibly made clothes or the groceries that I chose. When I got to business school and learned about the Spectrum of Capital, I realized I could direct even my minimal spending more purposefully.

David, our Purpose Seeker, had a real aha moment when completing his Dashboard. He had always known he wanted to achieve financial security and build enough wealth to enjoy freedom and pay that forward to his family, but he had focused only on accumulating wealth, never considering the values with which he wanted to grow or use it. Mapping his Dashboard helped him see the influence his money could have without compromising his wealth accumulation.

Now that they've been pointed out, perhaps you recognize these examples of surrendering financial power in your own case. So what can you do about it?

Counter Inaction with Choice. For most of us, a great starting point for harnessing our financial power is simply to buy less. Examine what you buy and why you buy it. Are you a user of retail therapy? Are there times that you shop when you could just call a friend, walk your dog, or do a kickboxing class for the same sense of relief? Then use the KonMari Method™ about each purchase: Does it bring you massive joy? If not, don't buy it![86] A next filter is whether you could borrow the item you need or buy it used. A major driver of our environmental threats is overproduction and overfilled landfills, so any time you can avoid buying something new, you're having a positive effect on our planet's well-being.

After paring down your buying, the next step is to start aligning your uses of money with your values so you are participating in the market in a way that shapes the world you want to see. If you do some research, you'll find that many, if not most, of your buying and investing decisions can contribute to making the impact you seek in the world or at least reducing their negative ramifications. Rather than accepting your IRA's default allocations, for instance, look for funds managed by investment professionals who identify as women and/or people of color. There are also ample funds you can choose with positive screens for environmental, social, and/or governance impact. Not only do these funds tend to have better-than-market performance because of their superior insights to market trends and risk, but they also help reduce the wealth gap that threatens our collective well-being and costs the global economy over $10 trillion annually.[87]

Aligning donations with your values is probably the most obvious step. But it's also worth reviewing to ensure that you're giving to organizations that address not only what you care about doing but also how you want to contribute to that change. Use the Spectrum of Impact and Spectrum of Capital to inform whether you donate only to not-for-profits or also to political candidates and/or for-profit social enterprises. Similarly, consider whether you want to support the huge global organizations that act at scale but may lose some responsiveness to local needs and/or efficiency or the small grassroots organizations with deep ties to the community but a narrower reach.

Finally, speak up as an investor and encourage others around you to do the same. Ask what funds are available in your retirement plan, and request the changes that meet your needs. Pay attention to what companies in your portfolio are doing about the issues you care about. Attend analyst calls, vote your proxies, and speak up on social media or directly to investor relations offices. Again, with increased democratization of investment, we do have a voice as individual retail investors to shape the market we want to see.

PITFALL #2: SHOULDING

Shoulding in the Money Sphere manifests as pressure to pay attention to financial-only metrics and goals and make and accumulate as much as possible. We're told by the vast majority of voices we hear that more income, profit, and GDP is better in the Me, We, and World dimensions. These shoulds are problematic both for their narrow focus on financial outcomes that exclude social and environmental consequences and their pressure to maximize our money. Let's look more closely.

Shoulding Leads to Bad Decisions. Very few outcomes are evaluated based only on their financial implications. If you make twice as much money this year but don't take a single vacation and miss all of your kids' activities, you may not consider that a win. An artist who charges as much as possible for a concert will not enjoy the most engaged audiences by virtue of having eliminated younger fans or other artists with less buying power. And a not-for-profit that chooses the least expensive way to serve its target audience may well not have the most profound or lasting influence on those people.

Yet we often feel pressured to focus only on the monetary elements when deciding what to buy, where to donate, and how to invest our money. When we make a decision for ourselves, our companies, or our communities, we should better integrate all the factors that influence our satisfaction with that decision, including the well-being of ourselves and other relevant stakeholders as well as the impact and duration of the outcomes.

Apart from causing a misguided, narrow focus, shoulding also leads to bad decisions because of the way we interpret risk and reward, a fundamental assessment in economic choices. There's nothing wrong with the concept of balancing risk and reward; the problem is that our notions of risk and reward are outdated for our fast-changing context. For example, graduates of the class of 2008 who got a job offer in the finance sector probably felt quite secure about their futures, as did their parents and career counselors. But within months or weeks of starting their roles, a startling number of those positions were made redundant when their employers were shaken by the financial crisis or even went out of business.

We could be at a similar stage regarding the environment. The Intergovernmental Panel on Climate Change has issued a Code Red, and the evidence of extreme climate with tangible and significant human and economic cost is piling up. Yet graduates continue to take jobs in the fossil fuel industry, product designers continue to build gas-guzzling cars, and consumers continue to buy them. Do those decisions properly account for risk and reward as they can be calculated today?

It wouldn't be surprising if the answer is no, given how our minds are wired. *Immediacy bias* is the psychological concept that we are more motivated by what we can have now even if it's less than what we could have later. We underestimate and undervalue future returns, such as more sustainable but modest salaries or fewer extreme weather events several seasons from now.

The latter example of making choices now that avoid extreme weather later is made even more unlikely because of *primacy bias*. This concept explains that we overvalue what we can directly see, such as our bank accounts, and undervalue less tangible things, such as global weather trends, particularly in far-away locations. So even though global weather trends will affect our children's well-being and the viability of our businesses far more than the money we may save now by continuing to use fossil fuels to heat our houses and drive our cars, we don't make these changes.

The loudest voices doing the shoulding—tradition, media, peer pressure, and self-imposed notions of success—are often too short-term and financially focused to support the decisions that are required to optimize our well-being and the impact we seek.

Shoulding Looks Like Dissatisfaction. Undue focus on financial factors and outdated calculations of risk and reward lead to suboptimal decisions that result in dissatisfaction with our lives. Unfortunately, this often has the perverse effect of driving us to seek more money in the form of income or revenue to provide that elusive sense of satisfaction, when actually the problem is nonfinancial.

Research in the 2020s shows that life satisfaction doesn't increase after achieving the baseline income level (about $95,000 in the US, with cost-of-living adjustments for different cities and countries), and our emotional well-being is optimized at an even lower level of income ($60,000–$75,000).[88] (Unfortunately, median incomes fall short of these levels in the US and most other countries, so there's an important conversation to be had about fair wages in another volume.) But many professionals earn well above these salaries. If we seek to accumulate wealth to improve our well-being and life satisfaction, going beyond these levels is useless unless we leverage that wealth accumulation to achieve some specific outcomes in the Me, We, and/or World dimensions.

The Great Resignation of 2021/2022 prompted research that suggests people were willing to give up tens of thousands of dollars in salary—or 23 percent of their lifelong earnings—to do work that's meaningful to them.[89] Our Purpose Seekers David and Lisa personify this dissatisfaction. David, as he looks forward to having a family, and Lisa, on the verge of at least partial retirement, are thinking more holistically about their earnings and uses of money. They've both realized that wealth accumulation in and of itself doesn't bring them satisfaction—or a sense of purpose.

Counter Shoulding with Holistic Decision-Making. Part of the beauty of doing the work to live and lead more purposefully is that it connects us to the nonfinancial outcomes of our work that are so much more powerful, if often less visible or publicized, than money. The important way to get over shoulding in your Money Sphere is to explicitly integrate nonfinancial factors into your financial decisions, which is the hardest place to do it. Consider, then, the impact you want your money to have—other than providing access to goods and experiences and making you more money. Do you want it to support clean energy innovation or equitable access to education for people with physical disabilities?

Also consider your activity along the entire Spectrum of Impact. Not-for-profits are often the primary way we think of solving big social problems, and donating money to them is the main way we think to engage. Donations are a great way to have influence with your money, but know that you can also *invest* in not-for-profits, getting a concessionary return on your investment alongside documented social and/or environmental sustainability. There are also not-for-profits that sell things you might want to buy, whether home furnishings from Goodwill or delicious treats from the Girl Scouts. (A lot of these purchasing options might be scuppered by orthodoxy about not-for-profits, so if you have objections or discomfort here, read on!)

On the for-profit end of the Spectrum, buy from or invest in companies that you see are making positive change. There's no perfect guide to understanding the complete and exact influences any company has, but there are some indicators of who's trying. Check out the JUST Capital rankings, signatories of the Business Roundtable Stakeholder Capitalism Pledge, and members of 1% for the Planet, Conscious Capitalism, and Pledge 1%. None of these credentials indicate perfect behavior, but they do each point to organizations that are trying, in one way or several, to turn around their massive operations and follow a new set of shoulds.

In the social enterprise range of the Spectrum, companies tend to be newer and smaller, but they have impact baked in from the beginning. Many have certifications for how they do business, with B Corp as the most holistic and rigorously audited overall view of a company's operations. Note that B Corp and similar certifications are difficult and costly to obtain, so many businesses that are deeply impact-conscious but less capitalized may not be certified even though they do run their businesses in an impact-optimizing way.

Finally, in the public sector of the Spectrum, municipal bonds are a powerful (and tax-free) way to invest in public-sector infrastructure such as schools, clean water, and green energy transitions. We can also buy from public entities, sometimes with a choice (such as school enrollment or national park destinations) and other times not (utilities). And many government agencies have ways to accept donations (school associations, National Parks Foundation) if you want to provide additional financial support.

PITFALL #3: ORTHODOXY

Orthodoxy in the Money Sphere tells us that profit is antithetical to purpose—that any activity that generates profit can't be good for the world. This means that on the collective level we make bad decisions about how to use our money, which has become a harmful orthodoxy. By over-indexing on short-term financial outcomes and failing to properly assess risk, we've built entire industries that now risk losing their licenses to operate because of their harmful environmental or social consequences. This phenomenon can be seen in mining as well as the oil and gas industries. Similarly, the way we've structured our systems to invest in businesses has resulted in the rise and fall of numerous personal transport and food delivery apps, while the US maternal mortality rate rises and remains the highest among industrialized nations.[90]

Orthodoxy is everywhere, but it announced itself to me particularly loudly one evening. A few months after I launched my company, I was working on its financial model. The model came up over dinner with my husband, specifically the target third-year salary of $125,000 for a key employee who was a recent MBA graduate. When my husband said it sounded high, I explained that it was Columbia Business School's (both my and the employee's alma mater) average for the last graduating class.

He hesitated and then explained, "But there should be some discount given the good work you're doing, right?"

I pushed him to explain this thinking further. After another pause, he said, "Well otherwise, everyone would want to do work that's good for the world!"

As we both fully processed his comment, we could only chuckle. He saw as clearly as I did that this common perspective wasn't productive in terms of making the world a better place.

> *Orthodoxy Leads to Restrictions.* The notion that an entity can only pursue profit *or* purpose results in unnecessary restrictions on human creativity. Perhaps this zero-sum approach to value creation was harder to escape during the Industrial Era, but in this world of exponential technology, there are countless activities that create more value than the sum of their inputs.

> Rather than limiting a given business or activity to generating profit *or* purpose, we now have opportunities to do good *and* do well at the same time. Yet there are still plenty of commercial activities that require limited natural resources, so, as Patagonia says, the world would actually be better off without them. Patagonia is clear to state that they're aiming to reduce their environmental harm while acknowledging that their very existence inevitably causes some.

> However, there are other businesses, such as Husk Power, that are building low-cost, hybrid power grids with a customer-centric payment system. The more business they do, the more access customers have to clean energy for light to study and work by and the more dignified jobs they create directly and indirectly. This is

the ultimate goal of social enterprise: to develop a business model that has inherent impact and is responsible and accountable to all stakeholders, including customers, suppliers, employees, and community members. In this case, businesses and their owners don't need to follow the common advice to give back—because they didn't take too much in the first place!

Orthodoxy Looks Like Blinders. When we think within the narrow confines of choosing profit or purpose, we lose the opportunity to have influence in our Money Sphere, outside of our donations. (And we lose the opportunity to have leverage in other spheres in the not-for-profit portion of the Spectrum of Impact.)

For example, Purpose Seeker Gabriela hadn't ever considered how her family's spending or investments could align with their modest donations to women's health not-for-profits. As she started reviewing her investment portfolio, she saw holdings of shares in several large companies that were lagging on paid parental leave. She worked with her advisor to reallocate those holdings to better reflect her values and not counteract the efforts of the not-for-profits she supports.

Similarly, other than accumulating the wealth he knew he wanted in order to raise his children comfortably, David hadn't thought about the values with which he wanted to grow and spend that money. He made charitable contributions that aligned loosely with his personal experience and hopes for the world his children would inherit, but his Dashboard provoked a much deeper examination of household finances with his partner.

By removing their blinders, Gabriela and David revealed numerous opportunities to leverage their wealth for their desired outcomes at no cost to their financial security and wealth accumulation. David is still at the beginning of the process, but he and his partner have started by taking a long-term view of the college savings fund they had already initiated for their future children. It felt particularly important to them that those investments, purportedly made for their children's future well-being, also account for their long-term social and environmental health.

Regardless of the size of your budget, when you realize the full range of possible uses for your money, you multiply your opportunities for impact. Without the profit-or-purpose blinders, money becomes a much richer instrument for the results you seek.

Counter Orthodoxy with Integrated Capital. To escape the orthodoxy that profit and purpose are mutually exclusive, get comfortable with using the Spectrum of Capital as an actionable guide for how you use money. Figure 21 presents a reminder of the types of organizations you can interact with all across the Spectrum. And even if you think you've broken free—or are married to a diehard social entrepreneur like me—keep looking for ways that orthodoxy influences your choices related to money.

Figure 21. A tiny sampling of the organizations across
the entire Spectrum of Impact.

After more than a decade of running, advising, and supporting Businesses for Good, I still find the influence of the profit-or-purpose orthodoxy in my own work and life. I see it in how I price my own services, evaluate vendors or competitors, or research and choose investments.

There's an interesting movement from within the orthodoxy to financialize nonfinancial outcomes like human lives and the environment. Brilliant economists are refining ways to value human lives and natural resources so that they can be built into financial reports alongside inventory costs and revenue. This is an interesting way to more accurately account for the positive and negative consequences of our businesses on the environment. That said, this approach still operates within the limited field of vision allowed by the profit-or-purpose blinders.

Ultimately, we have to remove those blinders to develop a new, holistic orthodoxy about money, one that recognizes we value things other than financial capital and performance metrics for companies or household worth must account for the human and environmental value we create—or destroy—alongside their financial dimension. The Spectrum of Capital helps take this step toward a new orthodoxy by presenting the outcomes of financial capital in a more integrated way.

In any financial targets you set, whether household budgets or goals for your retirement account or your business, include your desired nonfinancial outcomes. Consider how you want your salary to make you feel—other than the bills and savings you want it to cover. Thinking about the "so what" of how you use your money other than to make more money helps erode the orthodox thinking that limits us to one goal at a time, whether profit or purpose.

Factors That Influence Our Impact in the Money Sphere

For many of us, the main factor that influences our choice of activities in the Money Sphere is whether we acknowledge the range and extent of the power we have through our spending, no matter the volume. The simple inventory of the things we use money for will help bring our attention to the leverage we already have as well as other ways to do more. This mere awareness helps highlight our power as consumers and investors so we can make the impact we seek as well as what we're most comfortable with in terms of donations.

SOMETIMES ONE SIZE DOES FIT ALL

There are ample ways to use your money to address the specific problems that matter most to you, whether they involve a neighborhood school or theater, a city or country of origin that you support, or research to cure a disease that affects a family member. These are certainly worthy uses of your money. Beyond those unique interests your money can work on, however, there are some one-size-fits-all issues that deserve your money's impact. Environmental protection, for example, as well as human rights, equity, and healthcare are important for our collective well-being and prosperity.

The major and widening wealth gaps between genders and races in the US are bad news for all of us. Inequality leads to lost economic productivity, political fragmentation, and social instability. So it's in all of our best interests to buy more from local businesses, particularly those owned by people who identify as Black, Brown, Asian, LGBTQIA+, veterans, or having disabilities. Directing our purchasing power to those neighbors is a significant choice to make.

To find such businesses, there are certifications such as Women Owned, NGLCC, and Minority Business Enterprise. These organizations and their directories can be helpful starting places to find values-aligned businesses, but keep in mind that these certifications are demanding to obtain and renew, like B Corp and others. For businesses that are already undercapitalized, getting certified is sometimes an impractical luxury. So, simply walking downtown and chatting with a store owner is often the best search engine for local businesses that deserve your money.

There are other things we can all do with our money to advance our shared interests as well. For example, if the problem we care about is decarbonizing and reversing deforestation, we can buy less, especially single-use items and anything plastic; use less fossil fuel; and buy from companies that are responsible about the sourcing and disposal of their goods. (For more on this, Google "circular economy" and enjoy the rabbit hole.)

Crafting Your Money Sphere Cocktail

Now that you've learned about the Money Sphere, the pitfalls to avoid, the impact you can have there, and what influences that impact, it's time to apply the five-step model to this sphere. If you're using the playbook, turn to chapter 14 for a more detailed process.

STEP 1: BASELINE ASSESSMENT

Assess your investments in the Money Sphere by reviewing the activities you identified on your Impact Dashboard Excel Worksheet, the Purpose Party Playbook, or wherever you've been doing the work. Edit or add to that list so that it feels complete. When you're satisfied that you've captured the activities you do in this sphere, review the total number of hours you're spending there per week. You can also determine the percentage of time each week this sphere takes. Fill in whether you want to do each activity more, less, or the same, then rate these three statements as they apply to your Money Sphere now, last year, and a year from now:

I invest time, energy, and attention in the Money Sphere.

I am satisfied with the quantity and quality of my investments in the Money Sphere.

I see the outcomes of my investments in the Money Sphere.

STEP 2: WHAT DO YOU NEED IN THIS SPHERE?

Determine whether there's a change you can make in your Money Sphere that you really believe will increase your well-being and/or the well-being of your family, friends, workplace, or community. Identify a change in this sphere that you're willing to make over the next month, whether it's doing something you already do more regularly, stopping something you do, or trying a new activity. You might instead realize that it's really not the area you need to prioritize. Before you decide for sure, think through the questions from pages 162–163 of this book as they apply to your Money Sphere. When you're done, draft a simple, clear, and measurable belief statement about what you want to change in this Sphere. Remember that your belief statement doesn't include exactly *how* you'll achieve the goal you're setting; you're just identifying *what* you're going to do and *why* it matters.

STEP 3: YOUR ONE NEXT STEP

Once you believe *what* the outcome will be of changing something in your Money Sphere and *why* it matters, figure out *how* to achieve that change. Focus on choosing your One Thing for this sphere, then get really specific about exactly what this activity is going to look like (at least to start; you can revise the details as you learn). Here, in the playbook, or on the Excel worksheet, answer the questions from page 164 of this book as they apply to your Money Sphere.

STEP 4: SUPPORTING THAT STEP

Having a motivating belief statement helps keep you focused on why you're doing all this purpose work. Think about or write down your answers to the following questions that will help guide you in creating one.

- What's going to keep you from building this new habit, whether from the pitfalls we discussed in this chapter or otherwise?

- How can you overcome those obstacles?

Now write a simple, clear, and measurable behavioral plan to keep you on track. Be sure that this plan connects to the results you want to see from your financial activities.

STEP 5: KEEP AN EYE OUT

The only way to keep up with changes in your outlook, work, life, and the world and make the necessary adaptations is to keep an eye on what you're doing and the consequences it's having. Pick your preferred method of tracking change and use it. Remember, the point here is not to beat yourself up if you don't get exactly where you want to be. It's just to be able to see how it's going. Does the new activity actually have your desired impact? Does it fit into your life, or does it reveal something else you'd rather spend your time on?

Overlapping Spheres

In some ways, money touches all of our other spheres. It's the fundamental form of exchange that we've mostly settled on to trade efficiently. We use money to enhance the investments in our Self or Family and Friends Spheres by learning to meditate or buying experiences that facilitate quality family time. Similarly, our choices in the Job and Workplace Spheres—what we do and for whom—influence our wages and wealth, providing us with money to deploy in this sphere. Money can also be a powerful complement to your Community Sphere investments, allowing you to donate to, invest in, or buy from the organizations that you support as a volunteer, board member, or informal fan.

I've Got a Dashboard. Now What?

All right! We've had a party! With the Impact Dashboard, you've got a tool—a game, even—to clarify what you're doing, what you're not doing, and how much of it accurately represents you.

Your work with the Dashboard is designed to help you be healthier, have more impact, and build a legacy. The Dashboard gathers your efforts throughout all six Spheres of Impact and across the full Spectrum of Impact. That mapping is the foundation for leading and living more purposefully because it shows you how you're spending your limited time, energy, and attention.

Now that you've gotten familiar with the Dashboard and used it to map your current efforts, it's time to ladder up to the outcomes: the "so what" of all that effort. In the next and final chapter, we'll highlight the life-changing outcomes of your Purpose Party in the Me, We, and World dimensions. By recognizing these outcomes as well as sharing some strategies and tactics for achieving and maintaining behavior change, you'll be ready to throw your own Purpose Party, expanding your influence and inspiring others around you to do the same!

Reflection Questions

Given the potential for money to realize the impact we seek, and how little most people think about it, maybe this is the set of questions you want to download at www.inspiringcowgirl.com/goingfirst. Or maybe it's the one that makes you realize you want to keep going deeper, guided by the Going First Purpose Party Playbook! Find it and details on the book's homepage above.

- Consider your Money Sphere holistically. What are you doing to drive results by what you buy, invest in, and donate to? What are you not doing? Is the blend authentic to you and aligned with your desired impact?

- What blind spots did this section point out to you when it comes to the ways you use your money? How are you giving up your financial power as a consumer, investor, or donor?

- When was the last time you audited your grocery shopping process? Review your weekly purchases and ask yourself what you can buy from local shops or brands, which items you can replace with a B Corp or other certified "for-good" business, and what choices you can make that reduce the disposable packaging you buy. Repeat this process with the clothes, gifts, or entertainment that you buy.

- What choices are you already making about how to use your money to better align your spending, investments, and donations with your values and desired outcomes? What others occur to you that you can start making immediately?

- How distributed or concentrated is your money across the Spectrum of Capital? What's one use of money you can make today at a point on the Spectrum where you're currently underinvested?

- What nonfinancial outcomes do you want from your income or savings? What Money Sphere activities can you invest in that will lead to those outcomes? For example, is it important to you to learn a new language or visit your parents annually? Do you want to fund mental health care for a certain group of people or donate annually to candidates with an identity or platform you support?

- What are some examples of inaction, shoulding, and orthodoxy that are currently happening in your Money Sphere? Which would you like to let go of in this sphere?

- What area of investment on the Spectrum of Capital are you naturally curious about? What's one action you can take this week in that area, whether allocating money or just reading more?

- What connections do your current and desired investments in the Money Sphere have to the other spheres? How do you want to revise the investments in your Money Sphere or other spheres to optimize the connections between them?

Chapter 15

The Party Is Just Beginning

Congratulations! You've made it through my Purpose Party. Quite happily, I'd like to hope.

Thank you for coming! On behalf of everyone in your life and the future you're working toward, I'm so appreciative that you've gotten this far.

Now that you know what to bring to a Purpose Party and what exactly happens there (the Impact Dashboard), it's time to consider the ripples you create in the world by coming to my Party. You probably know me well enough by now to know that we're not just going to think about those ripples freeform—there's a framework here too!

Specifically, it's the three dimensions of the outcomes of living and leading with purpose: Me, We, and World. The final part of the Cs of our ABCs of purpose is the afterglow of a Purpose Party: by having gotten the *clarity* about the investments you want to make across the Spheres of Impact, the full Spectrum of Impact, and the Spectrum of Capital, you're already building the *confidence* and *courage* it takes to Go First.

So here we are at the D that follows the ABCs of purpose: *diving in*. Remember, purpose is a party that requires your active participation.

It's not a one-directional, switch-it-on-and-off performance. It's an interactive, day in/day out approach to your work and life. So I'll also give you tips (and two powerful activities) for the Es—the critical steps of *evaluating* and *evolving*—but how you implement them is really up to you. That's what happens in your daily, quarterly, and whatever other regular check-ins you schedule with yourself to review your Dashboard and your Me, We, and World outcomes.

The real magic begins now, as you take your reflections and commitments off these pages into your work and life and all the benefits of purpose that we discussed in chapter 4 start accruing.

How I Learned the Three-Dimensional Win-Win-Wins of Purposeful Leadership

After a decade of international not-for-profit work, business school was a massive learning experience for me in so many ways. I enjoyed being back in the classroom and learning frameworks, principles, and formulas to optimize performance (as understood narrowly in terms of profitability). As I hoped, these were not magic or proprietary tools available for use only by private sector wizards. They were just ways of thinking, analyzing, planning, and strategizing that anyone could learn and use. When paired with thoughtful consideration of all stakeholders involved, including people and the planet, they were certainly applicable to the problems I'd been focusing on in the not-for-profit sector.

On the other hand, my business school classmates revealed that they often missed a sense of "so what" in their outwardly very successful careers. They weren't sure why their work mattered to anyone beyond their analysts' review of their company's quarterly reports. And because of this missing piece—their *why*—many of them saw the MBA program as a way out of their current role to something different. They needed and wanted to continue accumulating wealth to raise their families, buy back time, and have unique experiences, but they also wanted to feel that they were part of something that mattered. They wanted their children to be proud of their work and enjoy the results of their efforts in more ways than the salary it provided.

My biggest takeaway from business school was the intoxicating possibility that if properly aligned, these two major problems—the urgent need for sustainable, strategic solutions to social and environmental problems and people's need to have positive impact in their work—could solve each other. The outcome would be win-win-wins: individuals would be happier, healthier, more motivated and fulfilled; their teams and organizations would benefit from a more engaged, inspired, creative, and collaborative workforce; and people and the planet would benefit from the positive results created.

Designing Win-Win-Wins

Don't ask yourself what the world needs. Ask yourself what makes
you come alive and go do that, because what the world needs
is people who have come alive.

~Howard Thurman

Howard Thurman's inspiring quote captures the win-win-win cycle, pointing out that individuals who do what they need in order to "come alive" are the ones who can heal the world.

Throughout my business school education, which unfolded in classrooms, small group projects, over coffee breaks, and on dance floors after class, I became increasingly more energized about facilitating this "coming alive" and its potential for win-win-wins. I knew that the not-for-profit sector was an inadequate solution for the major social and environmental problems of our time. Real solutions need the tools and scale of the private sector supported and guided by policy change. So it wasn't just about enrolling my classmates as donors or board members in not-for-profits (not that there's anything wrong with that); it was about finding ways they could contribute to a better future from the business roles in which they were *already* successful. My highly qualified business-professional classmates, like all humans, needed the satisfaction of doing work that matters. No bonus, promotion, or world-class learning opportunity was enough to keep them satisfied beyond the significant level of achievement they'd already reached 10 to 15 years into their careers. Indeed, one of the strongest indicators of life satisfaction is the feeling that one has done work that made a difference to other people.[91]

The opportunity I was excited about was connecting *all* of our work—whether investment banking, marketing strategy, product design, or otherwise—to the good it could do in the world. Helping professionals connect the dots in this way would enable companies to better engage and motivate their employees. Professionals would feel challenged and fulfilled, and we all would get scalable solutions to the existential problems we face.

My hypothesis is that if we support people in identifying the unique ways they're positioned and inspired to contribute and finding a path to follow that inspiration from their current seat, they'll be more motivated. Since that will be good for their organizations, it will lead to the engaged, innovative, and resilient workforce that's crucial for success in the rapidly changing 21st-century context. What's more, engaging people's sense of purpose will ultimately lead to more positive social and environmental impact. When presented with a choice they can understand, the vast majority of people choose to do things in a way that reduces harm and/or enhances the lives of the planet and people around them.

So I set about creating tools and experiences to reveal and catalyze these win-win-wins.

The Three Dimensions

We started with the inputs: those activities you do and want to start doing in the six Spheres of Impact. Now it's time to look at the outcomes of those purposeful activities. The consequences of your efforts—your "so what"—fall into the three dimensions of Me, We, and World.

Some of you will be more comfortable envisioning your desired outcomes than you were reflecting on or planning activities in the spheres. Great! Dig in here, and once you've clarified the why of what you're working toward, go back to review your Dashboard.

Others of you will have felt very comfortable with the concrete actions of tracking and planning the activities in your Dashboard, but your palms are already sweating as you think about planning, claiming, or tracking the resulting outcomes. That's great too. The content and tools in this final section are intended to reduce any anxiety about envisioning and expanding your impact.

WIN #1: ME

When you build the healthy blend of activities that activate your purpose in all the Spheres of Impact and across the Spectrum, you enhance your own well-being. You have more resilience to mental health challenges such as anxiety, depression, and dementia. Your heart is healthier, and your risk of premature death is reduced. And you feel engaged and fulfilled, with plenty of energy, creativity, and empathy to extend to others.

Positive change can only be created sustainably at scale by teams of Me's who have "come alive" in this holistic way thanks to the purposeful investments they're making in all six spheres.

WIN #2: WE

Your efforts in the Dashboard have potent effects on the people around you, including the formal and informal teams of which you are a part. By demonstrating and talking about your efforts across the Spheres and Spectrum, you build trust. People can see that you're working toward something beyond yourself. This outcome of your purposeful leadership alone is game-changing. Trust enhances the performance of teams in terms of efficiency, innovation, and resilience—prerequisite skills for teams to positively contribute in the 21st-century context.

But the wins in the We dimension don't stop there. You also set a powerful example for others around you, inspiring them to make efforts in whatever ways suit their unique profiles across the Spheres and Spectrums. In addition, you develop new ways of working based on that trust and contribution to a higher good.

Implicitly or explicitly, with formal authority or not, purposeful leaders innovate what their organizations do and how they do it. And their innovations line up with what's required for success in today's market. At Accenture, for example, Christie Smith sees and feels the "weight of the moment. We are putting humanity at the center of work in a way we never have. Which requires new ways of leading and living, specifically: access; agency, or autonomy; opportunity; and finally purpose. Employees, as well as consumers and investors, want to make a difference when it comes to the environment, diversity and equity, and health and well-being."

Notice we're still not talking about what people often think of as *impact*, whether that's teaching kids to read, collecting ocean plastic, or developing soil-enriching farming techniques. We're talking about building healthier and fairer organizations driven by thriving and inspired people. People, and the organizations of which they're a part, must be healthy before they can effectively drive external change.

We tend to overlook these more mundane elements of changemaking in favor of the glamorous direct sensation of saving lives and trees, but we do so at our own peril. Overemphasis on dramatic and measurable outcomes tends to favor paternalistic, top-down, ineffective or unsustainable interventions rather than the slower but lasting systemic change required to address root causes.

WIN #3: WORLD

If and when we're investing the time, attention, and money needed to keep ourselves and our organizations healthy, fair, and joyful—which, by the way, is a lifelong process rather than a single, summit-able peak—we earn the privilege to positively impact the people and planet around us. This isn't a hall pass to meditate your life away and remain oblivious to all the problems until you're enlightened; on the contrary, none of these dimensions move without the other. It simply means that you must ensure you're making the investments required in your Impact Dashboard to generate positive outcomes in the Me and We dimensions and ultimately achieve your desired outcomes for the World.

Outcomes in the World dimension might address any of our four major existential crises (racial equity, health, economy, and environment), with their myriad causes, symptoms, and spinoffs that merit attention. The important thing is that you identify the crisis and the thread of solution that you're equipped to pick up through activity in any of your Spheres of Impact.

> *Ask what makes your eyes light up. How can I elevate humanity, contribute to society in some way by what I'm doing? I didn't always see that . . . I was good at my work, but I wasn't jazzed up. Okay, so I built another $1M of business. I've realized that those narrow business metrics don't motivate me; it's about seeing people's lives transformed in some way.*

~Joe Kenner, president and CEO of Greyston Bakery

As Joe found, it's as important as ever in the World dimension to know yourself: what you care about, where you're positioned, what you have to give, and what you need in return. Only then can you choose your issues and desired outcomes accordingly. Are you addressing the one eight-billionth world problem that you're uniquely passionate about and suited for? You won't be surprised to find that I've got a tool to help you identify those passions. Read on.

Practicing in 3D

Just as the Dashboard is most powerful when we review it regularly to track our progress (evaluate) and make adjustments (evolve) to the investments we're making in each sphere, it's critical to regularly evaluate the outcomes of those actions in the three dimensions. The tenor of these evaluations is likely to be slightly longer because it takes time for action to add up to impact.

I've created a template that will help guide you through a simple annual review of the outcomes you're achieving in the three dimensions and what you'd like to do differently in the year to come. It's called the Annual Planning Template and is available from my website. I recommend using this template as part of your birthday celebration each year, which tends to be less crowded with other obligations (year-end reporting, holiday cooking, etc.). But like all of Going First, do you. Find a day or season that feels like a natural time for you to pull out this template and check in, and then get it on your calendar.

An Upward Spiral

Going First to change the world is slow, complex, and often frustrating work. Reflecting on our outcomes in the Me, We, and World dimensions helps us keep our focus on our motivation. "That meaning, purpose, and passion is what keeps you going when the times get tough. Which they do," said Lorie Valle-Yañez.

The good news is that the very process of envisioning these outcomes creates an upward spiral of win-win-wins. For example, let's say you recognize that you want to hold meetings in a way that invites everyone's participation regardless of their location or working style. This desired change leads you to do some reading and research, have a few conversations with your team and other leaders you respect within and beyond your company, and recall the best meetings you've been part of.

Over the next few weeks, you try out some changes. Even as some of those efforts flop, others seem to work. And ta-da! Your colleagues are more engaged and participation is more balanced from everyone, even the historically quieter folks calling in via video. Your team's dynamic improves, and you see people taking risks to speak up and interacting more readily than they used to. There's more laughter than there was before. You can feel tensions fade and see burnout start to recede. Individuals' well-being improves, and the team solves process problems more efficiently.

One day, after a few weeks of including personal check-ins as part of the regular meeting agenda, a colleague mentions having spent Sunday at a beach cleanup with his kids. Someone else asks for an invitation to the next cleanup. The following week, a third colleague shares a highlight of a conversation from a tutoring program they've volunteered with for over two years.

Fast-forward to a team conversation about which suppliers to renew with. Someone asks whether anyone knows which suppliers have started working with plastic alternatives. When a summer internship role is discussed, someone asks whether the tutoring program ever places kids. Your team has started to see their respective forms of desired influence, and they're starting to imagine ways to create that impact through the work they do.

Then, when the annual request for environmental, social, and governance data comes along, one team member pipes up that they've been reading a lot about the ocean plastics issue and would be glad to handle that portion of the reporting. Another shares their involvement with the Black employees resource group and offers to work on your team's reporting on diversity, equity, and inclusion metrics. You can feel a healthy blend of curiosity and envy from the others who don't speak up.

Your specific case may look more or less like this, and it may start with a different desired outcome or in a different dimension than We. But the upward spiral persists: When people are allowed and supported to be their best selves, they are more engaged team members. And teams of healthy, respected people do work that's good for the world. Doing work that's good for the world inspires people to be their best selves and motivates them to perform better. Therein lies the powerful win-win-wins of purposeful leadership.

Figure 22. The win-win-wins of purposeful leadership.

Where We Began

Take a minute to review your answers to the questions I asked you when we first began. As a reminder, here they are again:

- Why did you buy this book? Why did you start reading it?
- How do you think about purpose right now? Do you have a purpose statement? Even if it's not fully formed, jot some version of it down.
- What's your #1 question about purposeful leadership?
- If you could change *one* thing in your life after reading this book, what would it be?

Ideally, you have the answers handy that you gave then, before reading the book. Take a look or try to put yourself back in that mindset. Has your purpose statement evolved or emerged? Did I answer that #1 question of yours? (If not, feel free to submit it to me via my website and I'll do my best!) Perhaps most importantly, how close are you to changing that one thing?

Throw Your Own Party

My hope is that I've achieved the right balance of inspiration and reassurance to show you what's possible in terms of leading and living with purpose and that I've also offered you comfort that doing something is better than doing nothing. So let's talk about starting somewhere. You've shown up to my Purpose Party; now it's time to pay it forward and throw your own.

As you start doing these new activities, recognizing they will get you closer to the effects you want to have and help you stop doing the things that aren't aligned with those desired outcomes, you become a Purpose Party host in your own right. Without even trying, you set an example—a new should, if you will—for others around you. As you get more comfortable talking about your purposeful approach, you'll explicitly guide and inspire others to do the same, which is tantamount to inviting them to your Purpose Party.

Check out some tips and free resources to Play Along (page 341) and actually create your own Purpose Party Playgroup, with friends, colleagues, neighbors, family, or complete strangers! Remember, the best way to learn something deeply can be to teach it. Why not share the love and bring other people alongside you on your purpose journey?

For now, here are some guidelines for throwing an impactful and engaging Purpose Party. This includes some habit-formation tips because, once you get a taste of the Purpose Party atmosphere, you're never going to want to leave!

WALKING THE TALK

Jerry Colonna, CEO whisperer and dyed-in-the-wool purposeful leader, says, "I believe that better humans make better leaders." But evolving to be a better human doesn't result from talking, writing, reading, or reflection alone. In the words of Didier Elzinga, "You're spending time on talking or walking. I'd rather be walking."

You've done the talking: you worked with the Dashboard plotting current and aspirational activities across the Spheres and the Spectrum, and you've explored the outcomes of those efforts in the Me, We, and World dimensions. Now it's time to walk and take the actions that make up your own Purpose Party. We'll revisit the six One Things you'd like to do more of, less of, or differently. But first, a few tips from your host on throwing a Purpose Party that's sustainably impactful, rewarding, and engaging for you and your eventual collaborators and guests.

Purpose Party Host Tips

AVOID PERFECTION

It's easier for words to be perfect than actions. Now that you are walking your journey of purposeful leadership, it is essential to maintain grace for yourself and others around you. Because there's no excuse not to walk the talk, but it's critical to recognize that action is inherently flawed. You will never do enough. You won't do it as well as you realize you could have after the fact. At some point, you will do unintended harm.

~Minister and social justice advocate Donna Schaper

Ironically, we often let perfect be the enemy of good when it comes to our purpose. While we rarely overanalyze our grocery list on a normal shopping trip, once we decide that we want to shop more sustainably we lose hours down a rabbit hole comparing two kinds of fairtrade coconut water or the possible risks of organic versus free range eggs. We don't give much thought at all to our meeting agenda until the mandate to hold more inclusive meetings. Don't get me wrong; I'm glad you're thinking about such issues as inclusion and regenerative agriculture. But we have to recognize the complexity of these issues and the inevitability of a learning curve. We can't know "the answer" to issues like this now or handle them perfectly because we've all of a sudden started paying attention.

Nina Tandon, who as CEO and founder of EpiBone helps patients grow bones from their own cells, echoes these thoughts.

> Perfection is the enemy! We're not going to move the conversation forward by trying to design a world that would work better. We have to take the imperfect circumstances and be a little bit messy. That mess will be the catalyst for how we start to design things better. It's my role to bushwhack a little bit and get my legs cut up by thorns. These roads [to fairer and healthier work] don't exist, just like the pioneers didn't have train tracks. It can feel scary, but there

are enough of us who want it. So I suggest we push ourselves to be messy together, be willing to get judged for making nonconformist choices, and pray that our kids will forgive us.

ESTABLISH BOUNDARIES

Not only do you not have to be perfect, but your actions don't have to get it all done either. It's important to recognize the edges of your sphere of influence. Which actions and how much of them can you do in each sphere without incurring unacceptable costs in the other spheres? Even if the items in your grocery cart, your household compost, or your outreach to diverse candidates for a new role feel tiny or inconsequential, those actions are, by definition, *enough*.

Lara Galinsky, a longtime and wise thinker on purpose, laments "The pressure to have sizzle in the connection between what you do and its impact on the world around you" often leads us to bite off more than we need to. Lara knows from experience that "It can be small, simple actions that have great ripple effects and bring your purpose to life in its fullest form."

If you're burning out, I promise you're overreaching beyond those small, simple, but authentic and intentional actions and doing more than your fair share. So look for where you can dial it back and reallocate your time, energy, and/or attention to make sustaining investments in your Self Sphere.

Perhaps ironically, the deeper into the Purpose Party you get, the more you'll need these healthy boundaries around your levels of investment. Several interviewees share the perspective that purposeful leaders "define ourselves by what we do. It takes very thoughtful and firm boundaries to not merge yourself with your work, precisely because we find it to be so soulful." Similarly, first-time entrepreneur Jordan Taylor, cofounder and CEO of Medley, feels "grateful for the overlap of my purpose with my company's work, but it's also a lot of pressure."

So know that as you lead and live more purposefully, you'll need to up your game when it comes to setting boundaries on what you do (in all spheres) and when, how much, and with whom you do it. How do we set those boundaries? Great question. We'll practice identifying some initial boundaries in an upcoming exercise.

INVITE YOUR PEOPLE

No Purpose Party is a success without other people. You need guests who will listen to your journey, cheer you on, ask good questions, get inspired, and eventually go throw their own parties. That process is what drives the upward spiral.

Nina Tandon points out that this is "just like the dance floor at any party. Someone has to start dancing, and then a few others join them. Once you have three people out there, it's easier to get a crowd. The first inner circle had confidence to take that step and gave others the confidence to join. Courage is contagious. If some people show it, others are likely to stick their neck out more." That's why the first form of invitation to a Purpose Party is merely talking about your desire, plan, and initial attempts to lead and live purposefully. By sharing your purpose journey's curiosities, challenges, and successes, you're like that first dancer on the dance floor.

Marc Spencer, longtime purposeful leader, has learned that "[Purpose] is universal, but there needs to be a spark to get it going. And I don't see that spark being lit often. I didn't get it in my high school, college, or master's program or doctorate. Nobody's ever asked me what my purpose in life is. That's what it takes to change lives."

So who can you ask about their purpose? A colleague, old friend, child, sibling, parent? Merely opening the dialog about why they do what they do and what impact they aspire to have can be the spark that lights the fire already inside them.

It's also helpful to discuss your desired influence to better understand the problems you want to help solve. As Ward Vuillemot learned from his father during an impromptu and reluctant beach cleanup when he was a kid, "You don't have to be the person who caused the problem to step in and help solve the problem." When you notice a problem, ask the people in your team or community who are affected by it what they would like to see change, and let that inform the investments you make in your Impact Dashboard.

Since the best Purpose Parties are a team effort, Mauricio Gutierrez ensures that all of his teams at NRG have regular "open, candid conversations of where we are with our diversity initiatives, like any other important change process. We need awareness of the current state if we are to get to our desired destination, as well as an acceptance that we're not where we want to be yet." Successful Purpose Party hosts attract people from all the spheres of their lives to attend, co-create, support, enjoy, and replicate their parties.

Make the Party Last: Build Strong Habits

I warned (or enticed) you at the start of this book that purposeful leadership is a lifelong journey. It doesn't end. Therefore, it's not achieved by setting and meeting goals, even big, hairy, audacious ones. Leading and living with purpose is about building the habits that compose the investments you want to make in your Dashboard despite the pitfalls that none of us are immune from.

In the Workplace Sphere, for example, Deb Moroz, CHRO of Health-Ade Kombucha, knows "It's an ongoing effort to genuinely create an inclusive environment and understand what that means for different people. I believe in continuous improvement. This is a marathon, not a sprint. And so we build strong practices around performance reviews, for example, as well as our mission and values. Those are the organizational practices—the habits—that will get us where we want to be."

Habit formation is a science in itself, and one worth studying. I've included some great resources on habit formation in the Reader Resources section. For now, I'll share a few simple, well-established approaches for setting yourself up for success in making habits of the behaviors represented on your Dashboard, your unique version of leading and living purposefully.

START SMALL

Habits are, by definition, specific and discrete activities you do over and over. So it's not about saying, "I'll eliminate ocean plastic," but rather "I'll carry my own refillable water bottle when I travel to avoid buying bottled water." While these small habits can feel trivial in the face of existential global crises, they tend to initiate their own upward spirals within your own life. Once you stop buying plastic water bottles, you'll likely pay more attention to the other beverages you buy (or don't), what you stock in the office kitchen, and what packaging your lunch comes in. So start small.

SET PRIORITIES

It's important not to try to start a million new habits at once, even if they're all small, or even six new habits, which is the number of One Things you've identified you want to start doing. You know I wouldn't set you up to do something non-optimally! So it's time for our final activity: prioritizing those six activities that you said would get you closer to your desired impact.

- Open up the Excel template that you've been using for your Dashboard work, and go to the Purpose Party Planner tab. If you're using the Purpose Party Playbook, turn to chapter 15.

- Review your six One Things and prioritize them from one to six. There's no algorithm for these priorities, but I'd recommend starting with the ones you're most excited about in order to build momentum.

- In that priority order, assign one new habit to each of the next six months. Thirty days is a reasonable minimum time frame to start a new habit, and reviewing your progress and evolving what you're doing to build these new habits on a monthly basis is a good interval to start with.

PAIR HABITS

Habit junkies often recommend pairing new habits with another well-established habit. Can you do your target habit right before or after you brush your teeth, eat a meal, or commute home? Linking the new habit with something you're already doing often helps make it stick.

REWARD YOURSELF

We covered the topic of operant conditioning in chapter 8. The point is, carrots work! So give yourself a treat for completing a new habit the first few days you do it and then again each week that you do it at least six times. (Remember, perfect is the enemy of good, so you don't have to reach 100 percent to earn a treat!) Eventually, the inherent reward of leading and living purposefully does kick in; that eudaimonia buzz is hard to beat. But for now, you're pushing uphill against inaction, shoulding, and orthodoxy. So give yourself a pat on the back, whether it's in the form of a nap, a dance break, a cookie, or a five-minute break in the sun.

ANTICIPATE OBSTACLES

I spent so much time in this book on the pitfalls that I've encountered, seen, felt, and heard of because they're inevitable. We can't eliminate them, but we can anticipate which ones are most likely to trip us up and what form they'll come in. Review your answers to the reflection questions about the pitfalls in each sphere, and call those out on the Purpose Party Planning tab of my Excel worksheet or wherever you've been doing this work.

BOOK IT!

Finally, put your new habits on the calendar. Whether it's a 10-minute meditation each morning, a midday walk or stretch break, or an evening learning session about decarbonization or anti-racism, book it on your calendar. Ideally, these new impact-seeking activities go on your work calendar, where they are protected from competing priorities and inspire all of your colleagues who see them. Also, book a monthly session to evaluate the last month of effort and evolve your approach for the new habit in the next sphere in the month to come. You'll learn what days, times, and regularity works best for you, but start with this approach for now and adapt it to fit over time.

So When's the Party?

Speaking of calendars, when's the party? So glad you asked. It begins right now!

Just like that, you have what you need to throw your own Purpose Party. I won't keep you. Enough talk; now it's time to walk. And as you walk onward, remember that the tools and reflection questions in this book, as well as the accompanying activities in the *Going First* Purpose Party Playbook, are always here for you. Keep flipping through these final pages to get all the goodies I've provided, in the form of further reading, resources, downloads, and even an online community of other folks who are also Going First.

Leading and living purposefully is an ongoing, upwardly spiraling journey, with pitfalls and pitstops inevitably arising along the way. Coming back to these same tools and questions will never feel the same twice. They'll help you see new insights and aspirations each time, so keep them close.

In the meantime, share the frameworks, tools, questions, and insights you've gathered from this book and—if you're already into it, the Purpose Party Playbook. Teaching is the best way to learn, after all, and inviting someone to your Purpose Party is the best way to enjoy theirs as they create it!

Most importantly, Go First. In whatever way is appealing, authentic, just-the-right-amount-of-challenging, and inspiring for who you are and where you sit, take one action that will get you closer to having the impact you seek. Right now.

> *It is not the critic who counts; not the man who points out how the strong man stumbles, or where the doer of deeds could have done them better. The credit belongs to the man who is actually in the arena, whose face is marred by dust and sweat and blood; who strives valiantly; who errs, who comes short again and again, because there is no effort without error and shortcoming; but who does actually strive to do the deeds; who knows great enthusiasms, the great devotions; who spends himself in a worthy cause; who at the best knows in the end the triumph of high achievement, and who at the worst, if he fails, at least fails while daring greatly, so that his place shall never be with those cold and timid souls who neither know victory nor defeat.*
>
> ~Theodore Roosevelt

Acknowledgments

This book has been a few years—or a decade or a lifetime, depending how you look at it—in the making. It's the result of a lot of investments made by a lot of people across all of their spheres! My thanks here will surely miss people and activities that went into it, but perfect is the enemy of good, so here are the gratitudes I've been able to bring to mind and share within the final copy deadline.

Going First draws so heavily on the work I've done in the Inspiring Capital—and now Purposeful Growth Institute—communities. A huge thanks to the team who was there for the writing process, Nicolette Cabbell, Sarah Daniels, and Sasha D. Prince, and to all the past team members, particularly the strongest shapers among you: Yael Silverstein, Alex (Hanken) Russell, Kate Canfield, and Deb Lewison-Grant.

Deeply values-aligned investors leveraged their Money Spheres courageously and generously to support my work through Inspiring Capital. It disappoints me profoundly that I and the IC model were not able to provide a financial return on those investments. As we've discussed, I do hope you see the outcomes that your investments *did* have in the form of hundreds of now more purpose-driven professionals who have the tools, clarity, courage, and community to realize the change they want to see.

And those of you who have been fellows, interns, partners, speakers, mentors, event-attendees, and fans of Inspiring Capital, a huge thank you! I hope you'll follow the community and participate with the Purposeful Growth Institute in coming years.

In my relatively newly fleshed-out Family and Friends Sphere, a huge thanks first and foremost to my mom, for raising me as the securely attached spiritual warrior that I am.

To Grant, for your patient and unconditional support of everything in the last 10 years that has made this book possible, from morning meditations to flow on the ski slopes to weekend writing sessions, and *so* very much more. And thank you, deeply, for being the welcome catalyst of my increased family investments.

To Cameron, Charlotte, and Hallie, for being such satisfying givers and recipients of my family love and next-generation models of what holistic, purposeful lives can look like.

To my grandmother, Ann T. Debevoise, for being an inspiring model of pragmatically and thoughtfully purposeful work, as well as the source of the Will Rogers quote reminding me—and all of us—to keep moving.

My community beyond Inspiring Capital has fingerprints all over this book too. A big thanks to new partners Mark Griffin and Neil Turnham for creating PurposeFused and welcoming me in to shape its next chapter, even though we didn't go to middle school together.

Klay S. Williams, Sloan Leo, Janice Taylor, and Kelly Wendorf, you have shaped my thinking, warmed my heart, and inspired my persistence with your own respective brilliance and resilience.

Not all 152 (plus?!) purposeful professionals I interviewed in 2021 made it explicitly onto these pages, but you all shaped my thinking, encouraged me to write on, and inspired the ways I've sought to engage readers in their own purpose journey through this book.

I'm grateful to friends, family, and strangers who pre-bought the book and have now waited a full year to get it! I hope it's as useful now as you anticipated it would be then.

I certainly owe a shoutout to Greenwich Library and Gregory's for providing just the right balance of light, quiet, caffeine, breakfast treats, and anonymity to get this tome done!

Trevor Crane and the Epic team were essential players in turning a dust-collecting, two-year-old outline into what is now this book.

You, readers, whether you know it or not, and I both are deeply grateful to Mary Beth Conlee, Phoebe Miller, Kayla Henley, and Irena Kalcheva for making this reading journey everything that I hope it is: engaging, inspiring, and, at least in some concrete if small way, life-changing. Without their hands on my words, this book wouldn't have the clarity, readability, or interactivity that it does.

And to Jenn Grace, Nancy Graham-Tillman, and Bailly Morse, along with the Publish Your Purpose team, who were just the Sherpas I needed to get this book to its best and final state. Their depth of experience, loving guidance, and immaculate eyes and process oversight were a salve to my tired author self in the last stage of labor.

Finally, of course, thank *you*! I am grateful to you, the reader—if for some reason you're still here—for investing your time, energy, and attention in this action-oriented approach to leading and living more purposefully. It will be messy, hard, confusing, and overwhelming at times, but it's the only path to the world we want to be part of. Onward!

About the Author

Nell Derick Debevoise lovingly wrangles people, ideas, and horses to make work healthier and fairer for all of us. To activate that purpose, Nell facilitates courageous conversations that lead to growth and innovation and improve well-being and performance, advises on talent and social impact strategies, and coaches leaders and founders to expand their impact and build powerful legacies.

Since 2011, Nell has worked with hundreds of leaders from Fortune 500, startup, B Corp, and not-for-profit organizations to do the challenging but rewarding work of becoming the people their dogs and grandchildren think they are.

Nell has an interdisciplinary approach, gathering international, academic and applied perspectives that bridge sectors, industries, and generations. She has lived and worked on four continents and collaborated across sectors with Japanese executives, Palestinian community leaders, French high school students, and Mozambique education ministry officials, among others.

Nell studied leadership, innovation, and intercultural dialog at Harvard, Cambridge, Universita di Roma, and Columbia and London Business Schools. She is the Chief Wrangler of Inspiring Cowgirl PBC, a partner of PurposeFused, and cofounder and CEO of the Purposeful Growth Institute. Nell advises and invests in values-aligned startups across industries. She speaks and writes about this entire portfolio of work as a senior contributor for *Forbes* Leadership, and her first book is *Going First: Your Invitation to Find the Courage to Lead Purposefully and Inspire Action* (Spring 2023).

Visit www.inspiringcowgirl.com/about
to see and hear Nell's latest work, thinking, and news.

Work with Nell

If the tools, ideas, and examples in this book are appealing and relevant to your work or life, let's talk! Here are a few ways to engage further:

Read Nell's latest writing on *Forbes* or Medium.

https://www.forbes.com/sites/nelldebevoise/people/nelldebevoise/

https://nelldd.medium.com/

Engage Nell as a facilitator, coach, or speaker for your leaders, or learn more about her Equine-Assisted Learning practice and retreats.

www.inspiringcowgirl.com/services

Engage Nell and her partners in PurposeFused for your team. PF programs drive individual and team performance by helping professionals contribute at their best, more often.

www.purposefused.com

Join Our Community

The courage to Go First can be found more easily in community with other people who are Going First. Join our dynamic community of leaders across industries, ages, geographies, and backgrounds to set yourself up for success in the journey of leading and living with purpose.

Community members enjoy:

- Regular live sessions with me and other folks who are Going First;
- Curated and updated resources to support your purpose journey;
- Discussion and idea-sharing forums with other readers and Purpose Party hosts; and
- Latest news on the work of purposeful leadership, my work and thinking, and ways to engage and deepen or share your own purpose journey.

As a thanks to you for buying this book, you'll get a year of free membership in the community by using the code *Reader*.

www.inspiringcowgirl.com/community

Play Along

If you haven't already, get yourself the Going First Purpose Party Playbook.

And if you have, even better—now it's time to plan your party! My favorite way that people have engaged with this content over the last decade plus is in small, self-organized groups of colleagues, classmates, friends, family, or neighbors. Like a book group, but more action-oriented, your Purpose Party Playgroup can be a powerful forum to expand, deepen, and activate your learnings about Going First.

Being a purposeful leader is a team sport. And adults learn only when they practice and then reflect on the outcomes of that practice.

So putting this book down here would be tantamount to not having read it at all. Revisiting the reflection questions in this book, downloading and using the templates, or working through the Playbook are all great next steps.

But the best next step is to create or join a Playgroup. It'll enhance your learning (Me), inspire and support others around you (We), and greatly increase the likelihood and reach of your desired impact (World).

And it's as simple as wrangling a few other keen learners, and scheduling a first gathering when, where, and how you all are most comfortable.

Visit my website for additional support in forming your Purpose Party Playgroup (via the QR code and link below), including monthly Q&A sessions with me, peer discussions, and new topics and agendas to keep your group learning.

www.inspiringcowgirl.com/playbook

www.inspiringcowgirl.com/playgroup

Reader Resources

PURPOSE PARTY PREREQUISITES

- *Biased: Uncovering the Hidden Prejudice That Shapes What We See, Think, and Do*, Jennifer L. Eberhardt, PhD

- *Daring Greatly: How the Courage to Be Vulnerable Transforms the Way We Live, Love, Parent, and Lead*, Dr. Brené Brown (also a podcast called *Dare to Lead*)

- *Man's Search for Meaning*, Viktor Frankl

- *Mindset: The New Psychology of Success*, Carol Dweck

- *Minority Leader: How to Lead from the Outside and Make Real Change*, Stacey Abrams

- *The Power of Habit: Why We Do What We Do in Life and Business*, Charles Duhigg

- *Year of Yes: How to Dance It Out, Stand in the Sun and Be Your Own Person*, Shonda Rhimes

- *No One Is Too Small to Make a Difference*, Greta Thunberg

- Simon Sinek's books and online courses: https://simonsinek.com/

- Momentum Habit Tracker: https://momentum.cc/

- Day One customizable journaling tool: https://dayoneapp.com/

SPECTRUM OF IMPACT

- *This Could Be Our Future: A Manifesto for a More Generous World*, Yancey Strickler

- *Winners Take All: The Elite Charade of Changing the World*, Anand Giridharadas

Self Sphere

o *Flying Lead Change: 56 Million Years of Wisdom for Leading and Living*, Kelly Wendorf

o Podcast: *On Being*, Krista Tippett

o *Stealing Fire: How Silicon Valley, the Navy SEALs, and Maverick Scientists Are Revolutionizing the Way We Live and Work*, Steven Kotler and Jamie Wheal

o *The Body Keeps the Score: Brain, Mind, and Body in the Healing of Trauma*, Bessel van der Kolk

o *The Five Archetypes: Discover Your True Nature and Transform Your Life and Relationships*, Carey Davidson

o *Transcend: The New Science of Self-Actualization*, Scott Barry Kaufman

Family and Friends Sphere

o *Committed: A Skeptic Makes Peace with Marriage*, Elizabeth Gilbert

o Podcast: *Where Should We Begin?*, Esther Perel

o *The Five Love Languages: How to Express Heartfelt Commitment to Your Mate*, Gary Chapman

o *Warrior Rising: How Four Men Helped a Boy on His Journey to Manhood*, MaryAnne Howland

Job Sphere

o   Podcasts

  ▪ *Plan A Konversations*, Klay S. Williams

  ▪ *Hello Monday*, Jessi Hempel

o   *Reboot: Leadership and the Art of Growing Up*, Jerry Colonna (*also a podcast*)

o   *The Inclusive Leader: Taking Intentional Action for Justice and Equity*, Dr. Artika R. Tyner

o   *The Infinite Game*, Simon Sinek

o   *The Invisible Leader: Transform Your Life, Work, and Organization with the Power of Authentic Purpose*, Zach Mercurio

o   *The Lost Art of Connecting: The Gather, Ask, Do Method for Building Meaningful Business Relationships*, Susan McPherson

Workplace Sphere

o   *15 Commitments of Conscious Leadership: A New Paradigm for Sustainable Success*, Jim Dethmer, Diana Chapman, and Kaley Klemp

o   *A Great Place to Work for All: Better for Business, Better for People, Better for the World*, Michael C. Bush

o   *An Everyone Culture: Becoming a Deliberately Developmental Organization*, Robert Kegan and Lisa Laskow Lahey

o   *Better Business: How the B Corp Movement Is Remaking Capitalism*, Christopher Marquis

o   *Conscious Capitalism Field Guide: Tools for Transforming Your Organization*, Raj Sisodia, Thomas Eckschmidt, and Timothy Henry

- Hiring for Diversity: The Guide to Building an Inclusive and Equitable Organization, Arthur Woods and Susanna Tharakan
- Podcasts

  - Finding Humanity: B Lab Special Series, Hazami Barmada and Juan Pablo Larenas
  - WorkLife, Adam Grant

- The Regenerative Business: Redesign Work, Cultivate Human Potential, Achieve Extraordinary Outcomes, Carol Sanford

Community Sphere

- Care Work: Dreaming Disability Justice, Leah Lakshmi Piepzna-Samarasinha
- Disability Visibility: First-Person Stories from the Twenty-First Century, edited by Alice Wong
- Our Kids: The American Dream in Crisis, Robert Putnam
- Podcasts

  - Into the Mix, Ben & Jerry's
  - La Brega: Stories of the Puerto Rican Experience, WNYC Studios and Futuro Studios

- Radical Dharma: Talking Race, Love, and Liberation, Rev. angel Kyodo williams, Lama Rod Owens, and Jasmine Syedullah, PhD
- Restoring the Kinship Worldview: Indigenous Voices Introduce 28 Precepts for Rebalancing Life on Planet Earth, Wahinkpe Topa (Four Arrows) and Darcia Narvaez, PhD
- See No Stranger: A Memoir and Manifesto of Revolutionary Love, Valarie Kaur
- White Fragility: Why It's So Hard for White People to Talk About Racism, Robin DiAngelo

Money Sphere

o   *Doughnut Economics: Seven Ways to Think Like a 21st-Century Economist*, Kate Raworth

o   *Making Money Moral: How a New Wave of Visionaries Is Linking Purpose and Profit*, Judith Rodin and Saadia Madsbjerg

o   *Mission Economy: A Moonshot Guide to Changing Capitalism*, Mariana Mazzucato

o   Podcasts

   ▪   *Next Economy Now: For the Benefit of All Life*, LIFT

   ▪   *Economy Impact Briefing*, Impact Alpha

o   *The Soul of Money: Transforming Your Relationship with Money and Life*, Lynne Twist

DOWNLOADABLE RESOURCES (Available at www. inspiringcowgirl.com/goingfirst)

A Down and Dirty Purpose Statement Worksheet

This document offers a simple way to draft or update a purpose statement so that you have some sense of what you're working toward. It isn't meant to replace a thorough purpose-identification process, which some people find to be extremely powerful at certain points in life.

Impact Dashboard Excel Worksheet

This includes all of the work I led you through on the Dashboard, from the initial Baseline Assessment in chapter 7, through each of the spheres in part 3, and to a final review and prioritization of goals.

Annual Planning Template

This document guides you through reviewing the outcomes you've had in the Me, We, and World dimensions in the past year and reflecting on what change you want to contribute to in the year to come. It's flexible; it can be used on your birthday, Lunar New Year, January 1st, or whenever else you choose to look back and forward.

Weekly Purposeful Habit Tracker

This is the Excel sheet I use to compile my daily habit tracking with weekly reflections on how I'm doing in various spheres, capture quantitative metrics for the week, and add qualitative observations.

Notes

1. Though Mark Twain is often credited for this quote, Quote Investigator reports it likely originated from Blaise Pascal. Quote Investigator, "If I Had More Time, I Would Have Written a Shorter Letter," accessed September 30, 2016, https://www. lb7.uscourts.gov/documents/314-cv-921.pdf.

2. Brené Brown, "The root of the word courage is cor—the Latin word for heart," LinkedIn, 2019, https://www.linkedin.com/ posts/brenebrown_the-root-of-the-word-courage-is-cor-the-activity-6501865650728812545-Bg07?utm_source=share&utm_medium=member_desktop.

3. Brené Brown, Atlas of the Heart: Mapping Meaningful Connection and the Language of Human Experience (New York: Random House, 2021).

4. Dean Bokhari, "How to Find Your Why and Communicate Your Purpose," Personal Development Articles, November 6, 2017, https://www.deanbokhari.com/find-your-why/.

5. Patrick L. Hill and Nicholas A. Turiano, "Purpose in Life as a Predictor of Mortality across Adulthood," Psychological Science 25, no. 7 (2014): 1482–1486. https://doi.org/10.1177/ 0956797614531799.

6. Kath, "A Selection of Wise Prose from Rumi," For Reading Addicts, September 30, 2019, https://forreadingaddicts.co.uk/quotations/a-selection-of-wise-prose-from-rumi/.

7. Lisa Eadicicco, "Laurene Powell Jobs Says People Have Been Misinterpreting One of Steve Jobs' Most Famous Quotes For Years," Insider, February 28, 2020, https://www.businessinsider.com/steve-jobs-famous-quote-misunderstood-laurene-powell-2020-2.

8. Yi-Yuan Tang, Britta K. Hölzel, and Michael I. Posner, "The Neuroscience of Mindfulness Meditation." Nature Reviews Neuroscience 16, no. 4 (2015): 213–225, https://www.nature.com/articles/nrn3916.

9. Aliya Alimujiang et al., "Association Between Life Purpose and Mortality Among US Adults Older Than 50 Years," JAMA Network Open 2, no. 5 (2019): 1-13, https://doi.org/10.1001/jamanetworkopen.2019.4270.

10. Angelina R. Sutin, Yannick Stephan, and Antonio Terracciano, "Psychological Well-Being and Risk of Dementia," International Journal of Geriatric Psychiatry 33, no. 5 (2017): 743–747, https://doi.org/10.1002/gps.4849.

11. Nathan A. Lewis et al., "Purpose in Life and Cognitive Functioning in Adulthood," Aging, Neuropsychology, and Cognition 24, no. 6 (2017): 662–671, https://doi.org/10.1080/13825585.2016.1251549.

12. Gary Gensler, "Statement by Chair Gensler on Registration of Security-Based Swap Execution Facilities," Harvard Law School Forum on Corporate Governance, U.S. Securities and Exchange Commission, April 7, 2022, https://corpgov.law.harvard.edu/2022/04/07/statement-by-chair-gensler-on-registration-of-security-based-swap-execution-facilities/#more-145038.

13. Claudine Gartenberg, Andrea Prat, and Georgios Serafeim, "Corporate Purpose and Financial Performance," (working paper No. 17-023, Harvard Business School, Boston, MA, September 2016), available at http://nrs.harvard.edu/urn-3:HUL.InstRepos:30903237.

14. Lewis et al., "Purpose in Life."

15. Sutin, Stephan, and Terracciano, "Psychological Well-Being."

16. Alimujiang et al., "Association Between Life Purpose and Mortality."

17. Barbara L. Fredrickson et al., "A Functional Genomic Perspective on Human Well-Being," Proceedings of the National Academy of Sciences 110, no. 33 (2013): 13684–13689, https://doi.org/10.1073/pnas.1305419110.

18. Cynthia A. Bonebright, Daniel L. Clay, and Robert D. Ankenmann, "The Relationship of Workaholism with Work–Life Conflict, Life Satisfaction, and Purpose in Life," Journal of Counseling Psychology 47, no. 4 (2000): 469–477, https://doi.org/10.1037/0022-0167.47.4.469.

19. Neal Chalofsky and Vijay Krishna, "Meaningfulness, Commitment, and Engagement: The Intersection of a Deeper Level of Intrinsic Motivation," Advances in Developing Human Resources 11, no. 2 (2009): 189–203, https://doi.org/10.1177/1523422309333147.

20. Wesley A. Scroggins, "Antecedents and Outcomes of Experienced Meaningful Work: A Person-Job Fit Perspective," Journal of Business Inquiry 7, no. 1 (2008): 68–78, https://journals.uvu.edu/index.php/jbi/article/view/167.

21. Cynthia A. Lengnick-Hall, Tammy E. Beck, and Mark L. Lengnick-Hall, "Developing a Capacity for Organizational Resilience through Strategic Human Resource Management,"

Human Resource Management Review 21, no. 3 (2011): 243–255, https://doi.org/10.1016/j.hrmr.2010.07.001.

22. Viktor E. Frankl, Man's Search for Meaning (Boston: Beacon Press, 2006); Friedrich Nietzsche, "Maxims and Arrows," in Twilight of the Idols and The Anti-Christ, trans. Thomas Common (Kansas: Digireads.com Publishing, 2018), 12.

23. Gensler, "Statement by Chair Gensler."

24. "Transcript: The New Age of Billionaire Philanthropy | Sep 26, 2018," TVO Today, accessed February 10, 2023, https://www .tvo.org/transcript/2521804.

25. National Council of Nonprofits, Nonprofit Impact Matters: How America's Charitable Nonprofits Strengthen Communities and Improve Lives (New York: American International Group, September 2019), https://www.nonprofitimpactmatters.org/ site/assets/files/1/nonprofit-impact-matters-sept-2019-1.pdf.

26. National Council of Nonprofits, Nonprofit Impact Matters.

27. NCCS Project Team, "The Nonprofit Sector in Brief 2019," Urban Institute | National Center for Charitable Statistics, June 2020, https://nccs.urban.org/publication/nonprofit-sector-brief-2019#the-nonprofit-sector-in-brief-2019.

28. NCCS Project Team, "The Nonprofit Sector in Brief 2019."

29. Douglas F. Dowd, "Robert Own: British Social Reformer," Britannica, last modified November 13, 2022, https://www .britannica.com/biography/Robert-Owen.

30. "About Us," International Cooperative Alliance, accessed January 23, 2023, https://www.ica.coop/en/about-us/ international-cooperative-alliance.

31. Cole Hoover, "The 600 Year History of the Social Enterprise Movement and How the Next 6 Years Are Its Most

Important," MovingWorlds (blog), October 11, 2018, https://blog.movingworlds.org/the-600-year-history-of-the-social-enterprise-movement-and-how-the-next-6-years-are-its-most-important/.

32. "The Importance of Small Business to the U.S. Economy," in Exploring Business (University of Minnesota Libraries, 2010), https://open.lib.umn.edu/exploringbusiness/chapter/5-2-the-importance-of-small-business-to-the-u-s-economy/.

33. Lisa Reagan, ed., "Finding a Bridge to Indigenous Wisdom and Worldview: An Interview with Kelly Wendorf," Kindred Media, March 20, 2021, https://www.kindredmedia.org/2021/03/finding-a-bridge-to-indigenous-wisdom-and-worldview-an-interview-with-kelly-wendorf/#kanyin.

34. James S. Gouinlock, "John Dewey: American Philosopher and Educator," Britannica, last modified February 3, 2023, https://www.britannica.com/biography/John-Dewey.

35. Xun Kuang, "The Achievements of the Ru," in Xunzi: The Complete Text, trans. Eric L. Hutton (New Jersey: Princeton University Press, 2014), 64.

36. Although this quote is often attributed as a Chinese proverb, Quote Investigator notes that it's actually been misattributed, and the original source is likely unknown. Quote Investigator, "The Best Time To Plant a Tree Was 30 Years Ago, and the Second Best Time To Plant a Tree Is Now," accessed January 22, 2022, https://quoteinvestigator.com/2021/12/29/plant-tree/.

37. Jim Lucas, "Inertia & Newton's First Law of Motion," LiveScience, last modified January 19, 2022, https://www.livescience.com/46559-newton-first-law.html.

38. Hans-Otto Pörtner et al., Climate Change 2022: Impacts, Adaptation and Vulnerability (Geneva, Switzerland:

Intergovernmental Panel on Climate Change, 2022), https://www.ipcc.ch/report/ar6/wg2/.

39. Catarina Saraiva, "Inequality Has Cost the U.S. Nearly $23 Trillion Since 1990," Bloomberg, September 8, 2021, https://www.bloomberg.com/news/articles/2021-09-09/inequality-cost-u-s-nearly-23-trillion-since-1990-may-worsen.

40. Channel 4 News, "Greta Thunberg Full Speech at Extinction Rebellion Protest in London," YouTube, April 22, 2019, video, 2:52, https://www.youtube.com/watch?v=hKMX8WRw3fc

41. "Will Rogers Quotes," BrainyQuote.com, accessed February 18, 2023, https://www.brainyquote.com/quotes/will_rogers_104938.

42. "Number of Quits at All-Time High in November 2021," U.S. Bureau of Labor Statistics, January 6, 2022, https://www.bls.gov/opub/ted/2022/number-of-quits-at-all-time-high-in-november-2021.htm.

43. Mark J. Perry, "Fortune 500 Firms 1955 V. 2016: Only 12% Remain, Thanks to the Creative Destruction That Fuels Economic Prosperity," American Enterprise Institute, December 13, 2016, https://www.aei.org/carpe-diem/fortune-500-firms-1955-v-2016-only-12-remain-thanks-to-the-creative-destruction-that-fuels-economic-prosperity/.

44. Caitlin Johnson, "Cutting Through Advertising Clutter," CBS News, September 17, 2006, https://www.cbsnews.com/news/cutting-through-advertising-clutter.

45. Jon Simpson, "Finding Brand Success in the Digital World," Forbes, August 25, 2017, https://www.forbes.com/sites/forbesagencycouncil/2017/08/25/finding-brand-success-in-the-digital-world/?sh=174e79e0626e.

46. Margaret Atwood, "Beautiful View," in The Blind Assassin (New York: Archer Books, 2000), 428–432.

47. "This is Water by David Foster Wallace (Full Transcript and Audio)," Farnam Street Media | Philosophy, accessed January 23, 2023, https://fs.blog/david-foster-wallace-this-is-water/.

48. Takim Williams, "#InContext: Margaret Mead," Human Trafficking Institute, May 24, 2017, https://traffickinginstitute.org/incontext-margaret-mead/.

49. Samika A. Satterthwaite, "Advancing the Arts: African Proverbs Provide a Blueprint," Americans for the Arts, September 13, 2019, https://www.americansforthearts.org/2019/09/13/advancing-the-arts-african-proverbs-provide-a-blueprint#:~:text=3.,person%20can%20make%20a%20difference.

50. Marilynn B. Brewer, (2003). "Optimal Distinctiveness, Social Identity, and the Self," in Handbook of Self and Identity, eds. Mark R. Leary and June Price Tangney (New York: Guilford Press, 2003), 480–491.

51. Catarina Saraiva, "Inequality Has Cost the U.S. Nearly $23 Trillion Since 1990," Bloomberg, September 8, 2021, https://www.bloomberg.com/news/articles/2021-09-09/inequality-cost-u-s-nearly-23-trillion-since-1990-may-worsen.

52. Quentin T. Wodon and Bénédicte de la Brière, Unrealized Potential: The High Cost of Gender Inequality in Earnings (Washing DC: World Bank Group, 2018), http://hdl.handle.net/10986/29865.

53. Kirk Warren Brown, Richard M. Ryan, and J. David Creswell, "Mindfulness: Theoretical Foundations and Evidence for its Salutary Effects," Psychological Inquiry 18, no. 4 (2007): 211–237, https:/doi.org/10.1080/10478400701598298.

54. Michael Pollan, In Defense of Food: An Eater's Manifesto (New York: Penguin Group, 2009).

55. Tenzin Gyatso, Dalai Lama XIV, Worlds in Harmony: Dialogues on Compassionate Action (Berkeley, CA: Parallax Press, 1992).

56. Audre Lorde, A Burst of Light and Other Essays (Mineola, NY: Ixia Press, 1988), 40.

57. Damian F. Santomauro et al., "Global Prevalence and Burden of Depressive and Anxiety Disorders in 204 Countries and Territories in 2020 Due to the COVID-19 Pandemic," The Lancet 398, no. 10312 (2021): 1700–1712, https://doi.org/10.1016/S0140-6736(21)02143-7.

58. Peng Xiong et al., "Trends in the Incidence and DALYs of Anxiety Disorders at the Global, Regional, and National Levels: Estimates from the Global Burden of Disease Study 2019," Journal of Affective Disorders 297 (2022): 83–93, https://doi.org/10.1016/j.jad.2021.10.022.

59. C. Lindsay DeVane et al., "Supplements and Featured Publications, Anxiety Disorders in the 21st Century: Status, Challenges, Opportunities, and Comorbidity with Depression," The American Journal of Managed Care 11, no. 12 Suppl (2005): S344–353, https://www.ajmc.com/view/oct05-2158ps344-s353.

60. Jeffrey Pfeffer, Dying for a Paycheck (New York: Harper Business, 2018).

61. Kirsten Weir, "Life-Saving Relationships," American Psychological Association 49, no. 3 (2018): 46, https://www.apa.org/monitor/2018/03/life-saving-relationships.

62. Gus Wezerek and Kristen R. Ghodsee, "Women's Unpaid Labor is Worth $10,900,000,000,000," The New York Times, March 5, 2020, https://www.nytimes.com/interactive/2020/03/04/opinion/women-unpaid-labor.html.

63. "Inventory of Invisible Labor," Amy Westervelt, accessed January 23, 2023, https://www.amywestervelt.com/unpaid-labor-calculator.

64. Weir, "Life-saving Relationships."

65. Glennon Doyle, Untamed (New York: The Dial Press, 2020), 109.

66. Richard Weissbourd et al., Loneliness in America: How the Pandemic Has Deepened an Epidemic of Loneliness and What We Can Do About It (Harvard Graduate School of Education, Making Caring Common Project, 2021), https://mcc.gse.harvard.edu/reports/loneliness-in-america.

67. Charles M. Blow, "The Married Will Soon Be the Minority," The New York Times, October 20, 2021, https://www.nytimes.com/2021/10/20/opinion/marriage-decline-america.html.

68. Weissbourd et al., Loneliness in America.

69. Doyle, Untamed, 110.

70. Riane Eisler, The Real Wealth of Nations: Creating A Caring Economics (Oakland, CA: Berrett-Koehler, 2008), 8.

71. Sounds True, "Dr. Mario Martinez—Insights at the Edge Podcast w/Tami Simon PART 1 of 2 (#IATE 11/18/14)," November 18, 2014, in Insights at the Edge, produced by Tami Simon, podcast, YouTube video, 1:01:09, https://www.youtube.com/watch?v=vNpShovE5Vs.

72. Psychology Today Staff, "Learned Helplessness," Psychology Today, accessed February 14, 2023, https://www.psychologytoday.com/us/basics/learned-helplessness.

73. Alex Stajkovic and Fred Luthans, "Self-Efficacy and Work-Related Performance: A Meta-Analysis," Psychological Bulletin

124, no. 2 (1998): 240–261, https://doi.org/10.1037/0033-2909.124.2.240.

74. Katheleen Conte, "Companies Led by Women Have Happier Workers. What's the Secret?" The Boston Globe, November 14, 2019, https://www.bostonglobe.com/business/specials/top-places-to-work/2019/11/14/companies-led-women-have-happier-workers-what-secret/NQXNnRJ150gsP6Aibtzj5H/story.html.

75. Milton Friedman, "A Friedman Doctrine—the Social Responsibility of Business Is to Increase Its Profits," New York Times, September 13, 1970, https://www.nytimes.com/1970/09/13/archives/a-friedman-doctrine-the-social-responsibility-of-business-is-to.html.

76. Antoinette E. LaBelle, "Nonprofit Leaders and their Organizations: Routes to and Repertoires for Effectiveness" (PhD diss., Case Western Reserve University, 2010), 1–161, https://etd.ohiolink.edu/apexprod/rws_olink/r/1501/10?clear=10&p10_accession_num=casedm1568731826882939.

77. Robert D. Putnam, Bowling Alone: the Collapse and Revival of American Community (New York: Simon & Schuster, 2001).

78. Jerf W. K. Yeung, Zhuoni Zhang, and Tae Yeun Kim, "Volunteering and Health Benefits in General Adults: Cumulative Effects and Forms," BMC Public Health 18, no. 8 (2018), 1–8, https://doi.org/10.1186/s12889-017-4561-8.

79. Santomauro et al., "Global Prevalence and Burden."

80. "So Lonely I Could Die," American Psychological Association, July 27, 2017, https://www.newswise.com/articles/so-lonely-i-could-die.

81. Alexis de Tocqueville, Democracy in America, trans. Harvey C. Mansfield and Delba Winthrop (Chicago: University of Chicago

Press, 2002); originally published in 1835 by Saunders and Otley (London).

82. "Change in Segregation, 1990-2019," University of California Berkeley, Othering and Belonging Institute, The Roots of Structural Racism Project, accessed January 23, 2023, https://belonging.berkeley.edu/change-segregation-1990-2019.

83. Edelman, "Societal Leadership is Now a Core Business Function," in Edelman Trust Barometer 2022 Global Report, PowerPoint, slides 25–30, accessed January 23, 2023, https://www.edelman.com/trust/2022-trust-barometer.

84. Robert D. Putnam and Kristin A. Goss, "Introduction," in Democracies in Flux: The Evolution of Social Capital in Contemporary Society, ed. Robert D. Putnam (Oxford: Oxford University Press, 2002), 3–19.

85. Ilana Gershon, "'A Friend of a Friend' Is No Longer the Best Way to Find a Job," Harvard Business Review, June 2, 2017, https://hbr.org/2017/06/a-friend-of-a-friend-is-no-longer-the-best-way-to-find-a-job.

86. "What is the KonMari Method?" KonMari.com, accessed January 28, 2023, https://konmari.com/about-the-konmari-method/.

87. Wezerek and Ghodsee, "Women's Unpaid Labor."

88. Amy Patterson Neubert, "Money Only Buys Happiness for a Certain Amount," Purdue University, February 13, 2018, https://www.purdue.edu/newsroom/releases/2018/Q1/money-only-buys-happiness-for-a-certain-amount.htm.

89. Shawn Achor et al., "9 Out of 10 People Are Willing to Earn Less Money to Do More-Meaningful Work," Harvard Business Review, November 6, 2018, https://hbr.org/2018/11/9-out-of-

10-people-are-willing-to-earn-less-money-to-do-more-meaningful-work.

90. Eugene Declercq and Laurie Zephyrin, "Maternal Mortality in the United States: A Primer," The Commonwealth Fund, December 16, 2020, https://www.commonwealthfund.org/publications/issue-brief-report/2020/dec/maternal-mortality-united-states-primer.

91. Bryant P. H. Hui et al., "Rewards of Kindness? A Meta-Analysis of the Link Between Prosociality and Well-Being," American Psychological Association, Psychological Bulletin 146, no. 12 (2020), 1084–1116, https://doi.org/10.1037/bul0000298.

The B Corp Movement

Dear reader,

Thank you for reading this book and joining the Publish Your Purpose community! You are joining a special group of people who aim to make the world a better place.

What's Publish Your Purpose About?
Our mission is to elevate the voices often excluded from traditional publishing. We intentionally seek out authors and storytellers with diverse backgrounds, life experiences, and unique perspectives to publish books that will make an impact in the world.

Certified

Corporation

Beyond our books, we are focused on tangible, action-based change. As a woman- and LGBTQ+-owned company, we are committed to reducing inequality, lowering levels of poverty, creating a healthier environment, building stronger communities, and creating high-quality jobs with dignity and purpose.

As a Certified B Corporation, we use business as a force for good. We join a community of mission-driven companies building a more equitable, inclusive, and sustainable global economy. B Corporations must meet high standards of transparency, social and environmental performance, and accountability as determined by the nonprofit B Lab. The certification process is rigorous and ongoing (with a recertification requirement every three years).

How Do We Do This?
We intentionally partner with socially and economically disadvantaged businesses that meet our sustainability goals. We embrace and encourage our authors and employee's differences in race, age, color, disability, ethnicity, family or marital status, gender identity or expression, language, national origin, physical and mental ability, political affiliation, religion, sexual orientation, socio-economic status, veteran status, and other characteristics that make them unique.

Community is at the heart of everything we do—from our writing and publishing programs to contributing to social enterprise nonprofits like reSET (https://www. resetco.org/) and our work in founding B Local Connecticut.

We are endlessly grateful to our authors, readers, and local community for being the driving force behind the equitable and sustainable world we are building together.

To connect with us online, or publish with us, visit us at www.publishyourpurpose.com.

Elevating Your Voice,

Jenn T Grace

Jenn T. Grace
Founder, Publish Your Purpose

Printed in the USA
CPSIA information can be obtained
at www.ICGtesting.com
LVHW051223061223
765524LV00066B/1318